W9-BNX-024

# OPERATIONAL RESEARCH AND SYSTEMS

*The Systemic Nature of Operational Research*

# Contemporary Systems Thinking

**Series Editor:** Robert L. Flood
University of Hull
Hull, United Kingdom

## LIBERATING SYSTEMS THEORY
Robert L. Flood

## OPERATIONAL RESEARCH AND SYSTEMS: The Systemic Nature of Operational Research
Paul Keys

A Continuation Order Plan is available for this series. A continuation order will bring delivery of each new volume immediately upon publication. Volumes are billed only upon actual shipment. For further information please contact the publisher.

# OPERATIONAL RESEARCH AND SYSTEMS
## The Systemic Nature of Operational Research

*Paul Keys*

*University of Hull*
*Hull, United Kingdom*

PLENUM PRESS • NEW YORK AND LONDON

Library of Congress Cataloging-in-Publication Data

Keys, Paul, 1954-
    Operational research and systems : the systemic nature of
operational research / Paul Keys.
        p.   cm. -- (Contemporary systems thinking)
    Includes bibliographical references and index.
    ISBN 0-306-43642-6
    1. Operations research.  2. System analysis.   I. Title.
II. Series.
T57.6.K448  1991
620'.001'1--dc20                                        90-19443
                                                           CIP

ISBN 0-306-43642-6

© 1991 Plenum Press, New York
A Division of Plenum Publishing Corporation
233 Spring Street, New York, N.Y. 10013

Printed in the United States of America

# Foreword

*Contemporary Systems Thinking* is a series of texts, each of which deals comparatively and/or critically with different aspects of holistic thinking at the frontiers of the discipline. Traditionally, writings by systems thinkers have been concerned with single theme propositions such as general systems theory, cybernetics, operations research, system dynamics, soft systems methodology, and many others. Recently there have been attempts to fulfil a different, yet equally important, role by comparative analyses of viewpoints and approaches, each addressing disparate areas of study such as modeling and simulation, measurement, management, "problem-solving" methods, international relations, social theory, and last, but not exhaustively or least, philosophy. In a recent book these were drawn together within a multiform framework as part of an eclectic discussion—a nearly impossible task as I discovered (see *Dealing with Complexity—An Introduction to the Theory and Application of Systems Science* by R. L. Flood and E. R. Carson). Nevertheless, bringing many sources together led to several achievements, among which was showing a great diversity of approaches, ideas, and application areas that systems thinking contributes to (although often with difficulties remaining unresolved). More important, however, while working on that manuscript I became aware of the need for and potential value in a series of books, each focusing in detail on the study areas mentioned above. While modeling and simulation are served well in the scientific literature, this is not the case for systems thinking in management, "problem-solving" methods, social theory, or philosophy, to name a handful. Each book in this series will make a contribution by concentrating on one of these topics. Each one will offer a further interest beyond other available books because of the inevitable tensions that authors will have to deal with, between contrasting approaches that have all too often met in nonreflective adversarial mode as specialist takes on specialist. There can be no genuine victors emerging from that style of intellectual debate.

Yet an alternative critical and comparative study poses an interesting difficulty for authors in this series. Each author must consider how they can best deal with contrasting approaches. There are two obvious options: first, by adopting a monolithic isolationist position that makes no real distinction between approaches which stand apart according to their own principles; second, by taking the bold step of adopting a complementarist approach that operates at a meta-level and accepts fundamentally that different rationalities exist, each with its own theoretical and methodological legitimacies and limitations. I do not intend to dictate an isolationist or a complementarist position to the authors, but the reader's awareness of this issue sets up an extremely interesting tension that can be followed throughout the series.

ROBERT L. FLOOD

*Hull, UK*

# Preface

The ideas presented in this book emerged from a number of different roots to produce what is, hopefully, a coherent argument about what I see as an important aspect of the relationship between the systems movement and management science. Looking back after the completion of this project, I recognize some key events that have contributed to my present understanding of how systems ideas can be used to aid the resolution of problems in a variety of contexts.

Four years helping to develop a suite of microsimulation models, which could be used to analyze the behavior of urban systems, exposed me to the problems of working with socioeconomic phenomena and to the notion that different situations required different modeling styles and methods of analysis. The need to develop material for teaching students the process of operational research and its role in organizations forced me to approach that discipline from a perspective I had not considered before. This led to a concern with the relative strengths and weaknesses of a variety of methodologies and processes that has subsequently been the focus of a research program at Hull for the past seven years or so. The results of part of that program form the basis of the following pages. The work at Hull has been developed alongside a continuing interest in related issues in the U.K. Two major contributions which appeared after this volume was completed, and which would have received due attention if it had been possible, have come from part of the British OR community. Jim Bryant's *Problem Management* (Wiley, 1989) is a valuable discussion of the social processes of problem solving. Jonathan Rosenhead has edited a collection entitled *Rational Analysis for a Problematic World* (Wiley, 1989) which considers a range of methodologies, some of which are discussed in this volume.

My debt is therefore to many people: my colleagues at Leeds University, who introduced a raw mathematician to research, specifically in urban modeling and generally as a career; to Jim Morrison and the staff of the department I joined at Hull in 1980, who allowed me to establish my own research interests; to the students of that department, who were unwittingly involved in the development of those interests; and finally, to Mike Jackson and Bob Flood, who, in various capacities, have cooperated in and encouraged the growth of this research program. Without them I doubt that this book would have seen the light of day.

It goes without saying, but it must be said, that my greatest debt, as always, is to my parents and my wife, Anne, for their contributions, which are many, varied, and often intangible. To them this book is dedicated, a poor reward for the joys they have given to me.

PAUL KEYS

# Contents

## Part III. Operational Research in Systems

## 10. Operational Research and Systems: Some Observations and Issues

# OPERATIONAL RESEARCH AND SYSTEMS

*The Systemic Nature of Operational Research*

# Operational Research and Systems
## A Problematic Relationship

### Introduction

The material in this book is devoted to an examination of the relationship between two disciplines, operational research (OR) and systems. The two bodies of knowledge both emerged in the decade following the conclusion of the Second World War, and their common history is reinforced by the contribution subsequently made to both disciplines by certain important figures, notably Ackoff, Beer, and Churchman. The relationship is considered from a perspective which concentrates upon OR and systems in relation to problem solving and decision making. Thus an emphasis is placed upon the methodology and process of OR rather than upon the mathematical modeling techniques which have developed within it. Certain aspects of the systems movement equally are not directly addressed; for example, general systems theory, which seeks to provide a conceptual framework useful in many fields of interest, receives little explicit attention. This particular view of the relationship is adopted because it emphasizes a major area where the two disciplines overlap and offers a fruitful arena from which beneficial insights may be gained.

This first chapter gives an overview of the issues which are to be considered in the book and the approach taken to addressing them. The first part of this scene setting involves a review of some of the more recent pronouncements on the nature of the relationship between OR and systems. A more detailed discussion of some of these will appear in later chapters.

*Some Views on OR and Systems*

There has been an almost continual debate in the OR community about the place of systems within that discipline. The strength of the discussions has varied, but over the past five years or so they have been a dominant factor in the exploration of the nature of OR. A feel for the context of this situation can be gained from a reading of the comments made about two conferences held by the OR Society at Henley in 1983 and 1985. The first of these was entitled "Systems in OR" in deference to a view that "OR included systems anyway" (Stainton, 1983), and the proceedings were published as a special issue of the *Journal of the OR Society* in August 1983. The discussion that began at that conference was formally continued in the second meeting, entitled "Systems Thinking in Action." The second conference aimed "to maintain continuity with the concerns of the earlier conference while concentrating more fully on the practical applications of systems ideas" (Jackson and Keys, 1985, p. 753). The proceedings of this conference were published in the September 1985 issue of the *Journal*. Several comments have been made about these conferences and the issues they raised, and these are particularly relevant here as they illustrate the nature of the debate and the positions being adopted within it.

Hirschheim (1983) presents a thoughtful analysis of the first conference which seeks to characterize the meeting along different dimensions. Four particular dichotomies are identified: practitioner–academic, intellectually-rich–intellectually-poor, tools-and-techniques–underlying-concepts-and-theories, and OR-systems. In a detailed breakdown of the latter an overview of the differences between OR and systems is presented. OR is analytic and reductionist in its approach, which is often hard and technical and applicable to tame problems. It embraces the scientific method and hence is concerned explicitly with validation. A hierarchical approach to decomposition is used to find out how phenomena operate, and this approach leads to suggestions as to how things can be changed for the better. OR acts rather like a doctor, who, with little participation from the patient, indicates how health can be improved. Systems uses notions of synthesis and emergence, which are qualitative in character. Such methods can be used to address unstructured or wicked problems in a manner which is not seen as scientific by their proponents. As a result, effectiveness is seen as being more important than validation, and the methods lead to explanations of why phenomena are, rather than how they work. Thus, systems methods are seen as acting as devices for learning in a participative way.

The theme of two attitudes, fundamentally opposed along various dimensions, is also recognized by Rosenhead (1985). He remarks that in 1983 there was a sensation of there being two simultaneous conferences. Papers from the second (hard) conference seemed repeatedly to interrupt the primary (soft) conference, where the serious intellectual activity was occurring. By 1985, however, the "committed proponents of the 'hard' were significant by their absence, leaving a near walkover for advocates of soft approaches" (p. 849).

There were other, more analytic than descriptive comments to come from the two conferences. Jackson (1984) argues that OR is "a strand in just one of a number of different versions of the systems approach" and suggests that this is a better way to look at the relationship than as "systems in OR" (p. 155). Keys (1984) identifies three different ways in which systems ideas can be used in problem management, only one of which is widely adopted in OR.

The conference acted as a catalyst which resulted in both OR and systems exploring each other's disciplines to a much greater extent than had been the case in immediately previous years. The work which has resulted in the following chapters draws upon many of the analyses and observations made during the debate of which the Henley conferences were a part.

The aim of the analysis is to increase our understanding of some aspects of the relationship between OR and systems which have an effect upon the ability of these approaches to aid problem solvers and decision makers. In doing so, use is made of systems ideas in presenting a picture of what OR is and how it operates and in establishing its role within a broad systems approach to problem solving and decision making. The discussion here will not fully clarify the nature of the relationship; indeed it is likely to raise new issues to be considered. Therefore, the results of the analysis will reveal not only some suggestions as to how OR and systems are related but also some insights into those issues which need further consideration. The starting point, however, is to outline those matters which are to be looked at in the current analysis and to show how they will be tackled.

## Some Issues in OR and Systems

### The systems movement

is the set of attempts in all areas of study to explore the consequence of holistic rather than reductionist thinking. The programme of the systems movement might be described as the testing of the conjecture that these ideas will enable us to tackle the problem which the method of science finds so difficult; namely the problem of organised complexity. (Checkland, 1981, p. 92)

The United Kingdom Operational Research society defines operational research as "the attack of modern science on complex problems arising in the direction and management of large systems of men, machines, materials and money in industry, business, government and defence." It goes on to state that "the distinctive approach is to develop a scientific model of the system, incorporating measurement of factors such as chance and risk, in order to predict and compare the outcomes of alternative decisions, strategies and controls. The purpose is to help management to determine its policy and actions scientifically." Summarising this definition it could be said that operational research is concerned with allocation and planning in complex situations involving scarce or limited resources. (Moore, 1986, p. 2)

These views on the nature, purpose, and domain of systems, on the one hand, and OR, on the other, go a long way toward establishing the issues which will be tackled in later chapters. A consideration of the above reveals three apparent differences between the systems movement and OR. Each of these leads to significant questions being posed about the interaction between OR and systems.

A clear distinction appears to come from these "definitions" that OR is concerned with the world of action while systems is concerned with the world of ideas. A primary task of OR is to provide advice to decision makers about how to proceed in certain types of situation. The systems movement, in contrast, is motivated by the wish to construct theories about the behavior of entities which exhibit organized complexity. A fundamental distinction in purpose grounded in the theory–practice dichotomy appears to exist. Yet this dichotomy also suggests a synergy between the two components. A theory requires testing, and this involves interfering with the real world to a greater or lesser extent. A theory which yields understanding about the world will also have implications for how to address issues in the world. Thus the world of ideas has direct consequences for the world of action. Equivalently, in determining what type of action to take, some thinking about the possibilities and their effects usually occurs. Practice is usually accompanied by abstract analysis in some form or other.

A consequence for the current purpose is that it raises the issue of the relationship between the set of concepts informed by systems notions and the practical aims of OR. The straightforward concern is with the use which can be or is being made of systems ideas in OR. A less obvious issue is the relationship between the practice of OR and the practical consequence of systems ideas. A further aspect is the relationship between the theory generated by systems ideas and the theoretical implications of OR practice.

A second apparent difference between OR and systems is grounded in the relationship each of them shares with scientific method. The systems movement explicitly sets out to provide methods and tools which can succeed where science begins to fail. The problems posed by using scientific method to investigate situations which exhibit organized complexity are seen to be overcome by using systems-based methods of enquiry. Thus systems is complementary to and different from traditional science. OR, on the other hand, sees itself as being based on such scientific method. It uses science to attack problems and gains credibility from its use of a scientific approach. OR affiliates itself with science and makes no attempt to develop methods of enquiry which are not compatible with scientific procedures.

This difference in the attitudes toward scientific method held by OR and systems becomes a problem when it is realized that both OR and systems are concerned with complex situations. The systems movement takes as given the inability of scientific method to deal adequately with situations of organized complexity, while OR works within the scientific approach to tackle complex situations. The methodological issues which this apparent contradiction generates are several. They center upon the distinctions and similarities between systems, OR, and science, which can be revealed only by a thorough analysis of how each of these approaches inquires into the nature of the world and seeks to use the knowledge gained to change it.

A third significant point which results from a comparison of the above descriptions of OR and systems is the breadth of the phenomena with which the two disciplines are involved. Systems is concerned to spread itself over a wide range of behavior and processes, for it has at its core an interest in establishing connections between phenomena found in different contexts which might otherwise not be considered. OR focuses upon only one set of phenomena: those associated with the use of resources, often by organizations. Thus the area of interest of OR forms part of that of systems. The result is that OR is able to associate easily with only those parts of the systems movement which are involved with resource use or organizational behavior. The systems movement will, in turn, treat those issues considered by OR as part of its range of inquiry. Systems will be able to draw upon a wider variety of experience than can OR, and this extra breadth will be reflected in the perception, attitude, and treatment of situations exhibited by the two disciplines.

This difference in the phenomena of interest suggests that OR is, in some sense, embedded within the systems movement. The validity of this suggestion and the nature of any embedding, if it is shown to exist, warrant attention, for this issue is at the heart of the relationship between OR and systems.

This question of embedding helps to clarify and refine the issues mentioned earlier with respect to theory–practice and scientific method. The set of issues themselves form a complex of questions which are related in a nontrivial manner. In seeking to address one, the others are implicitly referred to, and in establishing a position on one, a particular view is likely to be adopted toward others. The discussion which follows cannot be seen as a linear progression of questions and answers but as a continuing exploration around a set of related topics. Consequently the structure of the chapters cannot follow a well-defined sequence, but it must exhibit some order and pattern. This structure and its relationship to the issues highlighted above will now be described.

### Structure of the Book

The broad issues to be addressed below focus on three themes: the theory–practice relationship in OR and systems, the role of scientific method in OR and systems, and the extent to which either OR or systems is embedded within the other. These three themes cut across each other in various ways, and no single ordering of material can guarantee the inclusion of all the possible connections and influences. By adopting an open structure in terms of the main themes, it is intended that most of the varied aspects of the interplay between OR and systems will be considered somewhere.

Before undertaking any detailed analysis of OR and systems, it is felt to be appropriate to consider the development of OR. The emphasis of the book is directed toward problem solving and decision making, and as OR has historically been more closely connected with these activities than has the systems movement in general, it helps to place the ensuing discussion in context if the emergence of OR is examined first. The factors which underlay the growth of OR are important in determining its culture and attitude and, indirectly, also influence the relationship of OR and systems. A discussion of OR and systems which is devoid of this historical context is likely to fail to consider certain directions in the history of OR which are still important today. The first part of the book looks at the early OR studies of the Second World War and some of the precedents of OR such as scientific management. It then goes on to consider the characteristics of classical OR which became established in the 1950s and 1960s.

The second and third parts of the book focus upon systems in OR and OR in systems, respectively. In the former, systems ideas are used to explore the nature of OR as a problem-solving process. In a series of analyses the nature of the OR process is examined at three levels. First, a detailed model of the process and its direct environment is developed. This is then embedded within an organizational system which hosts the OR activities in order to identify the way in which a set of OR projects is bound into an organization. Finally, the OR process is placed in a broad intellectual framework which illustrates the exchanges which occur in an OR process between the worlds of theory and practice.

The third part of the book takes as its topic OR in systems and involves an examination of OR in relation to other systems-based problem-solving methodologies. OR is placed within a family of such methodologies which share its fundamental approach and assumptions. This family is, in turn, located within a classification of methodologies based upon the effectiveness with which each can tackle certain types of situation. A means of choosing between different classes of methodology is developed which, in particular, shows the strengths of OR relative to other approaches and suggests when it should be adopted.

Throughout these analyses the three focal issues are continually being met in various forms. In a final chapter the insights derived from the different aspects of the study are drawn together around these issues to provide a thorough assessment of the relationship between OR and systems which it suggests. Here the connections between the different aspects of this relationship will become clearer and some observations on the ways of proceeding to clarify them further will be made.

## Conclusion

This chapter has laid out the main issues which the discussion following will address and the approach that will be adopted toward the analysis and the structure of the main body of the book. The theory–practice interaction, scientific method, and the primacy of OR or systems form a set of key related areas of interest which are looked at in the following chapters. The discussion is structured into three main parts concerned with the development of classical OR, systems in OR, and OR in systems.

# *I*

# *Background of Operational Research*

In order to develop a useful discussion of how contemporary OR and systems interact at a variety of levels, it is necessary to understand the paths by which they arrived at their present position. Since this book is one of a series aimed at the systems community, it is assumed that the reader will not need an overview of the history and themes of that discipline. What may be necessary for some readers, however, is a review of the major aspects of the development of OR. This need is met by the two chapters that form Part I of this book.

In Chapter 2 the origins of OR in the Second World War are traced, and some characteristics of the discipline that emerged from that period are noted. Taking these as a baseline, the question is then posed of whether any earlier work shares these characteristics, and consideration is made of the work of Babbage, Taylor, and various pre-War research associations in the UK.

Chapter 3 takes the development of OR into the 1950s and describes the growth of what might be labeled "classical OR." The emergence of OR in industry and commerce in Britain and the U.S. is described and compared, as is the growth of educational and professional institutions. The chapter ends by describing some common problems that this type of OR has been able to tackle and that form the basis of most popular classifications of OR.

# 2

# *The Beginnings of Operational Research*

## *Introduction*

Most disciplines or significant themes within a discipline which have stood the test of time can trace their origins back to an individual or group whose work is spread, if not over a lifetime, then over a significant number of years. Thus positivist sociology is usually taken to begin with the work of Saint-Simon and Comte in the mid-nineteenth century (Keat and Urry, 1982). A few years earlier than this, van Humboldt and Ritter were laying the basis of regional geography (Chisholm, 1975). The start of classical economics is usually associated with the work of Adam Smith (Barber, 1977). Many historians therefore find it difficult to be specific when considering the roots of a particular discipline. This is not the case to the same extent with operational research. It is possible, with reasonable accuracy, to refer to the first use of the term and hence to identify a starting date for the activity carried out under that name. In December 1967, a meeting was held at the Royal Society, London, to celebrate the thirtieth anniversary of the use of the term *operational research*. The first use of a label is clearly not necessarily equivalent with the introduction of the activity it is applied to, and at the meeting one of the pioneers of OR, E. C. Williams, noted the fact that although the first use of the name occurred in 1937, the activity of operational research predated this use by at least one year.

In this chapter we shall consider how the activity which became known as OR began and developed in the British armed forces in the period 1935–1945. There can be no argument that the term *operational research* was introduced in 1937 and that the specific activity to which it referred began sometime in 1936. It is, however, worthwhile to ask if there were any earlier activities which could be seen as being equivalent to OR. If there were, then we need to ask why these did not develop in the way that wartime OR did, and, if there were not, it is necessary to identify the particular conditions which existed between 1936 and 1945 to allow such a fruitful venture to emerge and develop.

In addressing these issues, the first step will be to outline the development of OR in the Second World War. This provides a reference point against which any earlier activities can be assessed. It is not possible to consider all such activities here, so three particularly important cases will be taken. Earliest is the work of Charles Babbage, who in the first half of the nineteenth century was responsible not only for innovative work in the development of the computer but also for the application of scientific methods to the operation of manufacturing concerns. Second is Frederick Taylor and the scientific management movement, which gained momentum in the United States in the first two decades of this century. Third, we consider the work carried out by the various research associations established since 1915 to aid British industry under the auspices of the government's Department of Scientific and Industrial Research.

## OR in the Second World War

### Bawdsey and the ORS Fighter Command

The story of radar and its relationship to the start of operational research has been told by various people for different reasons. The official record was laid down by the Air Ministry (1963). A detailed discussion of the work carried out in Coastal Command was given by Waddington (1973), and more personal recollections by, for example, Stansfield (1981, 1986) give a feel for the enthusiasm and commitment felt by those involved. Jones (1982), McCloskey and Trefethan (1954), Blackett (1962), and the obituaries of Williams and Larnder (Anon, 1980a; Stansfield, 1983) all add to the picture. Despite the different perspectives taken in the descriptions of the development of OR, there is little argument over the sequence of events which culminated in a number of operational research sections being in place in the armed forces of Britain, the U.S. and other allied nations at the end of the war in 1945. The first of these events was the decision taken by the British Air Ministry in 1935 to encourage the development of radar.

The early scientific work on the principles of the long-range propagation of radio waves which was applied to the detection of aircraft was carried out by R. A. Watson-Watt at the National Physical Laboratory in the early 1930s. In 1935 a committee of the Air Ministry under the chairmanship of H. T. (later Sir Henry) Tizard and including Professor A. V.

Hill, P. M. S. (later Lord) Blackett, and A. P. Rowe determined that this work should be actively supported in an attempt to upgrade Britain's defense against hostile aircraft (Air Ministry, 1963; Jones, 1982; Snow, 1961). Thus it was that in 1935 the development of radar as a military tool was begun at Orfordness. The work carried out in 1935 was successful, and further development was constrained only by the need to build larger aerial masts placed five to ten miles away from those already in place at Orfordness so that experiments with a chain of radar stations could be undertaken. A suitable site was found at Bawdsey, and Bawdsey Manor was purchased and subsequently further development took place in 1936. The potential of radar to both the army and the navy was recognized, and in 1936 representatives of all three arms were involved at Bawdsey.

The work at Bawdsey had shown that radar could work as an effective means of identifying the presence of aircraft at considerable distances from the receiving stations. The technical problems were therefore largely overcome, and radar as a military tool became feasible. The operational difficulties in its use remained, and in 1936 a team of RAF officers with Dr. B. G. Dickens as scientific officer was established at Biggin Hill to study how to use the radar equipment most effectively. This work continued at Bawdsey, and it was this group, headed by Larnder, that E. C. Williams joined in late 1937. Williams and Larnder were to go on to establish and lead OR groups for the duration of the war and afterwards. The work of the Bawdsey group was "to find out how best to use the radars in what we would now call the 'total system' for intercepting and destroying enemy aircraft" (Williams, 1968, p. 111). It was necessary to identify this group for administrative purposes, and so either or both of Watson-Watt and Rowe invented the label *operational research* for this purpose (Williams, 1968). The name arose from the need to distinguish Larnder's group from that of the more conventional research-and-development teams at Bawdsey. Their fundamental concern with operations rather than with equipment seemed to be the main distinguishing feature of the group, and hence the descriptive title of Operational Research Section (ORS) was a natural choice.

At Britain's entry into war in September 1939, two groups of the Bawdsey staff were transferred to Headquarters Fighter Command, Stanmore. One, headed by Williams, was initially responsible for aiding the command with the operation of the radar equipment and the interpretation of the information it gave. The second, headed by G. A. Roberts, was left in England when the remainder of the Bawdsey staff were evacuated to Dundee. Both groups were under the combined leadership of Larnder. This was the first formal attachment between civilian scientists and military personnel and set a pattern which was to be followed by other commands in the RAF and within the army and navy.

The successful work of the ORS Fighter Command in the first few months of the war was central to the development of OR in the following years. Had that group not been successful, it is questionable whether OR would have developed as rapidly as it did, if at all, and the subsequent postwar development would certainly not have been as dramatic. The early work was solely concerned with the investigation of the effective operation of the radar chain and the information it provided (Air Ministry, 1963, pp. 12–20).

Information on the location of enemy aircraft was gathered in two ways: by radar and by direct observation. The various radar stations which had been constructed reported to a filter room. Here the observations from several radar stations were plotted on a single diagram, and by finding the intersection of several sitings, the location of aircraft was found. As the information was never accurate because of the technology in use, a process of finding the most likely location was developed. This process was referred to as *plan position filtering*, hence the name of the room where it was carried out. The estimated locations were passed from the filter room to various operations rooms, at squadron, wing, and fighter command levels, for use in tactical, strategic, and coordination purposes. Direct observation was carried out from observer posts which reported to observer centers. These then fed information into the operations rooms to confirm radar-based expectations and to allow for any previously unobserved aircraft to be plotted.

The ORS was mainly concerned with the activity of the filter and operations rooms and the transmission of information between them. Work on the filter room had begun in 1937, and by 1939 significant experience in the use of the techniques had been gained. By investigating every case where enemy aircraft had failed to be observed, improvements in the plan-position filtering techniques were made. During the early months of the war the ORS was involved in continuous observation of the filter room at Stanmore. The development of filter room techniques was accompanied by improvements in the radar equipment itself, and although the difficulties of correctly estimating the location and size of aircraft formations were never completely removed, they were considerably reduced by the end of the war.

The ORS was able to influence policy on the staffing and organization of the radar system on a number of occasions. In 1940 they were asked to examine and report on its operations. At this time the enemy raids were at their peak and the system as it then stood was only just able to cope. The ORS provided a full report, which lead to changes in the organization of the radar stations and the establishment of further filter rooms to reduce the burden on that at Stanmore. The ORS had been involved with the education of those military personnel who were to staff the filter rooms since the first use of radar. In 1940 a recommendation was made that these staff should have certain qualities, and a series of selection tests were developed to help in the recruiting process, and a training school was created at Bawdsey.

As the war passed, the ORS expanded its activities to cover all those of Fighter Command. Various sections were formed within ORS. The first continued the original work on the coastal radar reporting system; a second devoted itself to night operations, particularly the coordination of searchlights with aircraft; a third section devoted itself to day operations; the procedures involved in operating ground radar equipment was the province of a fourth. A fifth section was concerned with the analysis of the movement of enemy aircraft, and a sixth section was attached to Number 60 (Signals) Group to monitor their performance. Conflict analysis and the analysis of armaments was the role of a seventh section, and, finally, the eighth section analyzed the effectiveness of day and night operations in order to assess the likely losses in operations and their implications for staffing (Air Ministry, 1963, pp. 11–12).

*Expansion into Other Areas*

The other two major commands of the RAF introduced ORSs after the success of that based in Fighter Command. That in Bomber Command was formally set up in 1941, although OR work had been undertaken since 1940, and that in Coastal Command also dated from 1941.

The main ORS work carried out in Bomber Command in 1941 was aimed at improving the success of night bombing raids. The ORS gathered information on raids from three sources: sortie raid reports, aerial photographs taken at the time of a raid, and reconnaissance photographs taken in daylight after the event. This information was assessed so that advice on tactics and improvements in operations could be made. A set of quantitative measures was devised so that comparisons could be made between raids. These were particularly useful in evaluating any new means of navigation and methods of undertaking bombing raids which were introduced (Air Ministry, 1963, pp. 47–68). In the later years of the war, ORS Bomber Command considered the cost effectiveness of bombing raids and investigated, with success, the effects of concentrating aircraft over target areas, the problems of collisions and other accidents, the loss or capture of air crew, and various other tactical issues.

ORS Coastal Command was established in 1941 with Professor P. M. S. Blackett as its director. Blackett had previously been involved in the organization of an ORS in 1940 to aid in the use of radar in connection with antiaircraft gunnery; this was to become known as Blackett's Circus. The major tasks of Coastal Command were the protection of convoys and the reduction of the mobility of enemy shipping by offensive operations against craft at sea and their home ports. This meant having to neutralize a main strength of the Germans, their U-boat fleet. Waddington (1943), who was involved with ORS Coastal Command for several years and was its director at the end of the war, has provided a thorough description of the work of this particular section.

The development of radar proceeded at such a rate that by 1940 it was possible to fit the equipment to aircraft and use it to detect enemy ships and submarines. This meant that one of the main weaknesses of the U-boat fleet, its need to spend significant periods of time on the surface, could be exploited. Radar made the likelihood of spotting U-boats, by day or night, much greater, provided it was used effectively. The earliest work of ORS Coastal Command was aimed at ensuring that the greatest benefit would be gained from the new equipment. A number of studies were carried out which investigated the effect on radar observations of various factors such as the height of the aircraft, the type of equipment used, and the fatigue of the operators. Each of these investigations was carried out by a rigorous analysis of data collected during sorties. Quantitative analysis was often used to provide measures of effectiveness which enabled meaningful interpretations of the information to be made.

When taking offensive actions against a U-boat, two problems occurred: the sighting of the craft needed to be efficient, and it was necessary that the aircraft remain unspotted by the enemy until attack was possible. In both cases analysis was able to provide useful advice. In the first case suggestions on flight patterns and heights were successful, and in the second the effectiveness of different types of camouflage was tested to yield significant improvements. Once the aircraft had observed the enemy and had remained unobserved sufficiently long to be able to attack, the remaining problem was the attack itself. Here the ORS was able to provide advice on how best to attack submarines by using depth charges. In particular, the depth of explosion and the distance between successive depth charges were found to affect the likelihood of the attack's success. Again, by analyzing data collected from air crew upon their return to base and developing appropriate measures of effectiveness, the best depth of explosion and distance between charges for differing circumstances could be provided.

*An Example of Wartime OR*

A feature which sets Waddington's description of the work of ORS Coastal Command apart from any other description of the OR work carried out in the Second World War is the detail with which the many and varied studies of that group are reported. It is useful here to summarize one of these studies in more detail than has been provided so far. The study chosen is the consideration of the best way to organize the flight schedules of Coastal Command within the available resources of aircraft and air and ground crews. This was begun in 1942 by a team headed by Dr. C. Gordon and is reported in Waddington (1973, pp. 41–57). Up to the time of this investigation, little knowledge was available on the relationship between hours flown, maintenance and repairs, and personnel and aircraft availability. It was recognized that there was some relationship and that improved efficiency might result from changes in the flight-planning and maintenance-scheduling routine. The ORS was asked to look at this issue, and their findings were eventually used throughout Coastal Command.

The first stage of the analysis was to examine theoretically the relationships between the relevant factors and to explore their impact on measures of performance. Abstract analysis had to be undertaken as insufficient relevant data were available to allow for the more usual quantitative analysis to be carried out. This analysis led to several insights of how the amount of flying time might be moved closer to its limit. These were then tested experimentally. The time span over which the analysis was carried out was a routine maintenance plan. This is the period of time between major inspections of an aircraft and includes within it seven minor inspections. The length of a routine maintenance plan was dictated by the number of hours which could be flown between major inspections. This time was set by the Air Ministry for each type of aircraft and in 1943 was between 320 and 360 hours and is represented by $q$.

The analysis began by calculating the relationship between two measures of performance: the intensity of flying, $I$, and the serviceability of an aircraft, $s$. It was assumed, initially, that an aircraft flew only one sortie per day and that an aircraft did not fly and undergo maintenance on the same day. Then the days in a routine maintenance plan can be broken into four groups. $F$ days will be spent flying sorties; this value is dependent upon the number of flying hours between major inspections and the length of a sortie. $D$ days occur when the aircraft is able to fly but does not, because of poor weather conditions or other reasons. An aircraft is actively maintained on $M$ days and so cannot fly on these. It also cannot fly on $S$ days if maintenance is impossible, either because there is insufficient ground crew or because they are awaiting delivery of spares.

The first measure of performance is the intensity of flying, $I$, and this is defined to be the average number of hours flown per day in a routine maintenance plan. Thus,

$$I = q/(F + M + S + D)$$

The second measure of performance is the serviceability, $s$, which is the proportion of the days on which an aircraft could fly in a routine maintenance plan. Thus,

$$s = (F + D)(/(F + M + S + D)$$

It is not difficult to show that the two measures are related,

$$I = q(1 - s)/(M + S)$$

and that therefore any attempt to change one will affect the other and that, assuming $q$, $M$, and $S$ are reasonably fixed, changes will be in opposite directions. Hence, any efforts to improve one measure of performance would result in a decrease in the other. Policy decisions therefore had to be made with this point in mind, and care had to be exercised to ensure that the full implications of any changes would be understood.

A maximum figure for the intensity occurred when no days were lost when flights could take place and did not ($D = 0$). By using realistic figures, it was possible to gain approximate values for $I$ and $s$ under such ideal conditions. If the amount of flying time between major inspections ($q$) was 360 hours, if 60 days were spent on maintenance ($M$), if 20 days were spent waiting for spares, etc. ($S$), and if 10 hour sorties were made so that 36 flying days ($F$) were necessary, then $I = 3.1$ hours per day and $s = 31.1\%$. If 5 hour sorties were made, then $I = 2.4$ hours per day and $s = 52.6\%$. Changes in the value of $D$, reflecting strategic issues on how to arrange flights and/or weather conditions, would affect the value of $I$ and $s$, and the effects of these could be evaluated in a similar fashion to the example above.

Thus the analysis shows that operational decisions affected significantly the measures of performance. Air Ministry decisions had previously been made in line with the expectation that serviceability should be about 70%–75% for a squadron operating efficiently. What this work showed was that such an expectation was clearly incorrect. Operational decisions influenced the levels of intensity and serviceability which should be achieved, and these varied between squadrons and, for a given squadron, depended upon its operating schedule. This conclusion meant that the problem of flight and maintenance planning was not to see each squadron operating with serviceability of 70%–75% but to establish the appropriate values of $I$ and $s$ and then to design flight and maintenance schedules to meet these targets.

In order to test this approach, a squadron was planned for over a six-month period by the ORS. Central to this plan was the concept of idle resources. The two constraints acting upon the squadron's operations were the amount of flying time set down by the Air Ministry and the time necessary for maintenance to be carried out. This meant that while, in theory, flights and maintenance schedules could be drawn up, which meant that all resources were being used most effectively, in practice this was never the case. It was always found that some aircraft would not be scheduled to fly when they were able to, or that some maintenance crew were idle as no aircraft were available to work upon. Despite having idle resources, the schedules which were put into operation resulted in a remarkable increase in flying effort. The flying effort per aircraft was 61% higher than the previous best for the squadron and 70% better than that of any other squadron over the period of the experiment. The approach was adopted for use in Coastal Command, and further work in the area resulted in further improvements.

*Further Expansion*

Operational Research, therefore, became an important element in the various parts of the RAF. It also became a valuable tool in the army and navy. Reference has already been made to the presence of army and navy staff at Bawdsey in 1936. The army took on the use of radar to aid antiaircraft gunnery, and Blackett's Circus, although formally under RAF Fighter Command direction, worked closely with army personnel. In 1942 the Army Operational Research Group came into being, and ORSs were subsequently established in various parts of the army. Blackett was appointed Director of Naval Operational Research in January 1942, and his group continued the work on anti-U-boat operations which Blackett had begun at ORS Coastal Command. Whereas the ORS in the RAF and army were in close contact with operational commands, often being attached to them, those in the Admiralty were less closely related and focused their efforts mainly on London-based activities (Air Ministry, 1963, p. 41).

The success of the ORS in the British military lead to their introduction in the allied forces. The U.S. Army Air Force had operational analysis sections associated with several of its commands. One of the earliest seems to be that of the Eighth Air Force, which was created in May 1942

(Air Ministry, 1963, p. 46). These sections worked closely with their British counterparts, as did the two American naval groups devoted to antisubmarine and mine warfare (Air Ministry, 1963, p. 185). The Royal Canadian Air Force introduced an ORS in August 1942 devoted to a range of issues covering radar, scheduling, and staffing (Air Ministry, 1963, p. 183).

By the final years of the war, operational research found itself being used in almost all areas of the military. As defense turned into offense, the character of the work carried out began to include ways of best attacking enemy positions and measuring success. The movements of the Allied forces out of Britain and into North Africa and the Mediterranean basin, Europe, the Indian subcontinent, and the Far East was accompanied by teams drawn from ORSs. This expansion both geographically and in areas of work created a demand for those people qualified to carry out OR work. Many individuals who were involved with OR from the early days of the war were used to head the new units, and they were supported by a steady flow of scientists into their sections. The result of this process of expansion was a dilution of the pool of experienced and well-qualified people among the different sections whereas a strength of the early ORS at Bawdsey was the concentration of qualified and experienced people. Many had research experience, although they were not academics, and this enabled the problems faced at that time to be assessed and the work to be carried out more efficiently than if the people had been less experienced. By the end of the war the close relationship between this group and the actual OR projects had lessened as the increase in the number of people involved meant that a greater degree of bureaucracy was necessary, and the experienced OR personnel moved into more managerial roles.

One person who noted the implication of this situation was Zuckerman. Working with J. D. Bernal, Zuckerman had spent the early years of the war investigating the effects of bomb damage on the human body. This work was carried out from the Research and Experiments Department of the Ministry of Home Security. Their work made important contributions to the decisions on bombing strategy when the British began to attack Germany in 1942 and also in the planning of operations in the Mediterranean and North Africa. While in North Africa assessing the damage achieved during attacks, Zuckerman first met army and RAF ORSs and was able to advise them on weapon effectiveness (Air Ministry, 1963, pp. 118, 122–125). He notes that he felt that these OR scientists were largely inexperienced in research and often tied to specific duties (Zuckerman, 1978, p. 162).

Despite these shortcomings, due entirely to the success of OR, it is impossible to overstate the importance of the various ORSs to the war effort. Without the early contributions to the use of radar, the German offensive in 1939–1940 may have proved successful, and in the later years the work of the ORSs was clearly important in the Allied forces' victory.

*Some Observations*

Some characteristics of the work of the ORSs in the Second World War can be identified by viewing that work as a process of increasing understanding. Characteristics of that process refer to the methods of gaining understanding used in the process, the subject of the process to which the methods will be applied, and the beneficiaries of the process who will gain from its existence.

First, the members of the ORSs relied to a great extent upon observation and quantitative data and on the logical analysis of the information these gave them. When data were unavailable, they would often collect them for themselves, and emphasis was laid upon the importance of accurate and meaningful data. In the early investigations, the level of analysis undertaken was low, partly because the urgency and novelty of the situation did not allow time to be wasted upon elegant but relatively unimportant abstract work. As experience was gained, urgency was reduced and more staff became available in the various ORSs, more rigorous analysis could be carried out. The methods used were soundly based in scientific method; observation and analysis were central to the process. Experiments were developed and carried out to test and support the conclusions of the analysis, although these were, of necessity, carried out in the field and not in the laboratory.

Second, the methods of observing and analyzing phenomena were applied and were used in predicting and controlling the use of existing resources rather than in the design and construction of novel resources. This distinction underpins that made at Bawdsey in 1937, when "operational research" was first used. Scientists were involved with the military in the design and construction of radar, navigational aids, aircraft, and other vehicles and weapons. They were acting as research-and-development personnel in a technological rather than an operational sense. The OR scientists were concerned with how to improve the effectiveness with which these new resources could be used and were therefore involved with a different set of issues from those addressed by the technologists.

Third, the beneficiaries of the analyses carried out by the ORSs were those people who decided how resources should be used. In the military, these people were the officers with responsibility for that part of the armed forces where the resources were based. Thus, although the ORSs worked closely with the operational staff, they reported their findings to the decision makers at a higher level of authority. Action was then initiated as appropriate by this higher command. The ORSs therefore serviced decision makers and the holders of authority and provided advice upon how those people could improve the effectiveness of the system under their command.

Thus there is a benchmark against which work carried out before 1937 and similar to OR can be assessed. It is now possible to examine some important examples of this work in order to place wartime OR in a historical context.

## Charles Babbage and Management in the Industrial Revolution

### Biographical Note

The Industrial Revolution, which took place in Britain in the late eighteenth and early nineteenth centuries, provided the impetus for many ideas which were to transform the character of the Western world and influence global development significantly. Major breakthroughs in the natural sciences gave rise to new products and the design of machinery to manufacture them. The processes of urbanization and industrialization changed the geographic, social, and economic structure of the British and European nations. Institutions set up to serve the needs of many groups, the creation of trade unions, employer's federations, and places of learning, for example, were all fueled by the dynamism of the period. Early in the Industrial Revolution was born one of the men whose contribution to that period has been lasting in its impact: Charles Babbage.

Babbage is mainly remembered for his work in developing the fundamental notions of computers. His designs for the analytic and difference engines embody many concepts central to the first electronic computers built in the 1940s (Morrison and Morrison, 1961). Babbage was also a mathematician of note and made several important contributions to the theory of calculus (Dubbey, 1978). A third strand of work which he developed was a focus upon the use of machines and the associated issues of mass production. It is this third part of his life which will be of major concern here, but to understand his motivation and attitude toward "the machinery question" (Berg, 1980), it is necessary to place this in the broader context of Babbage's life and of other developments in the management of factories and other concerns.

Charles Babbage was born to wealthy parents (his father was a banker and merchant) in Walworth, London, on December 26, 1791 (Hyman, 1982, p. 11). Apart from a period at a school near Exeter, he spent his early childhood in London. Later he was educated near Cambridge and at Totnes Grammar School before going up to Trinity College, Cambridge. While there, Babbage became close friends with a group who shared his commitment to mathematical analysis and who were also radical liberals. The group contained several men who were to become prominent scientists, John Herschel, the astronomer, and George Peacock, the mathematician, in particular. It was these years at Cambridge which were to lay the pattern for the remainder of Babbage's life, a belief in the scientific and mathematical method, and a strong reformist attitude which manifested itself in various ways.

Babbage married in 1814 and spent some time prior to his marriage and subsequently working on functional equations, and it was during this period that he did most of his mathematical work. In 1816 he was elected to the Royal Society and three years later took a trip to France with Herschel with the intention of meeting members of the French scientific establishment, such as Laplace, Fourier, and Berthollet. Hyman (1982, p. 43) suggests that it was on this visit that Babbage first came across the set of numerical tables constructed by de Prony. In the following few years Babbage began to concentrate upon the development of a machine to calculate tables. His first publications on this topic appeared in 1822, and although mathematics did not disappear totally from his work, the main thrust of his publications over the next fifteen year was the design and construction of the engines developed for this purpose.

Wealth and social position allowed Babbage to travel widely. His trips were often combined with visits to factories, in order to examine different machines and processes, and to other scientists, in order to exchange ideas. His travels took him throughout England and he revisited Paris in 1826. After his wife's death in 1827 he traveled through Europe. The European attitude toward science and scientists was very different from that in England. The prestige given to scientists and the importance given to the practical use of scientific ideas in Europe were not reflected in England. Babbage recognized that the European attitude was more likely to result in the development of the sciences and their use for practical ends. He returned to England in late 1828 determined to continue his work on the calculating machines and to strive for the reform of the scientific institutions of Great Britain.

Babbage was supported in his reformist ideals by many of his colleagues from Cambridge, and his efforts resulted in the publication in 1830 of his *Reflections on the Decline of Science in England, and Some of Its*

*Causes*. In this book the affairs of the Royal Society were attacked, and the controversy created threw the British scientific establishment into confusion. Babbage's support weakened as the main personalities went their separate ways, and eventually the bid to have Herschel elected as president of the Royal Society failed. The result was a failure to persuade the main scientific institution in Britain to alter its attitude toward science and to improve its relationship with industry and commerce. In 1831 David Brewster proposed that an alternative organization be formed: the British Association for the Advancement of Science. The direction to be followed was the bringing together of science and technology at a practical level and the fostering of relationships between science, industry, and commerce. The first meeting was held in 1831, and although Babbage could not attend, he was appointed a trustee (Hyman, 1982, p. 150). The strength of the British Association lay in the flourishing mechanics institutes. These were local societies, mainly in the new industrial towns and cities of the Midlands and the North, whose function was to provide a means of improvement for the emerging artisan class. Funded by middle-class reformers, this movement was important in diffusing and encouraging the skills and ideas necessary to develop industry (Berg, 1980, pp. 145–178).

## On the Economy of Machines and Manufactures

Work on the first calculating machine, the difference engine, proceeded at the same time as Babbage was attempting to reform British scientific institutions. In order that he might be as well acquainted as possible with the techniques necessary to construct the device, Babbage undertook a series of visits in England and Scotland to inspect factories. The information gathered, together with his concern with applying science to the practical, led Babbage to approach his visits with an attitude unique at the time. His reflections on these visits and their implications for the running of factories and the analysis of their business were published in 1832 under the title *On the Economy of Machinery and Manufactures*. It is this book which is of main concern to us here, for in it Babbage applied a scientific method based upon observation and quantification to the problems of organizing efficiently the operations of a factory aimed at mass production.

The book consists of two sections. The first accounts for one-third of the total and contains a discussion of the advantages to be gained from the use of machinery with many illustrative examples. These benefits fall into three main classes: the addition to power beyond that normally capable of being generated by humans, the savings in time gained by the speed at which machines can work, and the potential to convert materials to finished products in novel ways. The final chapter of this first section contains some notes upon how manufactories, as Babbage called them, should be observed. It is suggested that all information should be written down as soon as possible, and a *pro forma* is provided which contains general statements into which information specific to the case in point can be entered. This acts as an *aide-mémoire* and covers areas such as history, production methods, market conditions, and financial and sales data. Each process involved in production is taken separately, and Babbage requires information to be gathered on the number of people involved, the hours worked, the levels of skill needed, and the rate of production. Some difficulties in making observations are noted. For example, when measuring the productivity of a pin-making process,

> if the observer stands with his watch in his hand before a person heading a pin, the workman will almost certainly increase his speed, and the estimate will be too large. A much better average will result by inquiring what quantity is considered a fair day's work. When this cannot be ascertained, the number of operations performed in a given time may frequently be ascertained when the workman is quite unconscious that any person is observing him. (Babbage, 1832, p. 96)

In the final two-thirds of the book Babbage derives some more general implications of the observations he had made and discusses the political economy of the subject. During the course of a broad discussion, several issues and methods are considered which are still of current concern.

One topic of discussion is the relationship between supply and demand and how this affects the decision of how much to produce at what price. The point is made here that

> The importance of collecting data, for the purpose of enabling the manufacturer to ascertain how many additional customers he will acquire by a given reduction in the price of the article he makes, cannot be too strongly pressed upon the attention of those who employ themselves in statistical inquiries. (pp. 98–99)

This discussion is not naive; notice is taken of the need for perfect competition if the analysis is to be valid, and the effects of the durability of the good and of labor and material costs on price are explored.

Later Babbage considers the use of the concept of division of labor in some detail. Following Adam Smith, who introduced the concept in *The Wealth of Nations* in 1776, pin making is taken as an example. The various tasks involved in pin making are compared between the contemporary (1830s) British method and the French method used in 1760. The latter, not guided by the division-of-labor principle, is shown to be three and three-quarters times as costly as the former, which based on the division-of-labor principle. This is an excellent example of Babbage's ability to apply sound scientific principles to practical issues. The costing of the activities is carried out in a rigorous way which leaves no room for doubting the comparison of costs which he proposes.

Babbage also suggests an extension to the theory of the division of labor. The usual benefits of this way of organizing production, so that a whole production process is broken down into its component parts and each is then carried out by a group of workers devoted to that task, were taken to derive from four features. First, the time taken to learn the job was reduced because each worker needed to be able to perform only one task rather than several tasks. Second, time was saved as individuals did not need to readjust their mental and physical capacities to a series of different functions. Third, the specialization involved resulted in the acquisition of one skill to a greater extent than if a worker were required to perform several tasks, and consequently the whole process was better performed. Finally, by breaking the process into its constituent parts, it became possible to use machinery and tools where possible, which gave improvements in the efficiency and quality of the work. To these Babbage added the observation that the division of labor allowed an analysis of the skills and force necessary for each part to be made. Thus the employer could purchase only as many of these resources as necessary and no more. This observation was not original for, as Babbage (1832) notes, Gioja had made a similar point in 1815 (p. 138). However, it is indicative of the approach Babbage brought to the problem, for it shows how a theoretical concept could be directed toward important practical ends and, in so doing, was reliant upon precise observation and measurement.

These technical discussions of the detail of production processes are followed later in Babbage's book by a consideration of broader issues, including the implications for the management of large factories. It is suggested that before commencing to manufacture any article, information should be gathered on the costs of establishing the concern and the likely demand for the product. The question of when to use machinery is addressed by considering when machinery has advantages over human activity. Four categories are identified where this is the case: when mass production is required so that economies of scale can be taken advantage of; when accuracy and similarity between parts is important; when speed is vital in production, for example, in the production of newspapers; and finally, when conditions are such that humans cannot operate, for example, under water. As an aside, it is worth noting that it is in this context that Babbage refers to the use of machines to transport letters, which has lead to the suggestion that he, and not Rowland Hill, was the instigator of the penny post and that the analysis involved in this idea was another early example of operational research. I. D. Hill (1973) considers this situation and concludes that "Hill did his own operational research, produced his own plans in his own way, and that Babbage was in no way involved." Rowland Hill himself wrote in his autobiography (Hill and Hill, 1880, p. 243) that he first began to consider the details of the penny-post system in 1836, four years after Babbage's more speculative notions had been published, but he did not mention any knowledge of Babbage's work.

Returning to Babbage's consideration of the use and effective management of machinery for production purposes, the next issue to be tackled is the economic life of a machine. By analyzing the costs involved it is shown that in certain cases it is more efficient to sell a machine before it wears out and to replace it with one of newer design than to retain a machine of older style until it is unable to function. The final topic to be taken up in this general area is the observation that there exist within groups of workers rules and laws governing their behavior relative to each other and their supervisors. This observation has implications for the payment of workers and the introduction of machinery which are noted but are not addressed in any great detail.

In the final chapter Babbage discusses the future of manufacturing and science. The argument developed here is that centered upon the role of the scientific establishment in the growth of British industry. Babbage's belief in the British Association as the vehicle to bring together the scientist and the manufacturer is reaffirmed, the main benefit being the introduction of new products and materials and the design of new machinery and power sources to aid in their manufacture. The *Economy of Manufactures* had shown how operations could be investigated in a rigorous analytic fashion. Babbage was to continue to show an interest in the ideas he had developed for several years and in particular in his analysis of the Great Western Railway. The company began to construct the line from London to Bristol in 1835, and the first passengers were carried between Paddington and Maidenhead on June 4, 1839 (MacDermot, 1964, pp. 31–32). The engineer for the railway was Isambard Kingdom Brunel, and the gauge adopted for the route was 7'0", in contrast with that used by all other companies of 4'8½". The first passengers complained that the ride on the wide-gauge track was uncomfortable, and considerable pressure was brought to bear on the directors for the conventional gauge to be adopted. At a meeting on August 1, 1838, two investigators were authorized to consider the situation and report to the shareholders in October.

It was at this meeting that Babbage first appears on the scene. He had spent some time previous to this traveling on various railways and collecting data on the degree of vibration. This travel had been prompted by the fact that many of those attending the British Association meeting in Newcastle that year had traveled by sea because of the perceived discomfort associated with rail travel. At the October meeting, Babbage, as a shareholder, made a defense of Brunel, arguing that the comfort offered on the wide-gauge came, according to his figures, second of all the British railways. Further, the speed of the trains on that line was between two and three times that of other companies.

The final decision was delayed until December and, ultimately, the following January, as one of the independent investigators had not completed his work. Babbage took the opportunity to undertake further detailed studies and between October 1838 and March 1839 carried out a series of experiments. Equipment was designed to record the movement of various parts of a carriage while in motion. As in the structure of a seismograph, long rolls of paper were driven under a series of pens recording vibrations in three dimensions at the ends and center of the carriage. Supplemented by data on speed and force, this recording enabled a complete and permanent description of the carriage's movement to be kept and compared over different routes. At the January meeting, although his experiments were incomplete, Babbage was able to present a convincing argument in favor of the wide gauge, and Brunel was able to continue to build the line in that manner (Hyman, 1982, pp. 155–163).

## Babbage's Contribution

Babbage continued to work on his calculating machines for the remainder of his life. His continued efforts to bring science and industry together did not come to any meaningful end, and at the time of his death in 1871, the results of the British institutions' failure to act were beginning to be seen. The emerging industrial powers of the United States, Germany, and other European nations that had encouraged the coming together of science and industry were beginning to move ahead (see, for example, Armytage, 1976, pp. 230–250).

The above discussion of Babbage's work paints a picture of a man who was committed to his belief in applying the methods of scientific analysis to practical issues. His contribution, as far as the present purpose is concerned, falls within two streams of work. His uniqueness lies not so much in his work in each of these areas as in the bringing together of economic theory and the management of organizations.

As early as 1884 Toynbee recognized that the period between 1776 and 1848 had seen the birth of economic science (Toynbee, 1927, pp. 64–65). In 1776 Adam Smith's *Wealth of Nations* was published, and the consequent development of a rigorous theory of monetary value, its distribution, and its use as a resource set the basis for classical economics (Barber, 1977; Bell, 1967). The works of Malthus (*Essay on Population,* 1798) and Ricardo (*Principles of Political Economy and Taxation,* 1817) were landmarks in a period which concluded with John Stuart Mill's *Principles of Political Economy,* which appeared in 1848. The problems which focused the attention of these and other economists in this period were related to the contemporary processes of industrialization and urbanization. Changes in the ownership of wealth, and therefore power, and a redistribution of population from the rural to the urban areas caused a significant restructuring of British society, and the new science of economics sought to offer a rational analysis of the difficulties this posed. Berg (1980, pp. 2–3) particularly associates the growth of political economy with the machinery question and argues that the development of the new science, the emergence of a particular class structure, and the creation of manufacturing organizations dependent upon new technology were mutually supportive. The contributions of economics to the understanding of how industrial society and its component parts function provides one stream of work into which Babbage's work should be placed.

The second stream which needs to be considered is the emergence of a new profession, industrial management, and the ideas which were used by those individuals within it. Pollard (1968) gives a thorough discussion of this phenomenon and shows that it was first discernible in the late eighteenth century. The need for a specialized management function arose with the growth in the scale of the organizations involved in production. The availability of machines and mass production methods which entered into use in the second half of the eighteenth century fostered the creation of a managerial profession distinct from those who owned factories and the craftspeople and laborers who worked in them.

The new profession began to develop methods of working which were tailored to its members' needs. One recognized example was the systematic methods for organizing and administering the manufacturing operations of the Soho Foundry, Birmingham, built by Boulton and Watt in 1795. Constructed on a green-field site, the factory was designed to enable specific processes to be carried out within it, and its operations were controlled by the use of costing methods, production planning, and standardized components. The mix of skills used by the workforce was guided by applying the division-of-labor concept (Pollard, 1968, p. 98). A second example is provided by Benjamin Gott, whose woollen mill at Leeds was one of the largest and most mechanized of the time. Gott used a method by which managers regularly checked on work and the mill was organized around eleven departments, each of which was examined in turn (Pollard, 1968, p. 115). It is clear that the use of systematic methods was essential if the organizations of the Industrial Revolution were to be operated effectively. Babbage was to provide one contribution to the development of these methods, and hence he needs to be considered a part of this stream of work also.

Although Babbage is not now remembered as an economist, during the years following the publication of *Economy of Machines and Manufactures* his work was thought important. John Stuart Mill, while attacking certain of Babbage's claims, did recognize the importance of his use of the principle of the division of labor. The use of this concept to classify individuals according to their abilities and so open the way to a means of evaluating their contribution to a production process was seen by Mill to be of particular benefit (Berg, 1980, p. 331; Hollander, 1985, p. 204). Romano (1982) refers to the neglect of Babbage's contribution to economics and seeks to correct this by showing his position relative to the development of economic thought. Marx is also known to have been influenced by Babbage's work. He made a study of *Economy of Machines and Manufactures* in the period 1845–1846, and this informed his work of that period (Howard and King, 1985, p. 127; Oakley, 1984, pp. 13, 73). Rattensi (1982) remarks that Marx built on Babbage's analysis, which is significant in the way in which it made the concept of the division of labor appropriate to a social order "in which the patterns and rhythms of industrial labour are decisively structured by the requirements of capital accumulation" (p. 45).

Babbage was therefore recognized by the economists of his day as making important moves toward the application of economic theory. This view is compatible with Babbage's wider attitude in seeking to improve practice, as has already been seen. It is also worth noting that the economics of the classical period was perceived to imply a rational scientific approach to analysis. This was a method to which Babbage was naturally drawn, and he would not have found it inconsistent with his earlier work to apply economic theory to his studies of manufacturing.

Babbage's contribution to management thought is more difficult to evaluate. The reason is the lack of a developing body of theory into which his ideas may be placed. Unlike economics, management in the nineteenth century was dominated by the practical aspects of the profession. Babbage was one of several individuals who addressed in general terms the problems faced by managers in controlling the operations of factories. Boulton and Watt and Gott have been noted above as examples of such people, and Pollard (1968) gives many more. In the development of management theory, the period of Babbage's work was very much one of laying the foundations upon which theory could be later built.

Pollard (1968, pp. 296–301) suggests that a set of interrelated causes explains the failure of management theory, rather than its profession, to appear at this time. The emergence of a body of theory and the further development of those methods used in the Industrial Revolution were held back in three ways. First, although there was an emergent managerial profession and an understanding of its functions in an organization, it was difficult to differentiate clearly between this and other related activities, such as the technical and commercial functions. It was to take more time for significant differences to appear and so make management a distinctive profession and warrant specialized study and theoretical development. Second, the culture of the Industrial Revolution emphasized the characteristics of individual owners and their factories to the detriment of a concern with identifying the problems common to a number of organizations. Thus the pressure was to concentrate upon specific cases rather than to attempt to provide general assessments. Finally, the problem of how to treat labor was not yet clear. Two approaches were emerging: one in which labor was to be seen as a resource no different from any other and a second in which a more humane attitude was adopted. However, there was no clear view on how to deal with issues of labor management, which was a fundamental part of the managerial function.

Babbage, therefore, made important contributions to the development of economic theory and to the beginning of management theory. In both cases he was keen to show how theory could be applied to aid practice and based his analysis on empirical findings. Against this background it is now possible to assess how close Babbage's work came to that of the ORSs in the Second World War. First, Babbage shared the emphasis upon observation and quantitative data which characterized the wartime OR work. It has been seen that his commitment to the empirical methods of science was strong and influenced many aspects of his work. Second, he was concerned to show how the understanding gained by observation and measurement could be used to improve the efficiency of methods of production. He was not concerned, in his work on manufacturing, with producing novel methods of production or new products. He thus shared the ORSs' concern with the use of existing resources rather than with the design of new resources. Third, Babbage differed from the ORSs in that he was not producing his analyses to be used by decision makers. His goal, in the first instance, was to understand the processes that were being used and to investigate how they could be achieved more efficiently. This is a different motivation for working from that shown by the wartime ORSs. Babbage's work was of use to managers and decision makers in factories, but this was a secondary concern to him and thus sets his work apart from that of wartime OR.

The reasons for Babbage's work failing to develop into a form of OR lie in the reasons for management theory failing to develop. As Pollard notes, there was a set of forces which retarded management theory in Britain, and these at the same prevented the potential of Babbage's work from being realized. It is not a big step to see the development of a body of knowledge, methods, and techniques which could have followed from Babbage's work as being similar to OR. Instead, the potential was not realized, and it was not until the start of the twentieth century in the U.S. that the conditions for the development of such an initiative were such as to release much of the latent power of Babbage's ideas.

## Frederick Taylor and Scientific Management in the U.S.

### The Background of Scientific Management

The Industrial Revolution gave Britain a lead in global economic and imperial power. The trade made possible by the use of machinery to aid mass production drove the British economy to a dominant position by the 1850s. The second half of the nineteenth century saw the pattern begin to change. In the U.S. and in mainland Europe, the social and economic conditions which prevailed allowed several countries to move closer to Britain and, ultimately, to become stronger in terms of economic and political influence. In the U.S. the Civil War acted as a catalyst resulting in a rapid growth in ideas and in expansion of the geographic and economic boundaries of the nation. In Germany a series of educational establishments were producing a stream of people able to combine engineering skills with business understanding (Armytage, 1976, pp. 168–194).

It was in the U.S., however, that the growth was most rapid and large scale. Habakkuk (1962, pp. 215–220) has argued that several factors combined to allow the U.S. to expand much more rapidly than Britain in the forty years prior to 1914. In particular, three can be identified which show the relative position of the U.S. and Britain at that time. First, the rigidity of the class system and the status historically attached to the professions and ownership of land in Britain made it difficult for the majority of people to gain acceptance by those able to invest capital in new enterprises. In the U.S. these barriers to the creation of new enterprises did not exist, and the entrepreneurial attitude was strongly supported. Second, British expansion in the first half of the nineteenth century had slowed to a more steady rate, and economic growth was slower than in the U.S. Thus it was more difficult to develop new products, establish new companies, and implement new ideas. The expanding market of the U.S. made it easier to undertake these activities within an atmosphere of optimism and confidence. Third, the relatively high labor costs in the U.S. encouraged any moves to increase the use of machinery or reduce the costs of production. Consequently a continual stream of ideas was being proposed to improve the processes of production, and innovations were continually being made. In Britain this stimulus for creativity was not as strong and did not motivate the engineers and managers to the same extent.

In 1856, into the increasingly confident, expanding, and innovative U.S., was born Frederick Winslow Taylor. Taylor's life has been described by many authors, for example, Pugh, Hickson, and Hinings (1984), Urwick and Brech (1949a), and Person (1964). As with Babbage it is important to relate certain aspects of his background here also so that the origins and spirit of his work can be appreciated and an assessment of its relation to OR can be made in the light of this understanding.

Taylor originally intended to study for a career in law, but impaired eyesight and subsequent medical advice meant that this course could not be followed. He decided instead to take an apprenticeship as a pattern maker and machinist. When he had served his apprenticeship in 1878, a short-term depression in the industry made it difficult for him to obtain employment as a skilled worker, and he joined the Midvale Steel Company as a laborer. Taylor's career progressed rapidly, and by the time he left the company in 1890, he was chief engineer. He later worked for the Bethlehem Steel Company between 1898 and 1901 but spent most of the rest of his life working as a consultant for many different companies. His work centered upon a consistent theme, which was to establish a system of management for a machine shop which gave "each workman each day in advance a definite task, with detailed written instructions, and an exact time allowance for each element of the work" and which allowed payment of "extraordinarily high wages to those who perform their tasks in the allotted time, and ordinary wages to those who take more than their time allowance" (Taylor, 1906, p. 242). The method which emerged from this lifetime study is referred to as *scientific management* or the *Taylor system*. The specific objective of the method was "to secure the maximum prosperity for each employee" (Taylor, 1911, p. 119).

The incentive behind Taylor's wish to develop an ordered way of establishing working procedures was his experience as a laborer, machinist, and later supervisor at Midvale. As a member of the workforce he had no option but to work at the rate which was determined by his colleagues. He recognized that this was considerably less than he and others were capable of, and upon his promotion to supervisor, he determined to increase productivity. In so doing he directly confronted the common understanding that the work of craftspeople was guided by custom under their own and not managerial control. Taylor's use of coercive measures eventually led to his desired increase in productivity, but he felt that a better method must be possible.

The approach to organizing working methods which Taylor perfected involved the reduction of each process to its fundamental parts and then observation and analysis of how each of these was accomplished and related to other parts of the process. This approach led to an understanding of how each particular production process operated and allowed improvements to be made in the whole by improving, as far as possible, the component parts. Considerable experiments were made in order to establish the levels of improvement which could result. Eventually planning and production control systems based on this method were introduced in many factories, several of which are described in Thompson (1922).

*Two Examples*

An early example is the introduction of a piece rate system for the machining of steel tires for locomotive and carriage wheels. This work was carried out by Taylor for the Midvale company, and the system was introduced in 1893 and was described by Taylor (1911, pp. 83–85). The original means of organizing the machining process was a piecework system in which a fixed price was paid to a worker for completion of all of the work that could be done with a single machine setting. This had the advantages of leading to an easy method of fixing the rate for a job while not requiring detailed records to be kept of costs and the progress of work. The disadvantage was that the length of time taken to complete each piece depended upon the hardness of the metal, the size of the tire, and the amount of metal to be removed and so was not constant, as was implied by the fixed price being paid for the work. Taylor recognized this disadvantage and sought to remove it by undertaking a detailed study of the process. The single job was broken down into twenty-two individual tasks. For each task a proper time and price were evaluated dependent upon the nature of the task and the particular piece of metal. For each piece or group of similar pieces, workers were furnished with a card which told them the sizes to be cut, the type of tools to use, and the time and rate for the job. This procedure not only allowed for the variation in pieces but also allowed individual workers to assess their own performance against that expected of them. Taylor noted that this system operated for over twenty years at Midvale and its introduction led to an increase in output of at least 33%.

The calculation of time needed for a given job and the decision over which was the best method of machining a given piece were not straightforward. The early work Taylor did on these questions was mainly informed by observation and measurement. The data which were collected showed that twelve factors affected the decision about what speed to run a machine and what feed should be used for the operation (Taylor, 1911, pp. 107–108; 1906, pp. 243–244). This set of relationships was expressed as a set of equations which were rigorously solved by the use of slide rules by Barth (1922), who joined Taylor in 1899.

The implications of Taylor's approach were not restricted to the immediate management of production processes, for they also influenced the information-processing aspects of any company in which they were used. If the methods were to be as effective as possible, it was sometimes necessary to consider the organization of the planning process of the company concerned and if necessary changes were also made here. A second example of Taylor's work, described by Sterling (1922), brings out the broader implications of his method and shows how the system and the corresponding costing exercise in a manufacturing company work from the receipt of an order to its being shipped.

The basic structure of the plant in which this example is located took the form of a conventional hierarchy. A superintendent had executive responsibilities over a planning department, three shops, and two specialized service functions, one concerned with the setting of rates and the other with repairs and maintenance. The planning department was the hub of the operations as it was here that coordination of activities and decision making concerning production occurred.

The various items which were produced in the shops were classified by four types of order: those which required new designs or types of work; those which were regular and for standardized articles; those for silent gears and chain, which were a speciality of the plant; and those which were for standard items to go into store for labor use. Each type of order followed similar procedures, and so only one, in which new designs or work was required, is considered in detail. When an order of this type was received in the contract department, it was first of all passed to the drafting room, where all drawings necessary for its production were made and estimates of material costs were produced. The drawings were passed to the planning department for future use, and the bills of materials were given to the purchasing department, where orders were placed as appropriate. After the orders had been placed, the planning department received the bill of materials, and detailed instructions for production were drawn up on a route sheet. This identified the sequence of the operations which were to be carried out and for each operation defined a rate for that part of the job. Time cards were made for each separate operation, and when production could commence, these were posted, together with instructions for that job, on a board. These were issued to workers in order to initiate the work involved. Upon completion of a day, the cards were sent to the cost department for the calculation of earnings, information on which was given to each individual on the following day.

The set of procedures for planning and controlling the production process was supported by a set of procedures for monitoring levels of stock and for analyzing the cost of an operation. To aid both procedures, a sophisticated method of recording flows of material was established. Stock control was carried out by recording the individual changes of stock level, and when a minimum level was reached a requisition for additional stock was made. The cost department continually monitored information on material usage and costs and related these to wage levels. This department was also responsible for setting selling prices and monitoring expenditure.

It is clear from this example that scientific management was concerned not only with the establishment of a means of analyzing the production process but also with the creation of a management system which supported and was compatible with it. The Taylor system, in its completeness, was concerned with altering the environment in which both management and workers operated. This aim is compatible with Taylor's understanding of the contemporary situation in manufacturing concerns, where he saw both the management process and the production process being guided by intuitive rather than rational and informed methods and both being in need of improvement.

*The Scientific Management Movement*

Taylor attracted to him a series of associates who were to contribute to and further the development of scientific management. Mention has already been made of Barth, whose work on slide rules considerably aided the specification of efficient methods of machining. Gantt joined Taylor in 1877 and worked with him and on his own account for many years afterward (Urwick and Brech, 1949a, pp. 71–81). Gantt is remembered mainly for the chart used for scheduling production which bears his name, but this was only part of his activities, which spanned the spectrum of scientific management. The Gantt chart made its first appearance in 1903 (Gantt, 1903) and is a recording device for daily and total levels of production for different pieces. The ordering of the different operations in the production process is reflected in the layout of the chart, and allows a relatively easy assessment to be made of how balanced production is and where modifications may be necessary to restore balance if it is lost. This information is also related to the routing of pieces and the costing operations and so acted as a useful aid in these matters also.

Other major figures associated with scientific management were the Gilbreths (Urwick and Brech, 1949a, pp. 126–147). Frank Gilbreth was almost an exact contemporary of Taylor and had a similar background. He entered an apprenticeship to a bricklayer at seventeen and gained promotion to a managerial position within ten years. He established his own construction business, which eventually worked internationally, and in this company he developed innovative methods of management and control. The work for which he is mainly remembered is that in motion study, in which he was joined by his wife, Lilian. This work resulted in a method of analyzing the tasks necessary to complete a process and of organizing them so that the tasks were accomplished in the most effective manner. These developments gave further tools to be used in the name of scientific management.

Taylor and his associates developed their methods in major sectors of the American economy in the early twentieth century. The potential for applying the methods to other areas was recognized and Thompson (1922, pp. 544–579) showed how they might be applied to organizations in the retail sector. Here it is argued that scientific management may be applied to the development of costing, accounting, and stock-handling systems suitable for use in retail outlets. Clark and Wyatt (1922) argued that the methods might be used to improve working conditions for women. Their way of achieving this was to apply scientific management to the textile industry, one part of the manufacturing sector which employed a large number of women.

*Scientific Management and the Unions*

Scientific management was seen by many engineers and managers in the U.S. as a useful tool for improving performance. However, despite the continued arguments by Taylor and others that the methods were directed at improving the conditions for all involved, considerable resistance was shown by the trade unions to its introduction. By 1904 there were over 1.5 million workers in the American Federation of Labor and ninety affiliated national unions, mainly representing craftspeople (Peterson, 1963, p. 13). The employers' response to the increasingly organized labor movement was to become more hostile, and a range of measures, legal and otherwise, were used to reduce the unions' strengths (Karson, 1958, p. 33). Scientific management impinged on this increasingly confrontational relationship in two ways. First, the opposition in the unions to the increased rate of productivity and the reduction in job opportunities that they perceived as being due to scientific management reinforced the need for the unions to act as representatives of their members. Second, scientific management served to emphasize individual rather than group incentive schemes and so tended to act against the desire of the unions to create a strong, united workforce (Peterson, 1963, p. 15).

One of the better known examples of union action against scientific management was that taken at the Watertown Arsenal between 1910 and 1913. The use of scientific management in a number of government arsenals was first considered in 1909, when Carl Barth was appointed as a consultant to aid in the implementation of a trial of the methods (Thompson, 1922, p. 774). The manufacturing processes in selected arsenals were consequently reorganized along lines very similar to those described in the above two examples. A planning department was introduced, together with methods of costing, ordering, planning, and routing. Costs were reduced, the experiment was deemed a success, and the recommendation was made that the methods be used in other arsenals. The introduction of a piece-rate system at Watertown in May 1910 as part of the general reorganization was sufficient to provoke a strike. The strike was not long-lived, and the men returned to work under the agreement that the new system would operate but would be the subject of an investigation (Thompson, 1922, p. 780).

The unions involved made representation so strong that the House of Representatives appointed a special committee to investigate the use of scientific management methods, with particular reference to government works. The committee began its work on October 4, 1911, and Taylor himself gave testimony in several sessions between January 25 and January 30, 1912. In this testimony Taylor presented his most forthright explanation of the principles upon which his form of scientific management was based (Taylor, 1912). His concern with achieving improvements for both workers and employers is clearly recognizable. It is possible to see that he was interested in developing a tool which could be used for the good of all involved, provided the conditions existed for its proper use. It is equally clear that the potential for abuse was great and that the methods could be used to increase the amount of managerial control and exploitation. Taylor vehemently denied the notion that scientific management was a device for increasing efficiency per se but argued that it was a means of achieving change in the attitude of all involved in manufacturing. Time study, costing, and the other techniques of scientific management were a necessary means to the end of changing the emphasis from the division of existing surplus between employer and employee to increasing the total amount of surplus. In achieving this end, it was possible to see how all could benefit rather than one group having to benefit only at the disadvantage of another. The achievement of this end required that a radical change of attitude be adopted by both management and workers (Taylor, 1964, pp. 26–31).

The special committee found at the end of its deliberations that there had been insufficient time to allow for a proper finding on the allegations made against scientific management. The Committee did note its condemnation of the use of the methods for oppressive purposes and made clear the concern over this aspect of the approach. The result was that the Ordnance Department was able to continue its adoption of the methods. However, the unions continued to protest, and two further petitions were sent to the War Department in June 1913 (Thompson, 1922, pp. 741–771).

*Scientific Management and OR*

There is sufficient material documenting Taylor's work and that of his associates to allow comparisons to be drawn up between it and OR. First, scientific management is rooted in the belief, as is OR, that observation and measurement provide a secure basis for analysis. The level of sophistication of the tools of analysis used by scientific management is less than for OR, and this is an important difference between the two methods. OR is certainly more powerful than scientific management because it uses more powerful methods of analysis. Scientific management never succeeded in providing a general understanding of production processes and focused upon specific cases to a great extent. In contrast, OR was able to develop insights of a greater generality, as it had recourse to techniques not available to scientific management. Pocock (1954) points out that "Operations Research now brings to commerce and industry more powerful techniques of quantitative analysis and is an extension of Taylor's basic philosophy to possibilities probably beyond Taylor's vision, far reaching as it was" (p. 82).

The second and third characteristics of wartime OR were shared by scientific management. Both showed a concern with making the best use of existing resources and with the creation of new products or methods of production. The advice generated by the use of scientific management was used to aid and improve the managerial process. So the major thrust of scientific management is in the same direction as OR, the main difference lying in the sophistication of the techniques adopted. An explanation of this difference lies in the type of people who were involved in the development of scientific management and OR. In the former, the background of Taylor, the Gilbreths, and others, largely based in engineering and the practical aspects of manufacturing, led to their methods being derived from experience and governed by an intuitive feel for how to achieve an increased level of operational efficiency. In the latter, the individuals were educated in the use of mathematical and statistical methods and were able to conceive of operations in an abstract manner. It is not a surprise, therefore, to find these people using a more sophisticated approach than did Taylor and others.

Scientific management, despite its practical and unsophisticated techniques, was important in establishing the validity of using scientific methods to aid the management process. It laid the foundations for the profession of management consultancy, which developed in the U.S. between the two world wars. As will be seen in the following section, the nature of the relationship between science and industry in the U.S. and Britain in these two decades took very different forms. The nature of this relationship has important implications for the introduction of those OR techniques developed in the Second World War into the non-military sector after 1945 and more generally for the subsequent development of OR.

## Science and Management between the Wars

### Management Consultancy in the U.S.

Frederick Taylor died in 1915, leaving a legacy which was soon to develop into a major profession in the U.S. and to have a significant influence upon the postwar growth of OR there. In the same year the British government set in motion a process which was to have an equally important bearing upon the environment into which British OR emerged after the Second World War. These parallel developments will be considered with particular reference to their significance for the future development of OR.

Taylor, Gantt, the Gilbreths, and others involved in the scientific management movement each offered their skills to employers in the role of consultant. A significant proportion of their work was done on specific projects for companies of which they were not full-time employees. As the methods become better known and as the number of people able to use them increased, the profession of management consultant came into existence. Gallessich (1982, pp. 34–35) notes that this is one of several consultancy-based professions which emerged in the U.S. as it moved through a period of industrialization. Companies which employed consultants and offered their services were created, such as Arthur D. Little Inc. and Booz, Allen and Hamilton (Trefethan, 1954, p. 29).

The work undertaken by one of these companies, Booz, Allen and Hamilton, is described and related to OR by Pocock (1954). By 1954 the company employed 350 staff, who were involved in projects of a tactical and strategic nature spread over all functional areas. The work was carried out by project teams, which contained engineers, accountants, and other specialists, depending upon the nature of the task to be achieved. It is clear that this and the other large management consultancies had reached maturity by the early postwar years and that in reaching this state they had made American management aware of the concept of employing consultants to aid them in certain situations. As the consultancies were built upon foundations which included scientific management, it is also clear that American management developed a positive attitude toward a scientific approach to its problems. This attitude, coupled with a strong educational provision in management and business studies (many universities and colleges had a business or management faculty by the 1930s; Urwick and Brech, 1949b, p. 227), meant that when OR became known in the U.S. after 1945, it entered a receptive environment. OR was seen to be an extension of the existing methods used by management consultants and was rapidly accepted by them. Pocock (1954) writes that in Booz, Allen and Hamilton, "The application of operations research techniques to modern industry is high on the list for expanded development" (p. 85). However, OR did not necessarily open up further areas for enquiry, for Pocock also notes that the "problem areas susceptible to inquiry through operations research techniques today are also areas in which the management consultant has traditionally been active through many years" (pp. 80–81).

These points reinforce the earlier discussion about the relationship between scientific management and OR. The only essential change which occurred in the consultancies which included scientific management techniques in their portfolio when OR appeared was an increase in the sophistication of the analysis. The consultancies were using project teams for their work, and OR became another specialty among several represented in a consultancy.

The situation in Britain was very different in the midwar years. Taylor's work was not well known at the time of his death. Urwick and Brech (1949b, pp. 88–107) discuss in detail the British response to scientific management and argue that of the factors which prevented its development in Britain, the technical bias in the training of engineers was highly significant. They put forward four reasons why the British educational system failed to incorporate a significant element of management teaching and research (pp. 227–232).

First, there was considerable resistance within the major engineering institutions to any effort to dilute the technical aspects of their discipline. In contrast their American counterparts regarded management as an integral part of the engineering profession. There was therefore no stimulus from that section of industry which dominated the British economy at that time to develop management training.

Second, the professional bodies which did exist in Britain were small and often similar in all but specific matters of their areas of concern. This meant that any effort by those bodies to influence public opinion and decisions was diffuse and ineffective. In the U.S. two main bodies emerged, the American Management Association and the Management Division of the American Society of Mechanical Engineers, which were able to present a much stronger image of the management profession to the public and also to serve their members better.

Third, the general level of educational support for those subjects concerned with management was much lower in Britain than in the U.S. The resistance of the educational institutions to including management in the curriculum made it difficult for the engineering bodies to advise on course content and to encourage schools to include management in engineering courses.

Finally, government support for management in the U.S. was positive. A department of commerce existed to advise businesses and the Bureau of the Census provided appropriate statistical information. Franklin D. Roosevelt, when president, presented a report to Congress in 1937 which considered the bureaucratic and administrative structure of the U.S. government from a scientific management position (Urwick and Brech, 1949b, pp. 155–164). The British Civil Service appeared, in contrast, to show little understanding of how to provide and operate an effective service to industry and commerce at that time.

In addition to the resistance shown in Britain to accepting management theory as a useful guide to practice, scientific management also faced difficulties with the British trade unions. Just as in the U.S., the unions felt that the introduction of a piecework system was detrimental to their members' working conditions. Urwick and Brech (1949b) argue that this response was a "fraternal imitation of the American response and, as the methods had been little used in Britain, was almost entirely derivative and based on hearsay" (p. 223).

## Research Associations in the U.K.

Therefore scientific management in Britain was a victim of the failure of science and industry to create an environment in which both were mutually beneficial. Babbage had argued nearly a century earlier that the failure of science and business to work together was a hindrance to the positive development of British industry and commerce, and the case of scientific management supports the point. In 1915 this situation was recognized by the British government, and an advisory council was formed to advise on matters connected with the expenditure of government funds on the organization and development of scientific and industrial research. The first report of this committee (HMSO, 1916) noted that important benefits would arise when pure science and manufacturing industry were brought together. Several cases where successes had occurred were cited, and reasons were proposed as to why there was a lower level of research undertaken by manufacturing concerns in Britain than in the U.S. and Europe, notably Germany. Scale of operation was seen to be one reason; the small size of many British firms made the decision to invest in research an uncertain one with limited payoffs. The attitude of the financial and banking sector made it difficult to gain financial support for industrial research, as did the uncertainty over what the state of the economy would be at the end of the war.

On the recommendation of the advisory council, a department of scientific and industrial research was created which initiated action on the bringing together of scientists and industrialists. Within a year of the end of the First World War, individual researchers were receiving grants for specific projects, research was being coordinated toward ends perceived to be in the national interest, scientific and professional societies were being financially supported, and eighteen research associations had been created. The associations were a response to a situation in which it was difficult for single companies to sponsor a research project when they were uncertain as to its benefit. The research associations served an industry, or a significant part of an industry, and acted as a body able to undertake work which either was for specific organizations or would benefit the whole sector. The original intention was for companies to invest in an appropriate association to supplement government funding. This goal proved to be more difficult to achieve than expected. Early research associations served the woollen, cotton, iron, steel, and other industries.

Through the 1920s and 1930s the level of support given by the department, particularly to the research associations, increased. The work carried out in this period was mainly concerned with the development of new products and methods of production. Examples of particularly important results include the development and subsequent production of electric lamps and television sets and work in the plastics industry (HMSO, 1937). The work sponsored by the Department of Scientific and Industrial Research through the research associations was therefore not OR, as it was concerned primarily with the creation of new resources and methods and not with using existing resources more effectively. The potential for applying the resources of the associations to existing methods was recognized in 1935 when the advisory council to the department emphasized that "science can be of service in the workshop as well as in the laboratory, and it is this link between the workshop and the laboratory which is the real essential for the application of advances in scientific knowledge" (HMSO, 1935, p. 14).

The work carried out in this period also failed to meet fully the demand that OR be a process which serves the decision makers of an organization. This failure is a consequence of the concern with the creation of new products. While it is possible to see the desire for new products as the result of a management decision, the creation of that product is a process largely separate from the process of managing an organization which might make and sell that product.

The research associations and other work sponsored by the department are clearly scientific in character and so share with OR the characteristics of bringing scientific method to bear on problems in organizations. There is sufficient evidence to support an argument that the problems confronted by the two areas of work are significantly different to deny the claim that they are similar. Thus the argument made after the war that many of the research organizations of the department, as well as the research associations and research departments of industrial firms, had been engaged in industrial operational research since their formation (HMSO, 1949, p. 16) is not fully supported. There is a valid case to be made that the introduction of new products and processes requires attention to the way in which any machines associated with them are operated. In that sense research into operations was necessary. However, it is equally valid to argue that this was a secondary aspect of the work of the research associations, where emphasis was laid on work in the laboratory and not on the production process.

The industrial environment into which OR emerged in Britain in 1945 was very different from that in the U.S. There was no existing profession to which OR could attach itself and become easily absorbed into the managerial world. Thus OR had a much higher profile in Britain than in the U.S. It was seen in Britain as a radically new approach to managerial problem solving and not as an extension of an existing method. Consequently, in Britain OR developed from a very different baseline than it did in the U.S. The implications for the character and image of the discipline in the two countries will be considered in the next chapter.

## Conclusion

The starting point for the above discussion was the question of whether any activity prior to that of the ORSs in the Second World War corresponded to the concept of operational research, as it became known during and after that period. If it did, then it is necessary to show what unique features existed in the British military in the war years which allowed it to develop. What has emerged so far is the observation that in Britain and the U.S. two historical patterns were present which give different conclusions in this matter.

In Britain, the segmentation of science and industry, which dates from the Industrial Revolution, restricted the development of OR-type activities before the Second World War. The contributions of Babbage and others at the time of the Industrial Revolution were not allowed to develop to their full potential because the institutional environment was not conducive. The positive efforts to generate a suitable environment taken by government in the 1920s and 1930s went some way toward improving the situation, but cultural attitudes remained a significant barrier. Study of the contributions of Babbage and the research associations shows that a genuine coming together of scientific methods based on observation and a concern with aiding management in the decision-making process was impeded; thus the full application of scientific methods to management problems was prevented.

In the U.S. a clear association between the scientific management movement and OR is recognizable. Building on Taylor's conception of a method which can improve the benefits for both employer and employee, scientific management led to the profession of management consultancy. The environment in which this developed was supportive and encouraged the multidisciplinary activity necessary. Consideration of what scientific management meant makes it clear that its goals were similar to those of OR. A major difference between scientific management before 1939 and OR lies in the origins of the disciplines. Taylor, Gantt, the Gilbreths, and others were primarily engineers who were concerned with implementing and using technological resources. They adopted a scientific attitude but were not pure scientists. Consequently the methods developed in scientific management were derived from an engineer's rather than a scientist's perspective.

The reasons why OR did not develop into its well-understood form until the Second World War can now be better understood. The final question at issue is what conditions existed to allow it to develop at that time. These conditions were, in fact, those which were absent in both the U.S. and Britain in the years prior to the Second World War. First, there was a close proximity of scientists able to use sophisticated methods of analysis and management with difficult decisions. Thus, for the first time, it became possible to deal with such decisions with the aid of advice based upon scientific methods of analysis. Second, the impending war and eventually the actuality of war made effective operations of great significance which led to the lowering of the institutional barriers which in peacetime impeded the coming together of scientist and decision maker. The early success of the ORSs with radar operations did much to persuade people of the benefits of using scientific methods to analyze operations. After the war a situation then prevailed in which OR was able to move into the industrial sector in Britain with reasonable ease. In the U.S., of course, these barriers had never existed in any significant degree, and so OR could be accepted as an extension of management consultancy after 1945.

# *3*

---

# *The Development of Operational Research*

## *Introduction*

The emergence of OR as a novel discipline in the years immediately prior to the Second World War was not without precedent, as has been shown in Chapter 2. The application of a scientific approach to management problems had been undertaken previously and, in some cases, had been successfully developed. What OR brought to the fore was a greater degree of sophistication in the methods and techniques used. These enabled a broader class of situations to be tackled than had previously been possible, and as the approach became adopted by industrial and commercial organizations, advantage was taken of this potential. On both sides of the Atlantic the new management tool became established, and by the end of the 1950s the professional and academic discipline of operational research was widely recognized.

This chapter is concerned with tracing the development of the discipline in these formative years. The chapter consists of two main parts. In the first, the developments after the Second World War are described. The movement into industry is examined for the effect of the different business environments that were experienced in Britain and the U.S. The growing number of operational researchers and the demand for them gave rise to societies and educational programs, and these are also considered here. The emergence of a recognized group of people undertaking the activity and the requirements of educational programs made it necessary and appropriate to establish a common framework, which served to characterize the nature of operational research at that time. The second part of this chapter considers that framework, which emerged in the 1950s and has been retained, largely unchanged, to the present day.

## *The Growth of OR after 1945*

*OR in the Research Associations*

After the Second World War the British economy was in need of rejuvenation, and the election of a Labour government in 1946 led to a nationalization program over the next few years. Throughout this program, which saw coal, the railways and other important parts of the industrial base taken over by the state, the research associations of the Department of Scientific and Industrial Research (DSIR) remained and flourished. These associations formed a natural home for operational research in Britain, and their role and that of the nationalized industries will be explored below and contrasted with the situation in the U.S. There the established management and business schools in universities and similar institutions acted as a catalyst for bringing military OR expertise into industrial and commercial organizations. The results of this process and the existing use of scientific management in American companies led to a different attitude being adopted toward OR than in Britain, and this difference is manifested by the types of professional society which were set up in Britain and the U.S. and the development of educational provision for OR in the two countries.

The first reference to OR in the reports of the DSIR after the war occurred in 1949 (HMSO, 1949). Three research associations expressed an interest. The British Cotton Research Association—one of the earliest, dating from 1919—was keen to investigate how OR might be used in their industry (p. 100). The British Iron and Steel Research Association (BISRA) was using OR methods to look at problems of traffic flow in foundries (p. 131). BISRA was a relatively new research association, having been founded in 1944, although the industry had several bodies predating this time which provided it with scientific advice. An even newer research association, the Lace Federation Research Council, founded in 1949, reported the setting up of a small OR section to be devoted to the operations of the lace-manufacturing companies (p. 135).

In the report of the following year (HMSO, 1950), the interest in OR was maintained, and details of further projects were forthcoming. The Lace Federation Council, for example, was using its OR section to look at the problems of lighting machines and of maintenance (p. 134). The British Jute Trade Research Association was using OR in three areas, to explore the implications of different levels of moisture in bales and of the relative humidity in factories and to investigate the construction and materials used for sacks (p. 132). The Cast Iron Research Association had in that year set up a team of three operational researchers (p. 89). There was also general reference to the use of OR in the research associations in order to broaden the scope of their work (p. 12). More specifically,

> the British Cotton Research Association noted that there is enough in this borderline subject between technology, economics and management to require the continuous attention of a small staff, which not only deals with *ad hoc* problems, but is also building up a body of general information and methods. (p. 100)

In the early 1950s OR became recognized as an important tool in the research associations. The difficult economic climate made the efficient use of existing resources more important, and hence the role of OR took on added importance. In 1952 the DSIR established an industrial operations unit which had among its goals "to show to non-specialist staff how OR could be used" (HMSO, 1958, p. 22).

Of the many OR groups based in the research associations that associated with BISRA was possibly the largest. Sir Charles Goodeve was appointed director of BISRA at the end of the war, after being involved with the development of measures to counter German anti-shipping attacks and eventually becoming Deputy Controller of Research and Development at the Admiralty. His undoubted exposure to OR in the war enabled him to see its potential application in industry, and he was instrumental in bringing OR into BISRA (Anon., 1980b). Collcutt (1965) reported on the work carried out by the OR groups in BISRA in its first two decades, and it is appropriate to summarize that work here to illustrate its breadth and importance to the industry. The work was classified by Collcutt into three areas: industry problems, research problems, and company problems.

Industrywide problems were those concerned with issues which affected industry policy and which were usually under consideration by the industry's coordinating body, the British Iron and Steel Federation. Two main areas where such work was done were accident prevention and the importing and transportation of iron ore.

The importing of iron ore from the Americas, Africa, and Scandinavia was undertaken by an industry-controlled non-profit-making organization. BISRA carried out investigations for this company which led to changes in the management of the ships used and the unloading operations carried out at ports throughout the country. A computer-based simulation model of the operations involved was produced which could deal with tidal effects at the ports, different arrival schedules, and a variety of unloading methods. Use of the model allowed conclusions to be reached on the most cost-efficient way of organizing the shipping and unloading of iron ore.

Accident prevention was an important activity in all areas of the iron and steel industry. The BISRA OR group carried out a thorough investigation of the rate of injuries and ways of reducing them. An analysis of data on absenteeism in three works showed that there was less likelihood of injuries being caused when there was a low level of staff turnover. The people most likely to be injured were those who had not been in the works for a long time. Minor injuries tended not to be reported but would lead to the injured person taking sickness absence. Consequently the use of reported injuries as an indicator of accident prevention was unsound, and an alternative method was required. Such a method was developed to investigate the effect of safety posters on accident levels. The posters were designed to minimize the accidents caused by failure to hook back crane slings. The indicator of success was taken to be the increase in the number of times this activity occurred after the posters had been displayed. Posters of different designs and sizes were compared. This measure and the conclusions drawn influenced the industry's policy toward the use of posters.

Into the second class of problems, research problems, fell those which were common to several companies but which a single company did not have the resources to tackle alone. The extensive contacts by BISRA throughout the industry meant that staff in the research association were able to recognize such problems. This second class was common and provided a wide range of work.

An important characteristic of the iron and steel industry which distinguishes it from many other elements of the manufacturing sector is the size and composition of the equipment used in production. Furnaces are large and expensive items and, at the time when BISRA first began to analyze their performance, required relining with bricks about four times per year. The relining operation was costly, as was the loss of production which occurred if the lining collapsed because of wear. An analysis of the operation of furnaces in various works provided an understanding of how the relining policy was affected by the number of furnaces involved, the type of bricks used, the relining methods, and the rate at which the furnaces were worked. Recommendations on how best to operate the furnaces became available which led to considerable improvements in efficiency. BISRA also carried out a more general series of studies which assessed the probability of plant failures and the length of downtime under different maintenance policies. These studies gave insights into the relationships between these policies, the types of equipment, and the failure levels, and enabled more effective maintenance policies to be implemented.

A second type of research problem focused upon the planning of activities. A number of studies were carried out which were relevant to the decision of which mix of processes to use in the production of iron. As technology improved in the 1950s and 1960s, the range of possible processes grew. Production managers had to decide which combination of processes would yield a compatible and cost-effective set of processes. A model was constructed which was able to incorporate the various combinations and relevant factors, and its use generated information which was useful in production planning. Staffing planning was also looked at by the OR group in BISRA. By modeling the flow of staff, it was possible to establish the recruiting levels at various grades which were necessary to meet personnel requirements and the need for training that these requirements implied for new recruits and existing staff.

A final area in which the OR group was able to do work at a general level which benefited several companies was concerned with the introduction of computer-based management information and control systems. Three types of procedure were seen as being able to be supported by such systems: accounts and administrative procedures, production planning and control procedures, and information dissemination procedures. A series of studies resulted in general models describing the relationship between these procedures and the information system supporting them. These studies enabled analyses to be carried out which provided a structure for the effective introduction of such systems.

The third aspect of the BISRA OR group's work was to undertake consultancy for specific companies. Consultancy generated finance for the group and allowed the companies access to a consultancy team with specialist knowledge of their industry. The work under this heading differed from that in the previous two classes by being concerned with competitive advantage in the industry. The group itself worked on a wide variety of issues. The question of whether to buy in steel billets or produce them was addressed for one company. On a larger scale, the decision of whether to use an existing rail connection to a new plant or to install a more direct belt transportation system was analyzed. Production capacities and planning for a new plant were another area where confidentiality was important and the group found itself giving specific advice. Stock control was found to be an area where significant savings could be made by many companies. Advice on how to manage stocks of steel section and items used for repair and maintenance saved companies between 30% and 50% of their capital tied up in stock holdings. These and many other specific studies were able to build upon and contribute to the broader and less confidential studies carried out by the group.

The OR movement in the research associations, exemplified by that in BISRA, was successful in developing the activity and establishing its worth. The environment afforded by the associations was conducive to the development of OR. Contacts with industry were easily achieved, and the status given to OR by being part of the DSIR made it acceptable to client organizations. The consultancy mode of operating was common in the research associations and encouraged the specific and often confidential studies which were central to the work of an OR group. There were therefore few barriers to the growth of OR, and provided the industry served presented sufficient scope for work, the activity developed.

*Company-Based OR Groups*

While the research associations of DSIR provided an excellent environment for the development of OR groups, it became clear that it was useful for companies to have their own OR teams devoted specifically to their own management. Thus, for example, in the iron and steel sector, the Steel Company of Wales, Richard Thomas and Baldwins, the United Steel Companies, Guest Keen Iron and Steel, Stewarts and Lloyds, and Colvilles all had large OR groups by the early 1960s, and some of these dated back to the 1950s (Colcutt, 1965). The nationalized industries also provided an environment in which OR could develop; of these, the coal industry is the most significant and well documented in terms of its OR groups.

The National Coal Board (NCB) was formed in 1946 and took control of the coal industry on behalf of the nation on January 1, 1947. Sir Charles Ellis was appointed to the board in 1946 with particular responsibility for science. Supported by Donald Hicks, his executive officer, he played as important a role in establishing OR in the NCB, as Goodeve did at BISRA. Ellis was a physicist who had worked with Rutherford at Cambridge and who eventually became Wheatstone Professor of Physics at King's College, London. In the war he was scientific adviser to the Army Council and was responsible for the development of OR in the army. Just like Goodeve, Ellis was aware of the potential offered by OR and sought to bring the new management tool into the coal industry (Hicks, 1983).

Ellis introduced three types of scientific service into the coal industry. The implementation and management of these areas was the responsibility of Hicks, whose whole career had been spent in the industry and whom Ellis appointed as Director of Scientific Control in 1947 (Rivett, 1987). The Divisional Scientific Service was mainly concerned with science as it related to the production of coal. It was particularly involved in testing the atmosphere in mines and the quality of coal produced and had an interest in work on lubricants, water analysis, and the development of equipment. The Coal Survey offered a geological service to the industry. Its analyses were designed to assess the extent of coal deposits and the likely problems of its excavation. The Field Investigation Group (FIG) was the name given by Ellis to the group devoted to operational research. Hicks (1983, p. 847) suggests that FIG was used to prevent difficulties in defining operational research and also to prevent the activities of the group being limited by too specific a label. Tomlinson (1971, p. 2) suggests that OR, as a name, was not liked by all and so an alternative had to be sought.

The decision to implement FIG was made by the NCB on April 7, 1948, and three years later it had twelve scientists in post. The group was headed by Alan Evans between 1948 and 1951, and upon his departure Pat Rivett was appointed to replace him. Rivett was to see FIG grow in the 1950s until, in 1962, when the title of the group changed to OR Branch, it had over fifty staff. FIG provided a service to all coalfields and was intended to work on problems common to all. It was natural, therefore, that it should be initially based at headquarters, although later regional bases and groups were established. In 1953 Ellis set down three objectives for FIG: (1) to study existing practices and assess their efficiency and indicate where and how improvements could be obtained without any major change in equipment; (2) (following from 1) to indicate the fields of experimental research and development that were likely to be profitable; and (3) to act as an independent body to assess the efficiency of the results of research and development in actual practice (Tomlinson, 1971, pp. 3–6).

The work of FIG and the subsequent OR Branch has been reported by Tomlinson (1971). It is useful, as with the BISRA OR group, to outline their range of activity here. Tomlinson classifies their areas of investigation under four headings: production, marketing, planning, and personnel planning.

Most of the early OR work in the NCB was devoted to the production process. One reason is that it presented little difficulty to the analysts in its conceptualization and measurement. A further reason was the relationship between FIG and the other scientific activities. Production was one area where the scientific services and management had previously been brought into contact. It was easier to introduce the new application of scientific methods in this context than in areas where science had little or no previous applications. The use of OR in production was also attractive to the NCB because production costs were dominant, and hence their reduction was of significance. It was also found that the production processes at different coalfields were largely similar. This meant that investigations in this area had a wide range of applicability and could be justified on these grounds.

Three different aspects of the production process can be identified as offering different types of problem to the operational researcher. First, there were issues centered on the design and control of collieries. Here FIG worked on decisions about how best to transport coal from the face to the surface by conveyer belt and underground railway, how to organize shifts to achieve the best operational performance, and how to arrange for communications underground. Second, there were a set of decisions to be made about equipment on which the OR analyst could provide advice. Questions concerning operational characteristics, reliability, and maintenance all proved amenable to the style of analysis used by OR. The third area of work in connection with the production process was concerned with purchasing and stores. Here the main focus of attention lay on the control of stocks of equipment and spares. The problems facing an organization which had a vast amount of equipment at many different locations were considerable, and by analyzing the situation improvements in the inventory control system resulted.

Marketing in the NCB includes those processes by which coal is moved from the pit head to the customer's yard and supporting activities in addition to the usual marketing functions. There are some important differences between the marketing of coal and the marketing of other commodities. The specification of quality and grade of coal is not easy, and standards are likely to vary within one delivery. The demand for coal is relatively inelastic and is not easily increased, and substitution between coal and other products is difficult. The price of coal is dependent on use—industrial, carbonization, or domestic—and so restricted the ability of the NCB to be flexible in its sales strategy. In such a situation the role which can be played by an OR team is not clear. By the mid 1960s little work had been done in this area, but activity increased in the last half of the decade. Tools were developed to aid in the forecasting of demand and in the setting of targets. Central to this work was the construction of market models which enabled the influence of the various factors affecting supply and demand to be explored and their mutual interaction to be considered. Other areas investigated were the operations of the coal washeries, the process of quality estimation and control, and the distribution network.

The planning process also received little attention from the operational researchers in the NCB in the early days. However, by the 1960s the OR team was involved in planning at all levels in the board. At the colliery level the main issue was how best to work the various coal faces within the limitations imposed by staffing and equipment availability. An early way of dealing with this question was the provision of a manually operated system to help the planning activity. This was subsequently developed into a computerized method which was able to include more factors and provide more sophisticated information. Planning at the next level, of the area, was mainly concerned with commercial decisions on the levels of production and on the resource implications of these over the medium term. The OR analysts were able to provide information which supported the decision-making process. Finally, there was planning at the national level, where the OR team was able to assist in the production of models which focused on the longer term strategic issues and generated information appropriate to decisions at this level.

The final area where the OR team in the NCB was active in the period to 1969 was personnel planning. The levels of labor turnover and redeployment may be analyzed statistically, and several studies of this type were carried out. It was also found possible to undertake work which investigated the relationship between absenteeism, the shift pattern, and levels of productivity. The work which could be carried out in this area was limited by the lack of social scientists on the team, and "questions requiring this sort of expertise were deliberately avoided" (Tomlinson, 1971, p. 183).

The breadth of the work undertaken by FIG and its successors and its success in the first twenty years of the NCB are another indication of the relative ease with which OR entered the British industrial and commercial sector after 1945. In this case the support at the highest level given by Ellis was crucial, and the novelty of the organization, as well as the activity of OR, certainly helped. Preconceived notions and departmental boundaries were absent, and the positive contribution of OR to an industry central to the growth of the economy was recognized early. As with BISRA, the base of FIG at headquarters gave it access to the whole industry with relative ease, and its investigations were seen to be relevant at an industry level rather than being focused toward parts of it.

The success of OR at BISRA and other research associations and in the NCB is noted here because these are well documented. At the same time as these groups were establishing themselves, OR groups were being formed in many types of company. Goodeve and Ridley (1953), Gander (1957), and Rivett (1959) discuss this enlargement of OR's client base and show the extent to which it had grown in the decade since

1945. Not all organizations proved to be ideal for the new approach to grow and develop. Rosenhead (1989) describes how the Special Research unit headed by Cecil Gordon at the Board of Trade failed to introduce OR into the British civil service, for example.

## The Institutions of OR

The central role in the postwar development of OR in Britain played by the research associations and industrially based groups was not paralleled in the U.S. The differences in environment between the countries discussed in the previous chapter led to OR becoming established in different settings. In Britain the base was established in those organizations which provided a scientific service to industry. In the U.S. the strong network of business and management faculties in the higher education establishments provided a natural home for many operational research groups. This difference lead to distinctly different characteristics in the two communities which laid the pattern for the current state of the discipline on each side of the Atlantic. Two facets of this difference can be recognized. The first is the extent to which educational provision for OR was provided, and the second is the image which OR gained by virtue of the work published under that title.

The base for OR in the higher educational establishments of the U.S. enabled courses and training to be provided there at a much earlier stage and to much greater extent than in the UK. In 1953 the Case Institute of Technology had a master's degree curriculum established for OR, and the Massachusetts Institute of Technology was running a summer program (Education Committee, ORSA, 1953; Morse, 1953). In the following year, McCloskey (1954) reports, Columbia, Cornell, and John Hopkins universities and the Carnegie Institute of Technology also had courses. In 1956 ten institutions had courses leading to graduate degrees in OR (Educational Committee, ORSA, 1956). These were each offered by schools of industrial administration or engineering and built upon the earlier experiences gained from the teaching and development of scientific management.

In contrast to this rapid growth in education for OR in the U.S., the situation in Britain was one where initiatives were much less apparent. Gander (1955) gives details of a short course offered in 1955 by the Department of Production Engineering at Birmingham University. By 1958 this department had begun to offer the only master's course in OR in Britain, although a number of institutions had started to provide specialist short courses (Kendall, 1958). One reason for this tardiness in developing courses was the lack of suitable departments and schools which could provide a home for such a multidisciplinary activity. It was only when the new universities of the 1960s were created that OR particularly, and management generally, became established. Thus Lancaster University had a Department of OR created at the outset with Rivett, formerly head of OR in the National Coal Board, as its first professor (McClintock, 1974). Other new universities where OR and management subsequently flourished include Aston, Bath, Warwick, Sussex, and Strathclyde.

The difference in the amount of educational provision available had implications for the recruitment of OR personnel by organizations wishing to establish their own teams. In the U.S. the emphasis lay upon the recruitment of staff with some educational qualifications in OR. Morse (1955) called for more training courses and an increased effort to advertise OR as an attractive profession. Hovey and Wagner (1958) showed that a considerable proportion of OR workers in the U.S. had some formal qualifications in OR. In Britain the training of OR staff was largely carried out on the job and was supported by inhouse and short courses as necessary. It was only in the early 1960s that it became possible to recruit staff with formal OR qualifications in any numbers. This meant that the composition of OR groups in Britain retained the multidisciplinary character evident during the Second World War to a much greater degree than did those in the U.S. The FIG of the National Coal Board, for example, had a complement of thirty-three in 1957, half of whom were mathematicians and statisticians, the remainder being engineers, physicists, economists, and social scientists (Tomlinson, 1971, p. 5).

A second feature which distinguishes British and American OR was the type of work which was published in the journals of the discipline. In Britain the earliest journal devoted to OR was the *Operational Research Quarterly*, which first appeared in 1950. This was the journal of the Operational Research Society, which grew out of the OR Club, formed in 1948. The journal is now called the *Journal of the Operational Research Society*. The society was dominated in the 1950s by people practicing OR in organizations rather than by academics whose prime function was to teach and research the discipline. The membership of the society grew from 78 in 1953 to 317 in 1957 and had reached 3,381 by 1985 (Carter, 1987). The dominance of practitioners remains, with Carter reporting only 17% of the respondents to his survey being in education. Papers appeared on such pragmatic issues as the impact of scale factors in coal mining (Revans, 1953), the process of unloading iron ore (Eddison and Owen, 1953), the mechanization of ticket issuing (Eaton, 1955), and the provision of spare machines (Taylor and Jackson, 1954).

The Operations Research Society of America was formed in 1952, and its journal, *Operations Research*, first appeared in that year. By 1953 the society had 646 members, of whom 168 were in industry, and had a well-organized set of committees to manage its affairs (Malcolm, 1954; Morse, 1952). The early issues of *Operations Research* included many applications of mathematical and statistical methods, but over the following years a theoretical emphasis emerged. Many of the contributions to the techniques and analytical methods of OR which were made in the 1950s were included in *Operations Research*, for example, the new approach of dynamic programming (Bellman, 1954) and developments in stock control and production planning (Simon and Holt, 1954). Some important technical results were announced, by Dantzig, Fulkerson, and Johnson (1954), on a solution to the traveling-sales-representative problem, for example, and a Symposium on Modern Techniques for Extreme Problems was published in 1957 with papers by many leading mathematicians, including Tucker, Arrow, Hurwicz, Dantzig, and Bellman. In the same year a review of work in queueing theory was published (Saaty, 1957).

In 1953 the Institute of Management Sciences (TIMS) was formed, with the intention of identifying, extending, and unifying the scientific knowledge that contributed to the understanding and practice of management. The institute published a journal, *Management Science*, to achieve the dissemination of knowledge and to encourage research. The confusion over the boundary between management science and operational research was pointed out by Weinwurm (1954), and he proposed that "the concept of Management Sciences is much broader than that of Operations Research; thus the latter would have to be allotted its proper area within the framework of the former" (p. 275). While the broader scope allotted to management science seems to be widely agreed on, confusion still remains over the terms, and they are often used synonymously, or together as MS/OR. The historical roots of a "science of managing" in the U.S. and hence of the institute were laid out by Smiddy and Naum (1954), and Cooper (1954) argued that TIMS should act as a focus to broaden the understanding of behavioral science and management practice.

The broader concept of management science relative to operations research is shown by the inclusion of papers in *Management Science* on systems theory (Boulding, 1956) and behavioral science (Gomberg, 1957; Guetzkow and Bowes, 1957; Tannenbaum and Masarik, 1957). *Management Science*, however, has also included several important papers on the mathematical aspects of OR, by Charnes and Cooper (1954), Dantzig (1955), Ford and Fulkerson (1956), Holt, Modigliani, and Muth (1956), Markowitz (1957), and Orchard-Hayes (1958), for example.

Thus the literature which emerged from the British and American

OR communities reflected the dominant interests of those communities. The British operational researcher was typically employed in industry and read descriptions of applications of mathematical methods. The American counterpart was typically a research scientist, employed in a university or research laboratory, who was interested in developing the methods and techniques of analysis.

To a large extent this difference in the British and American journals remains today. *The Journal of the Operational Research Society* retains a strong theme of case studies and practice-oriented papers, while the American journals maintain an interest in the mathematical aspects of the discipline. The technical bias in the American journals has been redressed somewhat by the publication by TIMS of *Interfaces,* a journal devoted to the practice of OR and management science.

The developments of OR in the first decade after 1945 on each side of the Atlantic were largely independent of each other, but some cross-fertilization of ideas did occur. Rivett visited the Case Institute in 1954 and 1957 and noted the wider knowledge of techniques held by the Americans. Upon his return to FIG, he began to introduce significant changes in attitude in FIG, which resulted in improved understanding and training of the staff in the latest developments (Tomlinson, 1971, pp. 9–11).

Ackoff (1957) contrasts the situation in the U.S. and Britain at that time. First, there was a broader vision in Britain of how OR related to society in general. The reasons were unclear, but Ackoff suggests that one cause might be the prior existence in the U.S. of a niche into which OR naturally fitted. In the U.K. the discipline had to establish its own place and create a network of relationships around it. In the 1950s, it was possible to have to the impression that British OR was not as well connected with its environment as that in the U.S. and was consequently less clear in its conception. An alternative explanation might be that OR in Britain was entering an area where little experience had been gained and where many opportunities presented themselves. It was natural, therefore, for OR to attempt to act in a broad arena and to expand the scope of the discipline as far as possible. In the U.S. many other professions and disciplines existed which overlapped with OR's contribution. Thus OR had its potential area of application reduced and had to work within a situation where existing professions were well established. Its need and opportunity to lay claim to a particular field were much less than in the U.K.

Second, Ackoff notes the increased attention given to technical matters in the U.S. He suggests that the reason is that the previous uses of scientific methods in American industry meant that many of the problems of practice which were novel to the British had been dealt with previously in the U.S. Thus the key issues for American operational researchers revolved around the extension and development of techniques, whereas for the British a major concern was with the involvement of scientists with management irrespective of the tools used. The history behind the emergence of OR in the two countries played an important role in determining the direction and speed with which OR developed after 1945, and this role is reflected in the problems seen as significant by the two communities and addressed in their publications.

Third, the level of involvement by academics in OR in the U.S. was much greater than in the U.K. This distinction was due to the existence of business and management as academic disciplines in the U.S. before 1945 and its absence in the U.K. Thus there was a tradition in the U.S. of academics working with companies and using their experiences in their teaching and research activities. In Britain a divide existed between industry and education which prevented this collaboration taking place and thus hindering the growth of management and business studies generally. In particular it meant that OR groups in British companies had to depend on their resources to a much greater extent than they did in the U.S., where the support of the academic community could be called on if necessary.

The independent development of British and American OR began to come to an end in 1957, when the First International Conference on OR was held at Oxford. The conference had originally been suggested by ORSA and TIMS with the intention of holding a meeting in Paris (Hertz, 1958). The British OR Society was also involved and offered to hold the meeting in the U.K., an invitation which was subsequently accepted. The conference was successful in showing the extent to which OR had spread since 1945. Nearly 300 delegates from twenty-one countries attended, and sixteen countries were represented in a session reporting the progress of OR. Twenty-eight papers appeared in the published proceedings (Davies, Eddison, and Page, 1957), and in summarizing them Churchman (1957) identified five types of paper.

First, there were definitional papers where the author was concerned with defining the area of interest of OR. Second, a number of papers were presented which were programmatic. These set out a set of tasks which needed to be achieved in order to tackle an important but as yet unresolved problem. Third was a group of papers classified as expository. These sought to describe work on programs which had been successful. The papers in this category were concerned with efforts to refine technique, and Churchman expressed concern over this emphasis. In particular, he noted the danger that OR might become identified with those models and techniques which were successfully developed.

Fourth were a group of papers which concentrated upon specific techniques. Finally, there were a set of case studies which reported applications of OR methods to a range of management problems.

The British contribution to the conference was sizable. Of the twenty-eight papers, ten had authors with a British affiliation, and of these five were in the fifth category, case studies. Thus the industrial and practical emphasis of British OR was reflected by the contributions made at the conference. The major impact of the conference on British operational researchers resulted from exposure to the American view of OR. The members of FIG, for example, felt that the conference had had a "traumatic effect" on them as "the Englishmen and the Americans hardly spoke the same language" and "all intellectual complacency was shattered" (Tomlinson, 1971, pp. 9–11). All work in FIG was stopped for three months while its members educated themselves in the techniques developed by the Americans. A report of the conference in *The Economist* of September 7, 1957, observed the differences from a more detached standpoint:

> The American approach to operational research differs significantly from the British; the experts from the United States were concerned more with the elaboration of its techniques and with the study of large working systems in all their ramifications than with the practical case studies and applications British speakers described.

The effect on British OR of this conference was to open up a new dimension to the discipline. A framework of methods became available within which it could mature. The interest in applications was supplemented by an increase in the development of techniques and methods which could aid this practice. This framework was that used in the U.S. to form the core of that country's growing range of educational provision for OR. Churchman, Ackoff, and Arnoff (1957) provided a classification of problems and methods for tackling them which was to become a standard form of describing the common types of problem addressed by operational researchers. It is to this classification that attention is now turned.

## Classical Operational Research: Problems and Models

### Introduction to Operations Research

The main centers for education and research in OR in the 1950s were in the U.S., and it is not surprising, therefore, to discover that the early efforts to structure and explore the discipline were made there. The first textbook in OR was written by Morse and Kimball (1951) and was a published version of a 1946 technical report on wartime OR in the American military (Majone, 1985, p. 40). McCloskey and Trefethan (1954) is an edited collection of articles in two volumes which considers the history, organization, and concepts of OR and gives descriptions of its application in various contexts. Neither of these books presented a unified picture of a discipline; this was first done by Churchman, Ackoff, and Arnoff (1957) in *Introduction to Operations Research*. The material in the book derived from OR courses given at the Case Institute and had two objectives: first, to provide for potential customers of OR an opportunity to evaluate the field and understand its potential and procedures, and second, to provide practitioners with a survey of the field and a basis on which they could plan the further education required to enable students to show competence with the techniques.

*Introduction to Operations Research* is a book of nearly 650 pages which contain two types of material. The majority, nearly two-thirds, is taken up by a description of those models and their techniques of solution which had been found to be useful for the most commonly occurring problems tackled by operational researchers. The remaining one-third of the book considers the general nature of OR, the methods used to tackle problem situations, the character of the models used in OR, and its organizational aspects. It is fair to say that the majority of OR texts produced since 1957 have followed a similar pattern to *Introduction to Operations Research* but have shown an increasing emphasis upon the models and techniques rather than the more general environment in which they are used.

Churchman, Ackoff, and Arnoff recognized that there were several operational processes in which problems occurred regularly and for which models of a similar form were built when the problems were addressed by operational researchers. The search for methods of solution for such models became important, and particular areas of interest developed around them. These became so well established that they remain strong foci for educational and research work today. These processes, the models used to address them, and the methods of solution will now be considered to illustrate the variety of problems OR was dealing with in the 1950s and to show their current practical importance. Contemporary case studies will be used to illustrate these problems.

*Inventory Processes*

In many situations, resources are used and replenished in such a manner that it is necessary to have available a stock of the resources which can be drawn upon as needed. The management of the inventory or stock control process is often difficult if demand for the resource fluctuates or if purchase and storage arrangements constrain the level of stock in hand in some way. Two related decisions need to be made concerning this process: how much of the resources to order and when to place that order. Various factors influence these decisions, the most common being the time taken for an order to be delivered, the rate at which the resources are used, the cost of holding the resource in stock, the value of the resources used, and the cost of not having the resources available.

The earliest attempt to explore this situation mathematically was made by Harris in 1915, and by the mid-1950s the theory was well developed (Whitin, 1954). This work led to the economic-lot-size or economic-order-quantity equation. In this most simple model of the inventory process, the demand for a single resource is assumed to be constant and is deemed to be replenished by a fixed amount when the stock level has fallen to a specified level. In such a case the resource will never be out of stock, as the order will be placed at a time when there is enough stock to meet demand in the time before the order is received. The costs incurred by being out of stock do not therefore have to be considered.

The model is constructed by evaluating the total costs of the operation, $T$, over a given time period, usually annually. There are three components in this cost: the capital costs, the stock-holding costs, and the ordering costs. Capital costs are the value of the resources used. If each unit of the resource is valued at $C$ and total demand is $R$, then this cost is $RC$. Stock-holding costs are the costs involved in administering, storing, and maintaining any stock. This is expressed as a fraction, $I$, of the value of each item, and it is therefore $CI$ multiplied by the average number of items in stock. This average can be shown to be $Q/2$, where $Q$ is the number of items ordered at a time. Ordering costs are defined by multiplying the number of orders made each year (the total demand, $R$, divided by the quantity ordered, $Q$) by the costs of placing an order, $S$. Thus,

$$T = RC + CIQ/2 + RS/Q$$

A variable which can be chosen by management in this situation is $Q$, the order quantity. The problem then is to find that value of $Q$ for which $T$ is minimized for particular values of $R$, $C$, $I$, and $S$ which pertain to a given situation. This problem can be solved by differential calculus and yields a value of $Q$ given by

$$Q = \sqrt{2RS/CI}$$

This acts as a general model for setting the economic order quantity in situations which meet the assumptions made in the derivation of the equation for $Q$. Clearly there will be only a few cases which correspond closely to these assumptions. Demand is rarely constant, and the assumption that orders will be satisfied on time is sensitive to a host of practical difficulties. Many companies have tens or hundreds of items in stock and may wish to place orders for several at the same time in order to attract discounts and ease administration. Upper limits may be imposed on the number of items which can be stored by space restrictions and the desire not to tie up capital in unused resources. Companies with several plants at different locations may prefer to locate a single storage depot centrally rather than have one associated with each plant. The potential for complex inventory problems to arise is great, and the sophistication of the models built to address these situations and the method of their solution has increased correspondingly.

In many cases the analytical models developed from the simple case considered above and capable of providing exact solutions or approximations to exact solutions prove unable to reproduce the complexity of the actual situation. In these cases computer simulation models are used to explore the behavior of different inventory policies. A computer program is written which replicates the behavior of the system as stock levels fall and rise as resources pass through it. Changes in policy are explored by making changes in elements of the computer program, and it is possible to investigate the effect on the system of many different types and combinations of policy. The use of simulation models does not provide a policy which is best as the analytical models do but allows for the relative performance of different policies to be assessed in situations where analytical models are unable to be constructed. Johnston (1980) has shown how a simulation model can be introduced into the decision-making process to aid in the management of a complex stock control system.

The problem tackled by Johnston was centered on the stock control system of builders' and plumbers' merchants. Such companies stock a wide range of items used in the construction industry and so make it possible for individuals to purchase all their requirements at a single location. The analysis undertaken falls into two parts. The first is concerned with the strategic management of stock and focuses on the balance between the level of investment to be made in stock and the level of service provision. As investment increases, there is less likelihood of items being out of stock, and so service provision increases. As investment decreases, service provision will decrease, and a balance needs to be achieved between these two factors. The second part of the analysis looks at the tactical decision of when and which items to purchase, bearing in mind the decision on investment and service levels. The complexity of these decisions is made apparent by observing that many of the merchants carry about 10,000 different items from nails and screws to central heating systems. These are drawn from various suppliers, each with different discount rates, order procedures, and reliability for delivery, and are subject to different levels of demand.

The strategic decision on the balance between investment and service provision is explored by calculating the value of the return per year under different policies. The return is defined to be total income less stock-holding costs, ordering costs, and penalty costs on lost sales. Management specifies either the amount to be invested in a particular group of items, a buying family, or a stocking factor which defines the probability of running out of stock for each item in the family. A computer program then establishes the value of the unspecified variable which will result in the maximum return. Thus management can investigate the relationship between these two factors and determine the investment decision in an informed manner.

Given this decision on investment level and service provision, the purchase of stock needs to be made compatible. Demand for each item in a buying family is forecast, and this forecast allows comparisons with stocks available and on order. This comparison is carried out each night, and forecasts are updated as a result of the day's trading. The use of computerized sales records makes this task straightforward. Draft orders are produced which management can consider in the light of knowledge of discounts or special rates or circumstances and can issue if they wish.

The introduction of this system led to increased levels of service provision and lower stock levels, as it allowed for a better match of stock holding with customer needs than had previously been possible. The computer models were introduced into a decision-making process on a regular basis and enable both strategic and tactical decisions to be made consistent with each other.

*Allocation Processes*

A second commonly occurring process recognized by Churchman, Ackoff, and Arnoff is the allocation process. This arises when there are a number of activities to be performed, each of which may be completed in a variety of ways, but the resources available are insufficient to enable each of them to be performed most effectively. Decisions then need to be made regarding how each activity should be carried out within the constraints imposed by resource availability. The problem is to find that allocation of resources to activities which optimizes a measure of effectiveness.

This type of problem had been tackled by several people before the

Second World War, although their work did not become widely known until later. Leontief (1951) and Kantorovich (1958) had investigated problems with a similar structure from an economic perspective. In the 1950s Dantzig and his team on project SCOOP (Scientific Computation of Optimal Programs), established by the U.S. Air Force, provided a major breakthrough in the treatment of such problems. This was to utilize the power of the new computing machines in order to create an efficient method of solving models of allocation processes. Beale (1985) gives a summary of how these methods developed and stimulated progress in the use of computers by operational researchers.

The standard form of a model of an allocation process consists of two parts. A measure of effectiveness is defined which associates either a benefit or a cost with each allocation of a resource to an activity. The total benefit or cost is to be maximized or minimized, respectively. The second part of the model consists of a set of expressions which represent constraints on how resources may be allocated. Typical constraints derive from the limited amounts of resources which are available or from the infeasibility of negative amounts being allocated. If $x_{ij}$ represents the amount of resource $i$ allocated to activity $j$, $p_{ij}$ is the unit profit realized from each of these allocations, $r_i$ is the amount of resource $i$ available, and if negative allocations are not permitted, then a simple allocation model results:

$$\text{Maximize}_{\{x_{ij}\}} \quad \sum_{ij} p_{ij} x_{ij}$$

$$\text{so that} \quad \sum_{j} x_{ij} \le r_i$$
$$x_{ij} \ge 0$$

The solution of problems of this form is usually achieved by use of the simplex method or a variation, a method first developed by the SCOOP team (Dantzig, 1951). A special case of this problem, the transportation problem, had been provided with a solution algorithm by Hitchcock (1941), but the power of the simplex method stemmed from its power and computational efficiency. Since the 1950s, efforts have concentrated upon improving the simplex method to allow solutions to be generated to problems where nonlinear or integer expressions appear in the models and also to improve its efficiency.

A good recent example of this type of model which illustrates the improvements which have been made in solution methods is provided by Glen (1986). This example is concerned with the problem of how to manage an integrated enterprise which involves rearing cattle for beef and the production of crops to feed the animals. In this case the key management issue is how to balance the land use between cattle and crops, bearing in mind the need to purchase supplementary feed if insufficient is grown, the potential to sell excess crops, and the desirability of producing cattle of sufficient quality to meet regulations on its sale.

A model of a form similar to the simple example above is constructed which contains 640 constraints and 1,801 variables. The solution was achieved in thirty-five seconds of computer time. There are six types of variable which represent factors that can be controlled by the farm management: the number of animals fed on a certain mix of food to increase weight, the number of animals purchased at different weights at different points in time, the number of animals sold at different weights at different points in time, the number of animals kept at different weights at different periods, the amount of land used for crop production, and the amount of crops purchased for sale. Each of these categories has some implication for the income and expenditure of the enterprise, and by using suitable coefficients, their contribution to profit can be established. An expression of total profit which is dependent upon the values taken by each of the variables is constructed and is sought to be maximized. Several types of constraint must be recognized. Foodstuff from crops either produced or purchased must be sufficient to increase animal weight. The number of animals sold must be less than or equal to the total number of animals available. The number of animals bought and sold in any one time period defines how many there will be in the following time period. The amount of land available places an upper limit on the number of animals which can be supported. The combination of different types of animals, different feeding patterns, and a series of time periods rapidly increases the number of variables necessary, and the size of the model is typical of many practical applications of this approach.

Solution of the model yields a set of values which define how best to buy and sell cattle and organize crop production. Thus it can be used to assess how effective past management actions have been and to show how these could be improved. The model can be easily updated—to reflect changing prices, for example—and can be used to revise plans in the light of new circumstances. A strength of the model lies in its ability to bring together aspects of the problem—for example, the cattle and crop elements—in a single framework. The character of the model is typical of many used for production planning in various contexts where the linear programming approach has been found to be particularly valuable.

*Waiting-Line Processes*

Waiting-line processes are the third common situation identified by Churchman, Ackoff, and Arnoff. Such processes arise when resources are acted upon, either by machines or people, sequentially rather than simultaneously. Consequently, a queue of items awaiting service may appear, and this phenomenon leads to the alternative name of queuing processes. This process arises in manufacturing, service, and transport systems of various types. Early work on the study of this process was undertaken by Erlang in the first decade of this century. He explored the operation of telephone systems in which calls were queued before being transferred to their destination by an exchange. The generality of queuing behavior was recognized after the Second World War, and the complexity of the models and solution methods increased.

Four factors are central to the character of a queuing system and its behavior. The arrival pattern defines the speed at which the resources which are acted upon (the customers) enter the system. This may be a constant, as in a fully automated production line, or it may be random, as in the entry of patients into a coronary care unit. The number of servers who act on the customers affects the level of service provision. There may be one or more servers depending on the system being considered, and they may carry out the same or different tasks. The third factor is the queue discipline, which defines the order in which the customers are served. A common discipline is to serve customers in the order in which they arrive: first come, first served. In special cases a priority ranking may be adopted, in health care or housing provision, for example. Finally, the length of time which the server takes to carry out the activity on the customer is important. This may be constant or variable depending upon the specific case under consideration.

The task facing the management of queuing systems is to design a system in such a way as to provide an effective service. This requires using sufficient servers and a queue discipline which can cope with the arrival of customers without leading to excessive queue lengths and waiting times for the customers or to the servers being idle for periods of time.

The most straightforward queuing system to model is that with a single server operating with a first come, first served queue discipline in which customers do not leave the system until they have been served. The arrival rate of customers and the speed with which a server operates, the service rate, are defined by two values in the most simple model. The average number of arrivals in a time period is $\lambda$, and the average number of customers served per time period is $\mu$. These correspond to the likelihood of an arrival being described by Poisson distribution and the service rate by an exponential distribution. The behavior of the system in a steady state is defined by various functions of $\lambda$ and $\mu$ which are derived by analysis. The probability that there are $n$ customers in the system is given by $(1 - \lambda/\mu)\,(\lambda/\mu)^n$. The average number of customers in the system is $\lambda/(\mu - \lambda)$, and the average time spent in the system is $1/(\mu - \lambda)$. The likelihood that the server has no customers to serve is $(1 - \lambda/\mu)$. In cases where the assumptions made in establishing this model apply, the evaluation of these indicators is straightforward and provides useful information.

When more complicated queuing systems are considered, analytic solutions may still be possible. Work has been undertaken to explore those cases where more servers are used, different arrival and service rates exist, customers may choose to leave the queue before being served, and different queue disciplines from that above are in operation. Analysis is not always possible, and in these cases computer simulation is used. As with complex inventory processes, a computer program is constructed which replicates the behavior of the actual system. The program is used, as for inventory processes, to explore the effect of different policies upon the system and so to inform management of what might happen in different scenarios.

An example of the need for a simulation approach to a queuing problem is provided by Chiamsiri, Sculli, and Wong (1984). The problem is set in the office of the Hong Kong Trade Industry and Customs Department responsible for issuing export licenses. A representative of a company wishing to export goods from Hong King must go in person to the office in order to process the application. Thus a queuing system is formed in which the customers are the company representatives, the servers the officers of the department, and the activity the processing of applications. For many years the office had operated a manual system in which each officer had gained a high degree of knowledge on the classifications used and the details of the licensing procedure. The office had recently been computerized, and as a result, much of this information was available on the computer system and specialization was not so necessary, as all types of licenses could be issued from any terminal. The problem was to determine how many computer terminals should be installed to operate the new system effectively.

Observation of the system revealed that demand for the services was not constant. The late summer months of July, August, and September showed the heaviest demand, with a considerable reduction occurring in the following three months and in February. The daily demand also varied, with most customers arriving in late morning or midafternoon. The service rates varied as some customers would have more than one application or would have particular details to be clarified before a license was issued. The complexity of the situation made an analytical model impracticable, and a simulation model was constructed. The customers were assumed to form a single queue and to go to the first available officer once they reached the head of the queue. The average arrival and service times were established from observations, and by choosing numbers randomly, variations from the average were generated which conformed to the observed pattern.

The model was then run to reproduce activity over a period of 1,000 days with a different number of terminals in operation. The major criterion for choosing the number of terminals to introduce was the length of the queue at the end of the day. It was the policy to serve all of the customers in the office at the time of closing. A large number of customers would involve staff in excessive overtime and possibly in not being able to complete their duties before finishing work. It was desirable to have as short a queue at the end of the day as was compatible with efficient operations being carried out for the rest of the day. From the model's performance it was clear that three terminals gave too long a queue at the close of the office (nearly forty minutes were needed to clear it), and that six gave too much idle time (even in the busiest month, the office was empty for 45% of the day). Thus four or five terminals were to be used. The difference in performance indicated by the output of the model was not significant enough to suggest a definite preference, and the decision was passed on to management. They had to judge whether demand would increase, in which case five terminals would seem to be appropriate, or not, when four terminals would suffice.

*Replacement Processes*

The fourth class of commonly occurring processes centers upon the replacement of resources, usually physical resources. Replacement is necessary because performance falls below an acceptable level. Reduction in performance may be incremental (the blunting of a cutting edge) or dramatic (the blowing of a fuse). There are therefore two types of problem. For resources that deteriorate, a decision needs to be made about how often to replace them, bearing in mind the costs of purchasing new resources and maintaining existing ones. For resources that are susceptible to failure, the issue is to decide when to replace these so as to minimize the likelihood of failure, bearing in mind the costs of replacement and of failure.

The models developed to consider these types of problem origi-

nated outside OR. The machine-tool- and equipment-producing industries had a natural interest in these questions, and work was carried out
in these areas prior to the Second World War. The contribution of OR
was to develop this work and make it relevant to novel areas and to
management decision making. The models constructed for the simplest
cases, where single items of equipment are considered in isolation from
the system of which they are part, are reasonably straightforward. In the
case of items that deteriorate, the total cost of operating the item over
different periods of time is calculated. This cost involves amounts to
cover maintenance and any other necessary expenditure. It is then possible to compare the operating costs of different items over different time
periods and to choose that item and length of operation before replacement which are cheapest. Those items which are subject to failure, often
with an increasing likelihood with age, are subjected to analysis of the
likelihood of failure over time. It is then possible to determine the most
likely life span of the item and to use this to inform replacement decisions.

   An excellent example of how maintenance and replacement decisions are related and how analysis is undertaken to examine them is
given by Lamson, Hastings, and Willis (1983). They provide a study of
the maintenance and replacement strategy of a railway track used to
transport ore from mine to port in Australia. The climate and environmental conditions of the area and the size and weight of trains using the
line make the rate at which the track deteriorates high. The rail link is
vital to the success of the mining operation, and it is therefore important
that a safe and reliable service be offered. It was found that the nature of
the deterioration in the curved sections of track differed from that in the
straight sections. On the curved track, wear was mainly on the side of
the rail, so that regular replacement and maintenance were necessary.
The straight track suffered less from this problem, and metal fatigue,
leading to possible fracture, was the major problem. Thus two pieces of
analysis leading to two policies were required.

   For the curved track it was possible to regrind the rails to renew
their profile, and this regrinding formed part of the maintenance schedule for the track. Regulations and engineering data provided limits for
the rail characteristics, and consideration of these led to a maximum life
span for each rail of forty months. The maintenance of a rail is considered at regular intervals when a decision must be made to do nothing, to
regrind the rail, or to replace it. Each action has a cost associated with it
and has implications for the state of the rail at the next decision point. A
large number of combinations are possible. By searching through the
combinations in a structured way, it was possible to find the action with

the least cost. This involved grinding the rails every four months until they were twenty-eight months old and then leaving them until they were replaced after forty months. This strategy resulted in estimated savings of 23% of the maintenance budget compared with the previous policy.

Maintenance of straight track was possible in two ways. One was to replace a short section of rail (3.1 meters) manually whenever a fault was detected. The other was to replace a whole rail (400 meters) by means of a special machine. The existing strategy was to replace defective parts manually and, when fifteen faults had been so corrected in a one-kilometer stretch, to replace the whole rail. This effectively meant replacing a rail every twelve years. It was found to be considerably cheaper to replace a rail every eight years, irrespective of the number of faults occurring up to that time. This policy was estimated to save 55% of the cost of the existing maintenance strategy.

*Competitive Processes*

The final type of commonly occurring process noted by Churchman, Ackoff, and Arnoff is competitive processes. These differ significantly from the others in that the environment of the process is not passive. In each of the other processes, it is assumed that any changes in the process do not affect the way in which the environment behaves. In competitive processes this is not so; changes made by one actor in a situation influence the behavior of other actors. Two types of competitive problem are considered: games and bidding. In both cases theory was relatively well developed in the immediate post-war periods, but applications of that theory were sparse, and there is evidence here that OR in the U.S. was beginning to be driven by theoretical developments rather than by practical issues in organizations.

Game theory, inspired by von Neumann and Morgenstern (1944), is an analysis of the strategies that different players in gamelike situations should adopt in order to win or not to lose. Each actor takes into account the strategy of the others, and the outcome is a set of choices which optimize the benefits of all concerned as far as is possible. Recent developments of the theory (Bennett and Huxham, 1982; Howard, 1971) have expanded the scope of the analysis, but practical applications remain few.

Analysis of bidding situations is a second area where competition is central. Here a decision maker decides what amount to bid for an item and when to stop. The issue is to determine the level of bid which is likely to be higher than all the competitor's bids and to yield the highest return if successful. King and Mercer (1985) provide a recent application of this theory to the problem of bidding for contracts but note that there is still no generally agreed-upon approach to this type of problem.

*Discussion*

The framework which Churchman, Ackoff, and Arnoff chose to structure OR in the 1950s has remained at the heart of many subsequent efforts to discuss the methods used in the discipline. In many standard texts one still finds chapters devoted to inventory, allocation, queuing, replacement, and competitive processes and the methods of modeling them. Despite the apparent continuing success of this framework in structuring OR, its ability to define the scope and character of the discipline must be considered in the light of its limitations. These are not new and have been understood since the appearance of *Introduction to Operations Research* but can be overlooked in the search for a neat framework for defining OR.

First, the classification was intended to cover the commonly occurring processes and the methods developed to tackle them. It was not intended to be and is not inclusive of all problems and techniques. Certain types of problems emerged into the orbit of OR subsequent to the appearance of the book, and the techniques developed to deal with them form as important a body of knowledge as any of the original classes. An example is the use of network-based methods to tackle project-planning problems. The project evaluation and review technique (PERT) and critical path analysis (CPA) were introduced in the 1950s to help with the management of large engineering projects, originally Polaris and chemical plants. Decision analysis has developed as a tool to aid the decision-making process in complex situations at the strategic level. Both of these topics would now be presented in a standard text on OR. Many other problems tackled by operational researchers fall outside the categories defined by Churchman, Ackoff, and Arnoff and can be seen as one-off analyses of unique situations. The claim that OR deals with only certain classes of problems is too limiting, and a broader understanding of its interests is required.

Second, the presentation of a set of commonly occurring processes suggests that many problems will fall neatly into one of these categories. This suggestion falsely reduces the role of the analyst to one of identifying the type of problem with reference to this set of ideal types. In fact, it is likely that a situation will be perceived to be of different forms, as an example of work carried out at BISRA shows (Collcutt, 1965, pp. 27–33). An analysis was required of the strategy for repairing open-hearth furnaces. This problem might be seen as belonging to the class of problems of replacement processes and might be dealt with by comparing different strategies to find the most cost-effective. It was, in fact, conceptualized as a queuing process in which the furnaces "queued up" for repairs and were served by a maintenance crew. This approach yielded a different set of indicators to the management than simply total costs, and it allowed a different understanding of the situation. Therefore to attempt to locate problems uniquely within the classes of commonly occurring processes is to restrict the vision of analysts and to reduce the potential for gaining valuable understanding and information.

Third, following from the previous point, problems may not be sufficiently straightforward to fall into one category only and may show characteristics of different types of closely related problems. Williams (1978), for example, shows how problems in the petroleum industry have aspects related to the transportation of the crude oil from the well to the refinery, the production of different end products in accordance with demand, and the movement of these products to the point of sale. A manufacturing process consists of elements of a stock control problem, the allocation of resources to the production of finished products, the maintenance of the machinery involved, and marketing and distribution functions as well. When single, isolated classes of problems are presented, the complexity of many real issues is lost. Practical OR cannot simplify problems to fit a classification and must deal with complexity as it is perceived.

Finally, the classification into common processes and methods of modeling them leads to the view that OR is a set of techniques which can be applied to produce a solution to a given problem. There are cases where it is clear what the character of the problem is, and the application of standard techniques will yield useful information. However, in many cases this is not possible because the character of the problem is not clear or the assumptions necessary to apply standard methods may not apply. Then the operational researcher must develop methods particular to the case in hand. The view that OR is a set of techniques to be applied in a standard way omits the broader process of analysis in which they are embedded and the wider organizational context in which OR takes place.

## Conclusion

The conclusion to be drawn from the above discussion is that OR in the 1950s developed rapidly and, by the end of the decade, had established a set of problems and methods which it commonly dealt with.

This conclusion, however, does not define the full character of OR. It concentrates upon the technical aspects of the subject to the exclusion of the social system of which OR is part. In Part II of this book this aspect of OR will be considered. The focus will be upon OR as a problem-solving activity within organizations and will seek to provide a backdrop against which the commonly occurring processes and modeling techniques can be placed. This perspective will result in a broader vision of OR than has so far been presented.

# *II*

# *Systems in Operational Research*

The two chapters in Part I provide an overview of the history and scope of OR as it is normally understood. In Part II a rigorous analysis of the processes involved in OR is undertaken, with a particular emphasis on the role of systems ideas in and as aids to explanations of these processes.

Three levels can be identified at which OR processes operate, and these provide a structure for the following chapters. First, the processes that enable OR analysts to reach conclusions about problem situations are explored. Second, the interactions between an organization and the OR analysts who serve it are identified and discussed. Finally, in a broader discussion, the relationship between OR and the general set of systems ideas and methods is examined. These three chapters provide an internally consistent understanding of how systems ideas are embedded in a range of OR-based processes.

# 4

# Operational Research as Problem Solving

## Introduction

The purpose of the discussion in this chapter is to show how classical OR methodology can be interpreted as being a problem-solving system. The following two chapters will then consider how this system relates to the decision-making system in an organization and the extent to which it is scientific in character. The first task to accomplish here is to define what types of problems OR is deemed capable of tackling and from this definition to establish what it means to solve such problems. A problem-solving system is then seen to be a set of processes which can provide such solutions. The classical OR methodology is then described and illustrated. The various studies used previously to exemplify standard OR problems are used again here. Finally, systems thinking is used to provide a framework in which this methodology can be understood. The notions of hierarchy, emergent properties, communication, and control each highlight particular features of the approach.

## Problems in OR

It has already been seen in the previous two chapters that the intellectual and organizational motivation for the emergence of OR was the recognition that scientific methods could be used to improve the ability of management to control the parts of organizations for which they were responsible. As OR consolidated its disciplinary status in the 1950s, efforts were made to define the discipline and its methods. Although various attitudes toward this matter were adopted, Ackoff (1961) concludes that "most operations researchers are in substantial agreement" (p. 6) with Beer's suggestion (1959b) that:

(1) Operational research is the attack of modern science
(2) on problems of likelihood (accepting mischance)

(3) which arise in the management and control
(4) of men and machines, materials and money
(5) in their natural environment
(6) its special technique is to invent a strategy of control
(7) by measuring, comparing and predicting probably behaviour
(8) through a scientific model of a situation. (pp. 16–17)

The extent to which this list captures the accepted view of OR is reflected by the similarity between this view of OR and that included in each issue of the *Journal of the OR Society* from 1966 to 1984:

> Operational Research is the attack of modern science on complex problems arising in the direction and management of large systems of men, machines, materials and money in industry, business, government and defence. The distinctive approach is to develop a scientific model of the system, incorporating factors such as chance and risk, with which to predict and compare the measurement of factors of alternative decisions, strategies or controls. The purpose is to help management determine its policy and actions scientifically.

Without dwelling too long on these "definitions" of OR, it is clear, from the above discussion and the previous chapters, that OR is concerned with tackling management problems in a scientific manner. The issue arises, then, of what types of problems can be usefully addressed in this way. Ackoff (1962, p. 30) establishes as being five in number the minimal necessary and sufficient conditions for a problem which is capable of scientific resolution. The following features must exist:

1. An individual who owns the problem (the decision maker).
2. An outcome which the decision maker desires (the objective).
3. At least two unequally efficient courses of action which each have some chance of yielding the objective (the alternatives).
4. A state of doubt in the decision maker's mind over which alternative is best.
5. An environment in which 1 to 4 exist and that consists of factors which may influence them.

In this context, to solve a problem means to choose one of the alternatives. Which is chosen will depend upon the objective, the full set of alternatives from which the choice will be made, the measure of "best" (the criteria for choice), and the factors identified as lying in the environment. Thus OR as problem solving is a choice process and includes the activities of establishing the set from which the choice will be made, analyzing the situation to enable an informed rather than a random choice to occur, and providing information on the meaning of the choice in practical terms.

Before proceeding to explore the structure of this process in detail, some general points will be made about this particular view of problems and problem solving. First, it can be seen that if any of the five elements of a problem are removed, the problem-solving process is made unnecessary. A decision maker is necessary to allow a problem situation to be perceived as such. The objective gives the problem its purpose, that is, to achieve this desired state. If there is only one way of achieving the objective, then no choice needs to be made. Equally, if the decision maker is in no doubt over how to achieve the objective, then there is no need to solve the problem, for one does not exist. Finally, no situation confronted by decision makers is completely isolated from factors outside their control, and this point must be recognized if the problem is to include as many relevant factors as possible.

Second, the above statement of a problem is the simplest possible. Ackoff (1962) and Ackoff and Sasieni (1968, p. 24) consider various ways in which problems can become more complex and hence more difficult to tackle. These fall into six broad categories. When there is a group of decision makers rather than an individual, the number of objectives and views on what is the "best" alternative increases and making the choice is more difficult because of conflict and inconsistency over these matters within the group. The environment may be changing in rapid or unpredictable ways, so that its influence on the situation under study becomes more pronounced and difficult to account for. The set of alternatives from which a choice will be made may be large or infinite, so that the comparison of alternatives and the choice between possibly very similar ones is difficult and lengthy. Even if there is a single decision maker, the set of objectives may be large or may contain inconsistencies so that it is likely that one alternative will not be found which achieves all objectives to the greatest extent and compromises will have to be made. There may be a distinction between the decision maker(s) and those people who are responsible for implementing the chosen alternative, which introduces an extra channel of communication into the situation and hence an extra opportunity for alternatives to be misspecified or not carried out as anticipated. Finally, there may be reactions to decisions which could not be foreseen before they were introduced. Thus, problem solving does not finish once a choice is made. For successful implementation to be achieved, a monitoring process must be involved that assesses the extent to which implementation is as expected.

Third, the above definition of a problem does not distinguish between the person who solves the problems and the decision maker. It is unclear whether the decision maker is also the problem solver. A usual case is that the two roles are filled by different individuals, and that is the view taken here. This does not preclude the possibility that the same person is both decision maker and problem solver.

The above discussion raises some issues which are discussed in this and the two following chapters. In particular this chapter looks at how the choice process is structured and shows that this is a problem-solving system which exhibits the systemic properties of hierarchy, emergence, communication, and control. The following chapters tackle the issue of whether the claim that OR uses scientific methods implies that it is a science, and the relationships between the OR process, the part of an organization where it is based, and the remainder of an organization are explored. In the next part of the book the more general issue of the limitations of the OR process as discussed here is addressed, and systems-based methods which can overcome these limitations are discussed and compared with OR.

## Classical OR Methodology

### An Overview

It is already been said that the early operational researchers were trained as scientists. It is clear from this observation why the first organized efforts at OR should be seen as a science by those practicing it. They were applying their skills and expertise in the scientific method to a particular set of phenomena. Larnder made this point clear when describing the purpose of the ORS in the Second World War as being "to provide Commanders-in-Chief with a trained scientific staff who can collect data and undertake research into the analysis of technical, tactical and general operational factors" (Waddington, 1973, p. 20).

As OR developed in the military, efforts were made to formulate a framework within which the process used could be understood. The first such framework was given by Blackett in 1943 (Blackett, 1962). Blackett saw OR as being strictly practical in purpose and as being characterized by the limited number of numerical data available on the complex phenomena with which it was concerned (p. 177). In order to provide advice on future actions which involved these phenomena and which made the greatest possible use of past experience, Blackett identified three necessary stages. These formed his framework for the methodology of OR. First, past operations were studied to determine the facts of the situation. Theories were then elaborated to explain these facts and to enable the situation to be understood. Finally, the facts and the theories which sought to explain them were used to make predictions about future actions and so to enable better informed decisions to be made about implementing those actions.

Two methods of deriving scientific explanations of the facts were considered. One was the *a priori* method, which required a general solution to be found to a problem which was made simpler than it actually was. Simplification was carried out to the point where a general solution could be found. This solution was then used to explore the possible effects of actions under those circumstances most likely to prevail. This approach was limited by the need to simplify and, in particular, was least appropriate for cases where important factors had to be omitted during the simplification process. The second approach was referred to as the *variational method*. This was more commonly used and saw any future action as being a variation in the existing situation. Knowledge of how the present situation performed allowed the effects of the variation to be assessed and comparisons to be made between future actions.

Blackett's explanation of the OR process saw it was as a direct application to operational matters of those elements central to the scientific method of understanding phenomena. These elements vary slightly according to author. For example, Rivett (1980) states them as being observation, generalization, experimentation, and validation, while White (1985) refers to them as being observation, hypothesis formation, experimentation, and prediction. It is clear that Blackett's description of OR compares well with both of these, as does the more sophisticated version of the OR process described by Churchman, Ackoff, and Arnoff (1957), which is to be discussed shortly. The relationship between scientific method and the process of OR will be considered in detail subsequently. It is sufficient here to note the early, accepted view that OR was based in the scientific method of understanding, with all that this implied.

The move from military applications to industrial and commercial contexts did not see any change in the methods used in OR studies. Indeed the scientific character of OR gave it a credibility and status which eased its development and movement into nonmilitary organizations. The contribution of Churchman, Ackoff, and Arnoff (1957) to the development of OR has already been noted. Their text does not ignore the methodological aspects of the approach, and their description of the OR approach to problem solving will now be considered.

Churchman, Ackoff, and Arnoff, as noted above, perceived the role of OR as providing the optimum solution to the class of problems with which it deals. Thus OR is concerned not with marginal improvements in the existing state but with moving toward the best attainable state.

This is to be done subject to chosen criteria and within any constraints which exist. The OR group does not decide whether or not to implement this "best" solution; this is a task for those who are responsible for managing the resources involved. Hence OR is a service to management whose purpose is to provide a scientific basis on which decisions may be made and problems solved.

The process used by OR to provide such a basis is grounded in scientific method. In describing the method of OR, Churchman, Ackoff, and Arnoff distinguish between method, tools, and techniques. Although of little use beyond definitional purposes, this distinction does allow the level at which OR method should be considered to be identified. A method is a structured set of tasks or a plan which will enable an end to be achieved. In the case of OR, this end is the provision of advice to decision makers. Within this method, various tools are used. The way in which the tools are manipulated is defined as technique. Thus, OR method is a broad, procedural device which gives a general structure to the process by which OR achieves its purpose. While noting that a single method which will be agreed to by all OR practitioners is not expected, Churchman, Ackoff, and Arnoff propose six major phases which would receive general support as being the basis of such a method.

The first phase is to formulate the problem. This involves specifying the decision makers, their objectives, the system involved, the alternative courses of action to be investigated, and the criteria for measuring the effect of these on the system.

The second phase involves constructing a mathematical model of the system. This model expresses the measure of effectiveness as a function of the variables in the system and also contains any relationships which operate between the variables. The variables fall into two categories: those which can be controlled by the decision makers and those which cannot.

Third, the model is used to find the value of the measure of effectiveness given when each of the alternative actions occurs. It is assumed that each action corresponds to changes being made in the controllable variables. The ultimate goal is to identify the action which yields the best measure of effectiveness. In some cases, this action can be identified by mathematical analysis of the model, and exact results are found. In others, approximations and heuristic methods may be necessary if exact analysis is not possible. Results found by this method will not be as accurate as those obtained by the first method.

The next phase involves testing the model and the results it gives against reality. In particular those actions which yield the better measures of effectiveness need to be tested for the occurrence in practice of their predicted effects. If experiments show errors between predicted and actual performance, the model may be reconsidered and new analyses undertaken. If actual performance is satisfactory, then it is necessary to establish controls over any action likely to be implemented. These are a set of rules or mechanisms by which the action can be changed in response to changes in uncontrollable variables. The formulation of these rules is the fifth phase.

Finally, the actions yielding high measures of performance are offered to the decision makers together with their controls, ready for implementation. This handing over of advice should be supported by the details of any necessary changes in existing practice and by the provision of training in new procedures where appropriate.

These six phases are not presumed to occur sequentially and independently on all occasions. It is likely that some will take place simultaneously and that aspects of one phase will have implications for others. Thus it is preferable to see these as mutually supportive activities undertaken in the course of an OR project rather than as independent steps which are taken in order to reach the end of the road.

The extent to which this description of the OR process is more sophisticated than that of Blackett can be established by a comparison. Churchman, Ackoff, and Arnoff give a more detailed consideration of the early part of the process, the problem formulation phase. For Blackett this phase does not involve identifying decision makers or the system of interest; observations are made directly of that part of world under investigation. A reason for this extra emphasis in the later methodology is the increased use of OR in nonmilitary organizations, where different management levels and areas of responsibility are concerned. In such cases it is important to recognize to whom recommendations will be made. In military organizations, authority is more clearly defined and was not seen to pose as much of a problem to OR analysts. Problem formulation for Churchman, Ackoff, and Arnoff also includes reference to objective and criteria for effectiveness. The need to include these stems also differs from the need to be more aware of the ultimate recipient of the results of the investigation in nonmilitary applications. The objectives and criteria should be compatible with those adopted by the decision makers involved.

The modeling phase and the investigation of the effect of various actions are comparable in both approaches. At the latter stage, differences emerge where, for reasons similar to those cited above, Churchman, Ackoff, and Arnoff give more detailed consideration to implementation issues. This emphasis reflects an increased sensitivity to the difficulties of implementation in nonmilitary organizations than in military contexts, where a greater degree of authority eases any potential problems.

To illustrate the generality and explanatory power of the above framework, the applications of OR discussed in the previous chapter will be reconsidered within Churchman, Ackoff, and Arnoff's description of the OR process. The intention is not to show how the analysts involved apply the method, for it has already been argued that this is an inappropriate way to interpret their description. Instead, the discussion is intended to bring out the connections between the different processes involved in the method, to show how the investigations unfolded over time, and to identify the central role played in these investigations by a model of the situation being studied. Each of the six phases identified by Churchman, Ackoff, and Arnoff as being necessary for the OR process will be considered in turn, and their treatment in each of the case studies will be examined.

*Problem Formulation*

The first phase is problem formulation. This involves specifying the decision makers, the objectives to be pursued, and the alternative ways in which the objectives are expected to be achieved. Ramakrisha and Brightman (1986) note that errors have led to Type 3 errors: solving the wrong problem.

Problem formulation has recently received considerable interest in the OR community and has been reviewed by Wooley and Pidd (1980, 1981) and Pidd and Wooley (1980). They identify four approaches to problem structuring, as they call it, each of which indicates some ways of going about the process of understanding and structuring the situation that the OR analyst is confronted with. The checklist approach exemplified by Kepner and Tregoe (1965) seeks to give a step-by-step procedure by which the problem can be formulated and organized into a convenient structure. The definition approach illustrated by Ackoff and Sasieni (1968) requires the elements of the situation—the decision makers, objectives, alternatives, and measures—to be identified as a precursor to modeling their interrelationships. The science research approach places emphasis upon observing the situation, gathering data, and then using this empirical information to indicate the "real" nature of the problem. An example is given by Waddington (1977). Finally, the people approach understands situations to be the result of individual perceptions of the phenomena that the individuals observe. Cited examples which see OR analysts as organizational change agents include Boothroyd (1978), Checkland (1981), and Eden, Jones, and Sims (1983).

Each of these approaches to problem formulation results in the analyst's being able to understand the situation that must be tackled. They result in knowledge being available to the analyst about the objectives to be pursued and the factors which influence the ways in which these objectives can be achieved. The objectives, as can be seen from the following examples, are translated into quantitative forms which can be compared objectively. Thus any apparent element of bias or subjectivity is taken from the OR approach, and advice on how to achieve objectives in the best way is determined from a numerical comparison of performance indicators. It is also noticeable from the examples and the methods of problem formulation outlined above that the objectives are those of the clients or decision makers. The analyst is seen to have no role to play in choosing the objectives to be pursued; the task is solely to identify them, and various methods exist by which this can be done. This way of understanding the analyst's role also helps to increase the separation between the analyst and the problem and thus reinforces the view that the analyst's advice is unpredjudiced and objective.

The theoretical discussions of how to formulate problems, described above, are not necessarily reflected in the written accounts of applications of the OR approach. None of the five case studies viewed previously as illustrating standard OR problems gives much recognition to this aspect of the OR process. In each the problem is introduced in a manner which suggests that it is not difficult to understand its nature. While this is unlikely to be the case, in practice lack of discussion does hinder any assessment of the relative strengths of the different streams identified by Pidd and Wooley. Consequently a description of each of the problems tackled will now be given. In each case the decision makers and the organizational context of the problem will be identified, together with the broad objectives to be attained.

Johnston (1980) is concerned with a particular class of organizations: builder's and plumbers' merchants with a turnover of between 2 and 20 million pounds and one to five main branches. The aim of the investigation was to improve stock management in such organizations by designing and introducing a computerized stock control and purchasing system. Improvements were measured by the decrease in costs associated with the stock-holding function and the ability of the merchants to satisfy customer requirements from stock. By altering the purchasing of new stock and improving the monitoring of stock levels, these indicators are affected. Glen (1986) was attempting to construct a system which could help to manage the production and marketing of beef cattle. No particular decision maker was involved, but it is clear that the major user of the results would be farm managers. The objective is to identify that method of feeding, selling, and rearing beef cattle which is likely to yield the most profit. The decisions to be made center on the purchase and use of foodstuffs, the rearing and selling of cattle, and the use of land to grow crops and raise cattle. By changing the land use pattern, the feeding schedule, and the marketing of cattle and crops, the total profit is affected. That management strategy which maximizes profit is sought. Chiamsiri *et al.* (1984), in contrast, were involved with specific decision makers: the managers of an office which issues export licences. The management wished to improve the level of service and reduce operating costs by introducing a computerized element into the operation. A key issue was how many terminals to introduce in order to provide "reasonable" service. Lamson, Hastings, and Willis (1983) were involved with providing advice to the management of a rail link between mines and port facilities in Australia. The goal was to reduce maintenance costs by a rescheduling of the replacement and maintenance of the track while retaining safety of operation. Finally, King and Mercer (1985) were working for the management of a construction company and giving advice on how to improve its bidding strategy for contracts. The decisions to be made for any tender are the amount to bid for the work and the type of bid to make. On the basis of these decisions the strategy which results in the lowest bid which is likely to be successful can be identified.

*Model Construction*

The phase after problem formulation is model construction. It has already been seen how in each of these case studies one of the standard situations identified by Churchman, Ackoff, and Arnoff is modeled. Johnston builds a model of a stock control system using mathematical formulae to represent the levels of stock, the costs associated with their purchase and maintenance, and their dynamic behavior. Glen uses linear programming to express the necessary relationships between levels of foodstuffs, cattle at different ages, and land use and expresses a level of profit as a function of relevant variables. Chiamsiri *et al.* constructed a computer program which simulates the behavior of the export licence office which they were investigating. Lamson *et al.* used two approaches to arrive at a way of measuring the cost of different policies. A decision tree was used to build up a series of policy decisions and their total cost over a period of time. A mathematical expression was also used to provide the total cost of these decisions over a period of time. Finally, King and Mercer developed an expression which gives the value of the markup on a bid for a contract as a function of the time the job requires, its size, and the distance between the company and the site where the job is to be done.

In each of these cases the models constructed are not very different from the standard approaches which have been developed over many years for similar problems. The process of model construction lies at the heart of OR, and the classification of common problems indicates some useful types of model. Situations which do not fall into this category are dealt with in a manner which is specific to those cases. It would be exceptional to be able to use a standard model without some extensions and modifications to make it appropriate to a real world case. Thus, model-building activity in OR consists largely of the construction of a formal model of a real-world situation, often from scratch and occasionally with the help of a standard model from which to begin.

The process by which such models are constructed is often a focus of OR texts, and this emphasis can lead to the false impression that OR is solely a branch of applied mathematics. For example, Cohen (1985) makes the point that any understanding of the world gained scientifically must involve a model of that piece of the world. Models may be qualitative but OR "is concerned mainly with mathematical ones" (p. 2). Moore (1986) sees the use of models as a key characteristic of OR. These "are formulated in terms of a number of variables" and are of two basic types (p. 8). Symbolic models are those in which a mathematical representation is made to describe the system concerned. Analogue models are physical representations of the situation under consideration upon which analyses can be carried out. Williams (1978) notes that OR is concerned with abstract, as opposed to concrete, models and that these involve "a set of mathematical relationships . . . which correspond to some more down-to-earth relationships in the real world" (p. 3). Taha (1976) sees an OR investigation as consisting of "building a model of the physical situation" (p. 2). Further, "the most important type of OR model is the symbolic or mathematical model" (p. 5). Thierauf, Klelkamp, and Ruwe (1985) note that contemporary management scientists "make extensive use of mathematical models" (p. 8).

Despite the general agreement that OR makes use of models which are couched in mathematical language, there is relatively little written about the general process by which such models are constructed. It is not difficult to find details of models of standard and simplified operations and to grasp from these the fundamental behavior of such operations. What is more elusive is an outline of how models, in general, relate to the perception of the situation held by the OR analyst and the client who is being provided with advice. Two useful pieces of work in this area are those of Beer (1966) and White (1985).

Beer (1966, Ch. 6) understands the role of models in OR to be one which serves to bring together the OR analyst and the managers with whom they are in conjunction. In particular a scientific model acts as "a homomorphism on to which two different situations are mapped, and which actually defines the extent to which they are structurally identical" (p. 113). The two situations are a managerial situation and a scientific situation perceived by management and analyst, respectively. In perceiving each situation, a conceptual model is produced which is not rigorously defined and is held as a set of mental constructs by either a manager or an analyst. One task of an analyst is to bring these together to yield a deeper understanding and more rigorous statement of the situation to be tackled. The process by which this is achieved is to use the neutral languages of mathematics, statistics, and logic to formulate the conceptual models in precise terms. The two conceptual models can then be compared and brought together to give a single scientific model which is "shorn of mysticism and poetry" (p. 113). This model allows the situation to be examined objectively in order to establish how it can be improved. The basis for the scientific situation is derived by drawing analogies between the observed situation and others of which the analyst has had experience. Thus an OR analyst does not construct models to understand phenomena per se but as a way of formalizing conceptual models.

White (1985) also sees the OR process as involving two interlinked conceptual systems: the subject system and the object system. Here these represent the decision makers for whom an analysis is being carried out and the system about which decisions will be made. A model of the subject system is constructed in the first phase of the OR methodology, which is formulating the problem. The model construction phase is associated with modeling the object system. The systems are connected in two ways. First, the model of the subject system influences that of the object system, as the latter must be capable of being related to the objectives and policies specified in the former. Second, the decisions taken by the subject system influence the behavior of the object system, and this influence may lead to revisions in the models.

The model construction phase follows naturally from the problem formulation phase and is dependent upon it, for it is only when decision makers, objectives, and possible policies have been identified that construction of an appropriate model can begin. Beer and White imply to different extents the level of interaction which takes place between these two phases. Beer suggests that in understanding what type of model to construct, the analyst learns about the nature of the managerial situation to which it relates. Thus the two phases are almost in parallel. White does not go this far but still implies that the interaction is not serial but simultaneous.

The interaction between the formulation of the problem and the structure of the model can be illustrated by investigating the five studies noted previously. In each case the nature of the model reflects the concerns of the decision makers involved and makes them more rigorous by giving them specific form in terms of variables and equations. Johnston constructs a model of a stock control system which expresses the behavior of stock levels as a function of unit costs and profits, demand, and lead times for orders to be met. A set of equations models the phenomena which are to be controlled. The criteria for deciding how they should be controlled is the total expected return per annum of operating the system. This is given by an equation which measures the income from sales less stock-holding costs, ordering costs, and costs due to lost sales.

Glen's model of an integrated beef and crop operation is built around a set of relationships, inequalities, or equations, which specify conditions which must be satisfied in the operation. These refer to the availability of foodstuffs, animal sales, amount of livestock, and initial and terminal conditions for the planning period. Variables involved in these conditions measure factors such as the number of animals at different weights purchased at different times in the planning period, the amount of land used for various purposes, and the weight of crops produced for sale. Values of purchase and sale prices, the amounts of feed necessary to increase animal weight, the number of animals held at the start of the period, and the size of the farm are also included. Some of these variables are then used to construct an equation which represents the profit to be reaped from running the farm, which acts as the measure of performance.

In the third study, Chiamsiri *et al.* found that models based upon a set of equations were unable to cope adequately with the behavior of the system with which they were concerned. The assumptions which had to be made to allow equations to be constructed were not valid. It was decided to write a computer program which reproduced the behavior of the specific system under investigation rather than to work with an analytical model which yielded a poor approximation. The rate at which arrivals to the licensing office occurred was given by a probability distribution, and the time taken to serve a caller and the number of applications made per caller were measured. These factors were programmed to give an output which represented the state of the office, in terms of queue size, for half-hourly intervals. The program also calculated the amount of idle time in the office, that is, the amount of time during which no callers were present.

The study of maintenance policies for railway track carried out by Lamson *et al.* gave rise to two models because the nature of the problem for curved track was different from that for straight track. Curved track was subject to different patterns of wear from straight track, and thus different maintenance strategies had to be followed, as curved track needs to be replaced more frequently than straight track. For the curved track a decision tree was used to model the cumulative effect of different combinations of actions. Three possible actions could be carried out each month: nothing could be done, a rail could be maintained by regrinding its cross section, or a rail could be replaced. Knowledge of the engineering characteristics of the track enabled the costs of each action to be evaluated for the different possible states of the rail. It was also possible to define those states where the rail had to be replaced for safety reasons. The model thus consisted of a set of sequences of possible actions to be carried out every two months over a period of years, together with equations which gave the costs of carrying out those actions given the state of a rail. For straight track the possible operations were to replace either a small piece of a rail (a plug) or to replace a whole rail. An expression was constructed which gave the total cost of plugging and replacing a rail over its lifetime. Different values of this total cost were obtained if different lifetimes were used.

Finally, King and Mercer built a model which represents the strategy of companies bidding for contracts in the construction industry. Here the model attempts to describe the behavior of the successful bidders by analyzing that data available. By collecting what information was accessible, it was possible to construct an equation which gave the size of the lowest bid as a function of the factors thought to be significant: the distance to be traveled to complete the contract and the time and amount of work necessary.

*Solving the Model*

The third phase of the classical OR approach is to use the model constructed in the second phase in a predictive manner to examine the impact of various courses of action. This phase corresponds to solving the model. Methods used for solving models have been classified in various ways. Churchman, Ackoff, and Arnoff (1957) recognize three types of solution method—analytical, numerical, and Monte Carlo—which correspond, broadly, to manipulating the models algebraically, investigating their behavior by substituting numbers for the variables, and approximating their behavior by simulating them. This classification fails to bring out the relationship between the solution method and the type of model. Here an alternative classification is used which identifies two types of solution process, depending upon the relationship between the model of the system to be controlled and the objectives to be pursued in achieving that control.

It is useful here to define in general terms the structure of the models used in the OR process. Models consist of a set of relationships between variables which represent significant elements of the system of concern. These variables fall into two groups—controllable and uncontrollable variables (or parameters)—depending upon whether they represent factors in the system which can be directly influenced by the actions of decision makers or not. The behavior of the system is indicated by certain performance indicators. These are factors which can be measured and used to assess the state of the system. The controllable and uncontrollable variables are related in a model to give values of these performance indicators. Thus the relationships embedded in a model allow the value of performance indicators, $i$, to be calculated as functions of the controllable variables, $c$, and the uncontrollable variables, $u$. This can be written formally as,

$$i = f\,(c,u)$$

A model is used to investigate the effect on $i$ of changes in $c$ under certain conditions represented by $u$. If the model is a good representation of the real-world processes to which it corresponds, then the results of these investigations can be used to aid decision making by providing information about how to change the factors represented by the controllable variables in order to change the performance indicators in the desired manner.

There are, in principle, many, if not an infinity, of different ways in which $c$ might be altered to affect $i$ in a particular case. The decision-making process involves identifying that particular set of values for $c$ which will be implemented. The criteria for choosing this set of values are often specified with respect to an objective function which is a function of the performance indicators. The objective function is often a single value, $O$, to which several performance indicators might contribute in a particular way. Thus,

$$O = g(i)$$

Of course, $O$ is thus related to the values of $c$ and $u$ by

$$O = g(f(c,u))$$

One element of model solution is to carry out an analysis by an appropriate method, which results in the value of $O$ (or possibly its constituent parts, $i$) being given for different values of $c$. Having defined $O$ or $i$, they can then be used in a decision-making process to help inform the choice of which actions to implement.

It is possible in some cases to extend model solution to include a process by which a set of changes in $c$ are considered and that which gives an optimum value for $O$ is indicated. The information given in this case is also useful to decision making, as it shows which action will lead to optimum performance as measured by the criteria manifest by $O$. Thus a second element in model solution, which is dependent upon the first (without loss of generality), is to maximize the value of $O$ for a given set of possible values of $c$, that is,

$$\max_{\{c\}} O = g\ (f(c,u))$$

Model solution falls, therefore, into two major categories: that which consists only of the first element and may be labeled *predictive* and that which consists of both the first and the second elements and may be labeled *optimizing*. The two approaches provide different types of information for the decision-making process. It is instructive to see how this framework explains the solution procedures used in the five case studies discussed above.

The stock control model built by Johnston consists of controllable variables which correspond to service levels and the amounts of goods to be ordered. Other factors in the model are parameters which correspond to lead times, prices, and so on. The set of variables is used to produce various costs. These are then grouped together to yield a single objective which measures annual return. In this case it is possible to manipulate the set of equations using Lagrange multiplier techniques to give that set of order and service levels which maximizes the return. Thus this is a case of an optimizing-solution method.

The second example also yields an optimizing solution. The controllable variables in this case are the number of animals of different weights purchased in the planning period, the amount of land used for growing crops, and the weights of crops to be sold. The coefficients of costs, feeding rates, and capacities of a farm to support animal and crop production are the parameters which can be set at values appropriate to a given farming concern. The values of the variables are used to produce expressions for the various incomes and expenditures involved in operating a farm, and these are amalgamated to produce a single expression for profit, which is the objective. All of these expressions are linear, and thus manipulation of the expressions can be carried out relatively easily. The simplex method enables the optimal solution to be found quickly by computer, and by using this method, the values of the controllable variables which give the maximum attainable level of profit and which satisfy the set of relationships in the model equations are found.

Both of the above cases have sets of model relationships which are easy to manipulate because of their character, which considerably eases the process by which an optimizing solution can be found. In the third case this is not so, and a different type of solution is found.

It has already been seen that Chiamsiri *et al.* chose not to build a model of the system they were investigating which was in equation form. By building a computer program which simulated the behavior of the system, they were making it impossible to manipulate the model algebraically. Consequently the use of analytical methods to yield an optimizing solution was prohibited. Instead, the simulation model was run to give values of several performance indicators under different values for the single controllable variable: the number of service points to introduce. The performance indicators were measures of the average length of the queue at closing time, the utilization of the service facilities in a period, and the time taken to clear the office after closing time. Results were calculated for three, four, or five service points in an average month and for four, five, or six points in the busiest month. Investigation of the results shows that while four points is adequate for most times, five may be necessary for busy months. The important point here is that the decision over the optimal number of service points is made outside the model and on the basis of several performance indicators. The model here gives an example of a predictive solution method.

The fourth case is that given by Lamson *et al.* and consists of two parts. In the first, the study of curved-track maintenance, the controllable variable is the action to be taken in any given period of time. Three actions were possible: to do nothing, to maintain, or to replace. The model enabled the costs of following a combination of these actions over a time period to be calculated. The total cost was the objective, and this was expressed as a function of the actions to be carried out and various values associated with those actions. The structure of this model enabled a procedure to be devised which guaranteed that the least costly sequence of actions would be found. By using a dynamic programming method, the set of actions which gave the least costly maintenance policy for curved track was found. The second case study focused on the maintenance policy for straight track. Again the controllable variables were actions, here whether to "plug" the defective part of the rail or to replace the whole of it. An equation giving the total cost of a piece of track over the period of life of the railway was assessed for different lifetimes for single rails until a minimum was found. This equation gave the optimum life of a rail and indicated how often rails should be replaced rather than plugged. In both of these cases, an optimizing solution was found.

In the final case, King and Mercer used as the controllable variable the markup to be used in setting the bid price for contracts. The model expresses the markup as a function of variables which are fixed for a given contract. The objective here is to find the lowest bid which will be made by other companies in the market. The model here gives information on what the market is likely to bid for contracts so that the decision makers can assess what their bid should be. There is no objective as such to be defined in this case. Statistical analysis shows what the most likely lowest bid would be from competitors, and this is fed into the decision-making process. There is no place in this model for an optimizing solution, as no objective is specified which is affected by the controllable variables, and a predictive solution is obtained.

What emerges from this brief examination of five specific cases is the amount of interaction between the model solution process and the earlier two. First, it is clear that the type of solution procedure adopted and the information which can be obtained from the solution depends upon the nature of the model. Optimizing solutions can be obtained by different techniques for models specified in different ways. The ease with which an optimizing solution can be obtained is crucially dependent upon the ease with which models can be manipulated. Thus those models which can yield optimizing solutions are analytically more flexible than those which cannot. For example, Johnston's stock control model, Glen's linear programming model, and Lamson et al.'s maintenance models are each simpler in terms of their ability to be manipulated than Chiamsiri et al.'s computer simulation model.

A consequence is that it is likely that if an optimizing solution is required, the model to be used will be constructed in a way which allows one to be generated. The need to produce an optimizing solution will depend upon the nature of the advice sought by the decision makers, but the nature of the situation to be modeled may not make it possible to construct a useful model in such a way as to allow for an optimizing solution. This is the case in Chiamsiri et al.'s analysis. Thus model construction and model solution are intimately bound together and are each affected by the decision makers and the situation they seek to control. Thus, if an optimizing solution is required, the need to produce a suitable model must be balanced against the ability of that model to give an accurate representation of the situation under study. If a model cannot be built which is both accurate and capable of giving an optimizing solution, then either optimality must be sacrificed for a predictive solution or a model of a simplified situation must be produced which can give an optimizing solution.

It is now possible to understand more clearly why the classification of standard problems and other well-known forms of modeling are useful to an OR analyst. They give a set of models and procedures which can be used, directly or in modified form, to help build models and give solutions of either type. In particular they indicate what type of models can be built to give an optimizing solution and how to achieve that solution.

*Testing the Model and the Solution*

The phase following model solution is testing the model and the solution. Churchman, Ackoff, and Arnoff (1957) note four ways in which the model may be in error. First, the model may include variables which are not relevant and hence may emphasize relationships which are less important than their inclusion indicates. Second, the model may not include a variable which is significant and may therefore omit an important set of relationships. Third, the model may fail to show accurately the relationship between the variables and the measure of effectiveness which is used to determine which course of action is preferable. Finally, the numerical values which are used may be in error and hence may distort the ability of the model to reflect actual behavior. Testing the model and the solution offers the opportunity to evaluate the presence and the extent of these other sources of errors.

Testing of the model can be carried out with statistical tests that provide an indication of the degree to which each of the above causes of error is present. Such testing relies upon the accurate collection of information about the system which is being modeled. Collection of such information is not straightforward, as errors can be introduced in the measurements which form the basis of the tests. Another method of testing is to examine the solution generated from the model. This can be done retrospectively by assessing how well the model solution reproduces past behavior. Alternatively, the model can be tested by seeing how well its solutions work in practice. In both circumstances the assumption is being made that if the solutions are satisfactory, then the model must be a reasonable reflection of what happens in the situation.

This view of testing the model and the solution divorces the model and its analysis from the decision makers and the problem that they are attempting to tackle. Finlay and Wilson (1987) argue that validation is associated with two levels of modeling, one level associated with decision makers and the other with the model builders. Decision makers have a broad model of the situation, often general and lacking in detail but sufficient to indicate its structure. This structural model contrasts with the more detailed mathematical model built by the OR analysts. These two models should be consistent with each other if the decision makers are to accept the results of the analysis of the mathematical model. This perception is not dissimilar from that of Beer (1966) discussed previously.

Finlay and Wilson investigated the extent to which validation was carried out by decision makers and what methods they used by discussing this subject with twenty-five clients from various backgrounds. They found that, in general, validation was carried out rarely, and, that when it was, no common methods were adopted. Validation was carried out differently depending upon the nature of the decision makers. Decision makers who used an OR team based within their organization tended to want modifications in an existing situation. This meant that validation could be carried out more easily by the decision makers as they had a good understanding of the situation. Validation here was often undertaken jointly and took place throughout the modeling process. Decision makers who called in consultants from outside their organization often required advice of novel situations. In this case validation was not easy for them as they did not know what to expect. In these cases the decision makers validated the modelers, who were then left to validate the model themselves. Thus decision makers and modelers undertake some element of validation in both cases, but there seems to be little understanding of how best to proceed in either situation. Finlay and Wilson conclude by pointing out the need for increased attention to validation in general and for the development of validation methodology, in particular. This methodology should bring together the modeling and validating processes and not see them as independent activities.

Lanry, Malouin, and Oral (1983) went a long way toward developing such a methodology, which shares Finlay and Wilson's view that modelers and decision makers should both be involved in validation. They identify five aspects of validation which need to be incorporated into this phase of the problem-solving process. Conceptual validation assesses the relevance of the assumptions and theories which underpin the view of the situation held by decision makers and modelers. Logical validation is similar to that considered by Churchman, Ackoff, and Arnoff (1957) and is concerned with testing for the inclusion of relevant variables and relationships. The third type of validation is experimental validation. This is equivalent to testing the solution and is concerned with assessing the value of the solution and its accuracy. Operational validity measures the quality and applicability of solutions and recommendations. Finally, data validation evaluates the appropriateness, accuracy, sufficiency, and availability of the data necessary to the problem-solving process. When such a broad view is taken of validation, it is seen that it is dependent not only upon the model and its solution, which are essentially technical, but also upon the decision makers and their perception of the situation, which introduce a social element into the process. Validation is more than assessing the ability of a model to reproduce behavior; it also includes examining the usefulness of the model and the recommendations deduced from it. Validation must therefore be carried out in the context of the decision makers' purpose and requirements.

There is little in Finlay and Wilson's investigation which suggests that Lanry *et al.*'s framework reflects practice. It is a prescriptive framework which needs to be adopted rather than a description of what occurs. In order to explore a little further the extent to which validation does take place in practice, the five case studies being used will now be considered from within this framework.

The stock control analysis of Johnston contains no direct reference to validation of the models used in the analysis or of the relationship between the computer aid to stock control, which resulted from the analysis, and the needs of management. This is not to say that validation of some form did not occur, and there are indications in the description of the study that two types of validation did take place. First, the demand for the items in stock is described by a probability density function. A statistical test of how well the observed data correspond to the chosen function, a gamma distribution, indicates that the model gives a good account of itself in reproducing this aspect of the behavior of the actual system. Together with the confidence that the approach adopted in modeling the stock control system has proved itself over many years, and in many cases it has, it can be said that model validation has been undertaken. Second, in one case it was possible to specify the contribution made to the level of performance by the introduction of the new system. This measurement shows an increase in service level and sales combined with a decrease in stock levels. As this outcome corresponded to what management were wishing to achieve, the model was validated with respect to meeting its objectives. In terms of Lanry *et al.*'s framework this study included elements of experimental and operational validity. If other types of validity were examined, it would appear that this examination has been done subconsciously and is not referred to. The situation in this example also supports Finlay and Wilson's finding that when consultants are brought in from outside an organization, validation of the model tends to be left to the analysts. There is no reference here to the decision makers being involved in testing the model or the computer program in which it is embedded.

Glen was concerned with building a model which had general application to beef and crop farms. It is not possible here to expect that validation with regard to usefulness to management would be discussed. Model validation remains crucial—and particularly so, as the model was meant to be applicable to a wide range of enterprises. Glen discussed in detail the structure of the model constructed, and this discussion suggests that some form of logical validation took place. Experimental validation also occurred, as the maximum achievable actual gain of weight for cattle was compared with that predicted by the model under certain circumstances and was found to be close. The discussion of the model does not include reference to applications, and so conceptual, operational, and data validation, which require some input from decision makers, could not be considered. The lack of decision makers also means that it is not easy to see how well this example supports Finlay and Wilson's findings. It can be suggested that the model is most likely to be used by decision makers in organizations separate from the analysts. In such cases, Finlay and Wilson argue, validation is left to the analyst, and the decision makers are not involved. This view would seem to be supported in this particular case, as Glen indicated that the model would be best suited to use by consultants advising individual farmers. Data should be collected for specific cases and substituted for the variables in the model, and the model structure is assumed to be satisfactory and applicable to all cases without further model development.

The model of a queuing system built by Chiamsiri *et al.* was validated within its construction to the extent that certain functions and relationships in the model were directly based upon data collected from the office under study. As the model was being used to investigate a totally novel type of organization for the office, validation by comparing model performance with actual performance was not possible. Some retrospective validation was carried out four years after the study and revealed that the model predictions were reasonably close to what had actually occurred. Thus, in this case, logical validation and a form of operational validation were undertaken. As in the previous two cases validation appears to have been largely the province of the analysts, and the decision makers did not seem to play a significant role in it at all.

Lamson *et al.* followed the line adopted in the first two studies by combining a rigorous mathematical analysis, which ensures that a solution will be well defined, with the fitting of data concerning phenomena

to statistical distributions. There is therefore a built-in process of validation here that ensures that the data will match as well as possible the
distribution function chosen, in this case of Wiebull distribution. In both
of the cases studied, the savings to be gained were significant, and there
was no discussion of validating the solutions. This is an easy approach
to adopt, for even if there is an error, savings are likely. When the
indicated savings are not great, there would seem to be more need to
establish the validity of the solution. The usual picture of validation
emerges here. Logical validation had been carried out, again within the
study of the analysts, and the decision makers apparently were not
involved.

Finally, consider King and Mercer's examination of bidding strategies. In this case the model was constructed by fitting data to probability density functions. Thus the model was validated by ensuring that
an adequate match would be achieved. In addition, the model was compared with actual performance where possible and was found to be
sufficiently accurate to justify its use. In this case, aspects of logical,
experimental, and operational validation may be identified. As in each
of the other cases examined, this process was undertaken by the analysts with little apparent involvement by the decision makers.

A speculative conclusion to be drawn from this narrow analysis is
that there is a significant difference between the practice of validation
and the ideal which should be achieved. This conclusion supports Lanry
*et al.* (1983) and Finlay and Wilson (1987), who argued that more effort
should be devoted to validation and its role in the process of OR. In
particular, validation should be dependent upon the character of the
model and its solution and upon the purpose to which they are being
put. The process should be carried out by analysts and decision makers
in conjunction with each other. In contrast, the practice appears to focus
upon only those aspects of validation which are technical in nature and
can be done by the analysts in isolation from the decision makers. Logical, experimental, and operational validations are carried out with respect to the model and its solution and are thus largely independent of
the decision makers. In the above studies these forms of validation are
the types which are reported. Conceptual and data validations which
attempt to evaluate the model against the perceptions and purposes of
the decision makers appear to be given little consideration.

*Establishing Controls over the Solution*

The fifth phase of the OR process is to establish controls over the
solution. It is recognized that a solution is derived for a given set of
uncontrollable variables, those which apply at the time when the analy-

sis is undertaken. This phase accepts that the values of the uncontrollable variables may change and that, when they do, it is not certain that the original solution will remain valid. Therefore it is necessary to know how to control the solution when the uncontrollable aspects of the situation change. An alternative way of defining this phase is to see it as establishing how sensitive a solution is to changes in the uncontrollable variables. A solution which is valid for wide variations in the uncontrollable variables will be more easy to control than one which is not.

Churchman, Ackoff, and Arnoff (1957) see that three stages are necessary in this phase of the process. First, a list of variables and relationships which are included in a model, or which should be if values change, needs to be drawn up. Second, a procedure for monitoring the uncontrollable variables and identifying significant changes needs to be designed and implemented. Third, that action which needs to be taken to alter the solution if significant changes occur should be specified. These tasks refer almost exclusively to the model and its solution. White (1985) identifies the problem as determining "the extent to which solutions (in terms of actual decisions and objective function levels) depend upon the parameters of the problem" (p. 191). In his discussion of the topic it becomes clear that much of the work is of a mathematical nature and is concerned with finding the changes in the objective functions and solutions of models caused by change in the value of the uncontrollable variables or by the values used being different from the actual values.

This process played very little part in four of the five case studies considered here for different reasons. The stock control model developed by Johnston was embedded in a computer program which was being continually updated with new information on prices and demand. Thus the model was producing optimal solutions on a daily basis. There was no need for controls to be established as solutions did not last for a long enough period to allow the uncontrollable variables to change. The model of beef and crop production built by Glen was designed to be used in different contexts, and the variables in the model were set to appropriate values for each application. Although linear programming, the method used by Glen, is one area where extensive works has been undertaken in sensitivity analysis (see, for example, Williams, 1978), there is no reported use of sensitivity analysis in the case study. It would not be expected to be a major problem to undertake the analysis in this case. Chiamsiri et al. explored the variation in the solution they developed to the extent of considering an average level of demand for export licenses and the highest demand. In both cases the solution they recommended is thought to be adequate. It is noted that in the four years of operating the solution, total growth in demand for licenses was small and the arrival pattern of customers in the office had not changed significantly. Thus the uncontrollable variables had not changed to any degree, although this lack of change could not have been foreseen at the time of the analysis. King and Mercer did not consider any changes in the market in which bids for contracts were being made, it being assumed that the timing and size of contracts would have the same influence on bids as previously. As this was seen to be a small influence, the assumption did not appear to be unreasonable.

The fifth case study, that of Lamson *et al.*, did include a discussion of the sensitivity of the recommended replacement and maintenance policies to changes in various costs, in the case of curved track and, to technical and financial conditions, in the case of straight track. In both cases a reasonable degree of stability was shown to exist. The values of certain uncontrollable variables were changed by 50% and 100% for curved track and by 25% for straight track, and, within these limits, the optimal solution showed little change. This example reinforces the view that establishing controls and investigating sensitivity are largely an extension of analyzing the model and its solution. The decision makers and the form of the problem have very little to do with this aspect of the process.

*Implementing the Solution*

The sixth, and final, part of the OR process is to implement the solution. This involves passing the recommendations to the decision makers in such a way that they can act on them and authorize the changes to be made. In particular, as Churchman, Ackoff, and Arnoff (1957) point out, information on how to implement the solutions should be provided. This information should indicate who should do what and when, as well as the information and facilities that are required to do it. There are two good reasons why OR analysts should be involved in implementation. First, the translation of an abstract set of concepts into practical action is important, and the analysts are the people who know most about what the concepts should mean in actuality. Errors in implementation are less likely if the OR analysts are involved in some way. Second, in implementing the solution, shortcomings in the way it will operate or the need for extra data may become apparent. In both cases it may be necessary to make minor changes in the solution, and these can be more rapidly and effectively made if the analysts are closely involved. These authors noted that "at the current stage of development of OR no well-formulated methodology of implementation is available" (p. 616). It is fair to say that the situation has not altered much in the intervening thirty years. What has been learned is a great deal about how to implement recommendations in organizations, by those OR groups based within them. The bringing together and structuring of this information have not been adequately attempted and indeed may prove not to be possible.

One reason why an understanding of implementation has been slow in appearing is the failure of those people who provide descriptions and discussions or OR work to reflect on how the results they provide have been used. In all of the five cases studied here, implementation received only marginal consideration. It is likely that in all cases the results were used successfully, but the process by which they were handed over to the decision makers involved and then the way in which those decision makers used the information are ignored.

Despite the lack of insight into implementation in the five cases studied here, it is possible to identify some useful understanding from that work which has been done on the topic. The view remains, however, that there is no recognized body of knowledge on how to achieve successful implementation, or indeed on how to define implementation (Hildebrandt, 1977; Huysmans, 1979; Tomlinson, Quade, and Miser, 1985). Schultz and Slevin (1975a) outline a variety of perspectives on implementation, including the views that it is the selling of solutions and recommendations, the involvement of decision makers in analysis, the mutual understanding of analysts and decision makers about their roles, and the changing of organizations by having results accepted. Each view contributes something to the understanding of the implementation process, and Hildebrandt (1977) sees a necessary task as bringing these views together into a suitable framework.

The study of implementation gathered pace in the 1970s, and Hildebrandt (1980) provides an excellent summary of the work up to that date. While many different classification schemes have been developed, a common view is that model building is affected by giving consideration to implementation issues. Huysmans (1970) points out the need for an implementation strategy to be considered at the beginning of a project. Implementation is crucially dependent upon managerial processes, and these act as a constraint upon what recommendations are likely to be managerially feasible. These constraints are as important as, if not more important than, those due to technical and financial factors. Despite the increased amount of theoretical interest in implementation, it is questionable whether it has lead to changes in the practice of OR analysts. Schultz and Slevin (1982) note this and call for implementation research to take on an increased practical dimension.

*Classical OR: Sequence or System?*

The classical view of the OR process emphasizes that although the above phases of the process are, at first glance, sequential, they do, in fact, interrelate in a more organic fashion. As one phase is completed, others may need to be revised and may influence other aspects of the investigation. The intimation is that the six phases discussed above are components of a system for problem solving, and to interpret them in this way may be beneficial and may lead to an emphasis on the organic rather than the logical aspects of the process. In the following section, this perspective is taken up in more detail.

## A System for Problem Solving

*Why a Systems Approach?*

Systems thinking is often taken to be concerned with wholes rather than parts. The focus of the approach is to understand phenomena by adopting an expansionist rather than a reductionist method (Ackoff, 1974b, 1979a). Such an approach to generating knowledge and understanding emphasizes the larger environment in which a part of the world operates rather than looking at its internal components and examining each of them in isolation. Systems thinking, according to Ackoff, uses the notions of producer–product to explain processes rather than the more mechanistic and reductionist notion of cause–effect transformations. Importantly, systems thinking places the responsibility of behavior within the system itself, which is seen to be teleological. The view that all behavior is determined and preprogrammed, which is compatible with the cause–effect explanation of behavior, is not accepted, and systems are seen to have the capacity to set their own goals and to behave in a purposeful manner in an effort to achieve them.

Systems thinking acts as a complement to the longer established and reductionist-based scientific method (Checkland, 1981). It offers a way of understanding those situations where scientific method runs into difficulty. Checkland identifies the major problems for scientific method as being due to complexity, occurring when social rather than natural systems are being investigated and when managerial activity, interpreted in a very broad sense, is involved. The OR process under consideration here is complex because it involves a high degree of interaction between the component parts and between the process and its subject. It is social in nature, for it is a process undertaken by individuals or groups, and so behavioral and political factors play a significant role. It also involves a managerial process in that a study must be planned and controlled.

Scientific methods cannot cope with complexity because in isolating parts of a system important connections are omitted from consideration, are assumed to be weak, or fail to be noticed. It is also the case that definition of the parts is arbitrary, and thus to claim to have *the* correct process of reduction is impossible. When social phenomena are under consideration, experimental methods, reliance on data and measurement, and the ability to state and test general laws, which form the basis of scientific methods, are particularly difficult to adopt (Keat and Urry, 1982; Pratt, 1978). The difficulty of providing such a scientifically grounded set of knowledge of behavior means that those involved in the management of situations in which individuals and groups have a role to play cannot fall back on the same amount of accepted theory as can engineers and others managing natural behavior. Thus science cannot offer much support to those individuals involved in planning, controlling, and implementing action in social systems or to those attempting to understand the processes these people use. A systems approach to this study offers one way of gaining an understanding which is potentially more beneficial than an analysis grounded in scientific method.

*OR: A System in Its Environment*

Given that systems thinking may be able to help one to understand the complex social process by which OR solves problems, the first task is to establish the OR process as a system of interrelated parts, the parts being the six phases discussed above. Then the concepts of systems thinking can be brought to bear on this system in order to highlight certain characteristics.

Here the OR process is interpreted from the viewpoint that it is a problem-solving system which is open to its environment (Lilienfeld, 1978; von Bertalanffy, 1950). It is seen as a system designed to yield information to decision makers on how to achieve improvements in the behavior of a particular part of the world: the system under study. The decision makers are associated with an organization which is also seen as being open to an environment. Thus the environment of the OR process, the subject system, consists of the decision makers being served, the system under study, the organization that the decision makers are associated with, and an environment relevant to that organization. Table 4.1 gives the above information in tabular form. The task now is to establish how these two systems are related.

TABLE 4.1
Problem-Solving and Subject Systems

| Problem-solving system consists of processes | Subject system consists of entities upon which the processes act |
|---|---|
| 1. Formulate the problem | 1. Decision makers |
| 2. Construct a model | 2. System under study |
| 3. Solve the model | 3. Organization associated |
| 4. Test the model and | with decision makers |
| its solution | 4. Environment relevant to |
| 5. Establish controls | system under study |
| 6. Implement the | |
| solution | |

The detailed discussions of the components of the problem-solving system have indicated to a degree the amount of interaction between them. These are now summarized, and additionally it is shown how each of the six phases relates to the various components of the subject system. The result of this analysis is the set of interactions involved in the OR process. This is given in diagrammatic form in Figure 4.1.

The first phase, formulating the problem, involves acquiring information about its relevant environment. The result is a collection of information on what comprises the problem. This information-gathering pro-

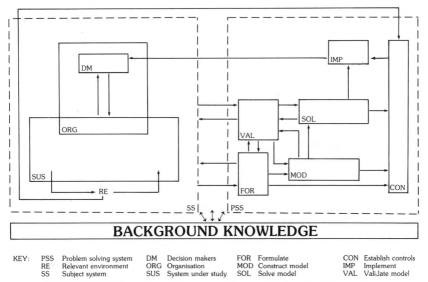

BACKGROUND KNOWLEDGE

KEY:  PSS  Problem solving system   DM   Decision makers      FOR  Formulate        CON  Establish controls
      RE   Relevant environment     ORG  Organisation         MOD  Construct model   IMP  Implement
      SS   Subject system           SUS  System under study   SOL  Solve model       VAL  Validate model

FIGURE 4.1. Interactions between problem-solving and subject systems.

cess may also generate knowledge within the organization and among the decision makers about the nature of their situation. It is therefore possibly a two-way interaction, with both elements giving information to the other. The problem formulation is used to give a foundation to the model construction phase. The type of model which is built depends upon the nature of the situation which it is meant to represent and the sort of solution and information which it is required to generate.

Once the model has been constructed it may be solved; the method of solution is dictated by the form of the model to be solved. The validation process compares the model and solution—and hence, implicitly, the formulation—with actual behavior in order to assess their relevance to the decision makers. This comparison process will generate information on how the formulation, the model, and the solution may need to be modified in order to meet more closely the needs of the decision makers. Thus the validation phase can lead to further formulation, modeling, and solution activity. As in the formulation phase, this bringing together of the understanding gained through the modeling and solution phases and the subject system may generate understanding within that system of its own character, and there is also, therefore, a two-way interaction here. If the validation process is satisfactory, the next phase is to establish controls on the solution. The extent to which controls are needed is influenced by the solution which has been generated. In order to identify the controls, information is needed on the nature of the environment of the system under study. The type of controls required is explored by using the model and solution methods previously established. Finally, the result of the analysis of controls and the solution are brought together to yield the method for implementing the solution. This method is then fed to the decision makers, who, hopefully, will use it to guide their intervention in the system under study.

None of the above processes takes place in a theoretical vacuum, and each is guided to some extent by previous experience, acquired either directly or indirectly. This experience is referred to here as *background knowledge*. It consists of information, guidelines, and understanding relevant to the various elements of the problem-solving system; how they interact with each other; how the OR process, generally, relates to the subject system; and how to conceptualize the subject system itself. The background knowledge therefore is continually being supplemented by activities within the problem-solving system; each action contributes something to the background knowledge available for future reference. Such knowledge has two main categories. Formal knowledge which is available from various sources such as textbooks, journals, and reports is often concerned with those aspects of the OR process which can be well defined. Specific examples include technical details on model construction and solution techniques. Informal knowledge is held about the more intangible forms of experience. This has often to do with the attitude of a particular set of decision makers or an aspect of organizational culture which is not amenable to written description. Both are important sources of valuable information for the OR process.

The description of the OR process has so far reinterpreted the phases of the approach as a system in the sense that these phases are seen as a set of interrelated parts which form a whole. Systems thinking can go beyond this and provide insights into the character of the problem-solving system which stem from this systems perspective. Checkland (1981, p. 75) argues that systems thinking is founded upon two pairs of ideas: (1) emergence and hierarchy and (2) communication and control. Each of these concepts can tell us something about the character of the problem-solving system.

The expansionist idea central to systems thinking emphasizes that as systems come together to form a larger system, properties emerge which can be identified only when systems are joined together. This joining together of systems leads to a hierarchy of systems, each level of which has different properties associated with it. For the hierarchy to be maintained, communication between the levels and within them is necessary. The information which flows within the hierarchy is such that the structure can be regulated or controlled, and hence it protects the hierarchy and its component parts from collapse and destruction. Systems thinking, in general, is concerned with exploring these ideas and showing how they arise in various situations. The purpose here is to show how they can be used to increase our understanding of the OR process.

The first task is to define meaningful levels in a hierarchy of systems. As the focus of the current discussion is the OR process, it is sensible to start with this as one level. The problem-solving system of Table 4.1 and Figure 4.1 is one level of the hierarchy and can be seen to have its own features, as discussed below. The level below this consists of the six separate phases which constitute the problem-solving approach. Each phase can be defined as a system for formulating a problem constructing a model, and so on. If desired, each can be investigated more fully than it has been here to reveal its systemic character. The problem-solving system joins with the subject system to form a further level in the hierarchy, which is above that of the problem-solving system itself. There are therefore three levels in the hierarchy based upon the problem system: A substratum consisting of the six phases of the approach, the stratum of the interest containing the problem-solving system itself, and a superstratum which adds the subject system to the problem-solving system. The structure of the hierarchy is given in Table 4.2.

As the elements of one level are aggregated to produce the higher level, properties emerge which can be identified only at the higher level. The adding together of the individual elements creates phenomena which are not identifiable in any of those elements on their own. In the present case, two occasions where properties emerge need to be considered. The first of these is the aggregation of the six systems corresponding to the phases of the OR methodology to produce the problem-solving system. This occurs in moving from the substratum to the stratum of interest. Only when these six separate processes are brought together is it possible to structure and analyze the situation under study and to provide useful information on how to achieve the desired improvements. If any of the processes are excluded, then it is impossible to provide the necessary information. If the problem is not formulated, the type of information needed cannot be identified. Failure to build or solve a model means that analysis of the situation will not proceed. Validation of the model and the solution give some confidence in the value of the information produced, and if validation is not done, the results are thus essentially meaningless. It is necessary to carry out some investigation of the sensitivity of the analysis to changes in uncontrollable factors or assumptions made in the analysis if the results are to be of full use to the decision makers. Successful use of the information is likely to be improved by involving the analysts in the implementation and by monitoring their recommendations, and so these are also necessary for a successful conclusion to a project. Any one phase or system from the substratum cannot provide the required information on its own; all six need to be present to ensure that such information is produced.

The second occasion on which properties emerge from the aggregation of systems is in moving from the stratum of interest to the super-

*TABLE 4.2*
*A Hierarchy for the Problem-Solving System*

| | |
|---|---|
| Superstratum | Problem-solving system + subject system |
| Stratum of interest | Problem-solving system |
| Substratum | Problem formulation system |
| | Model construction system |
| | Model solution system |
| | Validation system |
| | Control system |
| | Implementation system |

stratum. The adding of the system consisting of decision makers, their organization, and their environment to the problem-solving system results in a system which is capable of making decisions on an informed basis and of changing the form and content of the situation under study. The problem-solving system provides information concerning the situation under study and the impact of possible changes, while the subject system is responsible for deciding which changes to make and how. Without both of these systems, changes would not take place. Decisions cannot be made without information, and, unless the information is acted on by people in order to produce decisions, the changes will not be introduced.

It is appropriate to return at this point to an earlier observation concerning the separation of the OR analysts and the decision makers. It was assumed for the above discussion that decision makers and OR analysts have separate roles. These can now be seen to correspond to the two elements of the superstratum. Decision makers play a role in the subject system and OR analysts in the problem-solving system. The reflection of the structure of the superstratum in the roles of the two sets of actors identified is not necessary. A person may act in both the problem-solving system and the subject system. This possibility reinforces the view that the specification of systems is a device for understanding the processes involved, and not for defining the organizational structure in which they take place.

The concepts of hierarchy and emergent properties allow a structure to be placed in the OR process and give an explanation of this structure. The concepts of communication and control, which will now be considered, provide an explanation of how that structure is maintained. Systems whose structure is not maintained either undergo significant changes or disappear. The apparent stability of OR and its success would suggest that its structure is strong and able to survive in many different situations. The concepts of communication and control should give some explanation of how such strength and adaptability are achieved.

That part of systems theory which is concerned fundamentally with control and communication, whether in animal or machine, is cybernetics, as originally defined by Wiener (1948, p. 19). For Beer, cybernetics is the "science of effective organisation" and has formed the basis of a model to which all viable systems should conform (Beer, 1959a, 1966, 1979, 1981). Control and communication, understood within cybernetics, explain how complex systems can maintain themselves in the face of disturbances being caused in their environment. The mechanism which accomplishes this maintenance is a self-regulating device embedded in the structure of such systems. Feedback loops facilitate self-regulation by allowing systems to reflect on the results of past behavior and to modify current and future actions in response. Essentially, feedback loops allow systems to learn from past events and to modify future action on the basis of this knowledge.

The basic structure of a feedback loop is given in Figure 4.2. There are several different ways of classifying feedback processes. Schoderbek, Schoderbek, and Kefalas (1980), for example, describe three orders of feedback, differentiated by the sophistication of the decisions which are influenced by past behavior. Bogart (1980) emphasizes the different locations of the feedback loops in relation to a system, in order to produce a different classification. What these two examples and many other classifications share is the idea that in a feedback mechanism, the results of a process are fed back into that process in order to influence its future behavior. Feedback is a flow of information which is used to influence future actions.

The circular structure gives the system of which it is a part an ability to maintain itself. Once the structure is in place and functioning, the process will continually monitor its own behavior and will modify its behavior accordingly. Forrester (1968) sees the feedback as a fundamental system building block and argues that for a system to be understood fully, the set of feedback loops which constitute it must be recognized and understood as a whole. It can be seen that the OR process as a problem-solving system contains such sets of feedback loops at two levels: the stratum of interest and the superstratum. To understand the self-regulating properties of the OR process requires an understanding of these sets of feedback loops.

Within the problem-solving system itself, the richness of the relationships among the six phases has already been noted. What can now be established is that each of these relationships is part of a feedback loop. For example, the model construction phase is related to the problem formulation, model solution, and validation phases. The result of the model construction phase influences each of these: it gives explicit

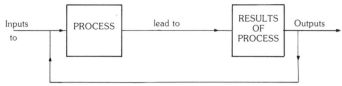

which are fedback to act as inputs

*FIGURE 4.2.* Processes and feedback.

form to the perception of the problem, it establishes what types of solution are possible, and it defines the criteria upon which validation may be achieved by indicating where comparisons between modeled and actual behavior are possible. In their turn, each of these three phases then acts in response, with possible consequences for the model construction phase. The model may not reflect the desired formulation and may need to be reconstructed. Solutions of the desired type may not be available, and modification of the model may be deemed necessary. Validation may show the model to be inadequate and to require further attention. Thus, through these circular routes, the results of model construction feedback into the process, in order to improve model performance and to allow the OR process to achieve its goal of providing useful information to decision makers.

A similar analysis could be repeated for each of other phases. What is clear is the complexity of the feedback loops and the mutual influences they create between the phases. To separate any phase and treat it independently means that crucial elements of control which are built into the process will be omitted from consideration. It also becomes clear that it is difficult, and probably unbeneficial, to attempt to lay out a procedure for moving through the process. The problem-solving system is an organic whole bound together by the complex of feedback loops within it. These loops enable the system to maintain itself and to adapt to change by acting as communication channels between the various phases.

If the problem-solving system is taken as a whole alongside the subject system (see Figure 4.1), then a different feedback loop can be recognized. The feedback loops discussed above act during the operation of the problem-solving system. A further loop which runs through the background knowledge held by the OR analysts acts over a longer time period. This loop relates to the overall results of the problem-solving system to the organizational system which it serves. The result of any investigation by the OR process will cause change in the organization and the decision makers being served. These changes supplement any existing background knowledge held about that organization. In future projects this knowledge can be used to influence the work undertaken and to increase the value of that work to the organization. This loop also helps the organization to learn about the contribution of the OR process to its activities and can help the decision makers to understand this support to their work.

Control and communication, understood within the notion of feedback, help to maintain relationships within the OR process and between that process and the decision-making process it supports. Failures in these loops mean that self-regulation is weakened and that the performance of the problem-solving system decreases. This reduction in performance is manifest in the short run by a failure to provide adequate information on a specific issue to the decision makers. In the long run it results in a lack of information being available in the background knowledge, with subsequent difficulties in the OR process itself.

The above discussion has investigated the systemic properties of the OR process. In so doing, it has emphasized the holistic nature of that process and has shown that the process has a structure which is organic rather than sequential. The systemic notions of hierarchy, emergent properties, communication, and control play an important part in the understanding of the process from this perspective, and each has been shown to bring some insight into the discussion.

## Conclusion

This chapter has focused upon the process by which classical OR solves problems of a specific kind. Previous discussions of this matter have concentrated on the constituent parts of this process, either individually or as a set. Little has been said of the way in which these parts combine to form the process or how that process relates to the decision-making process it supports. The above discussion has shown that systems thinking which emphasizes an expansionist rather than a reductionist approach, leads to an explicit consideration of these issues. What emerges is an appreciation of the degree of interaction which takes place between the various phases of the approach and the mechanisms which bind them together and which ensure that they will act in a self-regulatory and mutually supportive manner—in other words, an appreciation of what makes the OR process a system.

# Operational Research in Organizations

## Introduction

It emerges from the analysis of the OR process in the previous chapter that it provides a strong interaction between the operational researchers and the organization to which it is relevant. In this chapter the character of this interaction and its implications for the practice of OR groups based in and primarily serving a particular organization are examined. The processes concerned operate at two particular levels. First, there is a set of connections which need to occur if a particular study, or project, is to be successfully carried out. These connections are partially described in the previous chapter and are associated with the various stages of the OR process as discussed there. Second, there is a more complex and sophisticated set of interactions between the OR analysts in an organization and the other parts of that organization which are concerned with the broader role of the OR group. These connections are not captured by the discussion in the previous chapter, and their nature will become clearer after the first level has been considered in detail below.

The material in this chapter falls into three areas. First, the nature of the interactions between an OR analyst and an organization which relate to specific projects is considered. Then the higher level interactions which operate among projects are explored. Finally, the systemic quality of the full set of interactions is examined in order to expose the necessity for both levels to be managed effectively if an OR group is to operate successfully in an organization. This discussion also provides a further argument for the case that OR acts as a system and exhibits systemic properties.

## Projects and Their Implementation

*Background*

The material in this section focuses upon the implementation issues which operate at the level of a project. A project can be seen as a set of activities carried out to achieve some specified ends. A project team is usually formed to undertake these activities under the management of a project leader. The team would be dissolved at the completion of a project, and therefore the internal structure of a group undertaking OR work is fluid, although consisting at any one time of a set of teams working on particular issues. This pattern of work dates back to the military OR sections in the Second World War, and Waddington (1973, pp. 18–25) describes the particular structure of the section in Coastal Command.

A recent survey of OR practitioners (ORS, 1986) shows that only 10% of them are consultants working outside of OR groups based in organizations (p. 848). It is therefore appropriate to concentrate here upon the inhouse OR group serving the organization in which it is based. Mercer (1981) notes some key differences between the activities of the external and the inhouse consultant. Hence, in the following, the term *consultant* will be taken to refer, as far as possible, to inhouse operational research analysts. Inhouse OR groups vary considerably in size, with a small percentage being over fifteen in number. The median size of those groups who responded to the survey noted above was six, but over 85% of all practitioners belong to groups larger than this figure.

The usual pattern of work for such groups is based in project teams, each project having a sponsor who is a member of the management of the organization. The sponsor is a person who has either been involved in setting up the work being carried out in the project or been allocated the task of acting as a contact by the organization's management. The survey of OR groups showed that 75% of groups have at least some of their work sponsored, with two-thirds of groups having at least 70% of their activity organized in this way. The number of projects in hand varied as the size of the groups varied. The average per group was twenty-two projects, which is equivalent to two projects per group member (ORS, 1986, p. 882). Thus each member of an OR group works on several project teams at one time, usually involving different sponsors in different parts of the organization.

The discussion below concentrates upon the relationship between the OR group and the rest of the organization and in particular that between a project team, the consultants, and the sponsor associated with the project, the client manager. An appreciation of this relationship helps one to understand the nature of one level of interaction between the problem-solving and decision-making systems and goes some way toward explaining the conditions under which projects are successful. It therefore provides some guidance on the management of projects.

*Consultant–Client Relationships*

It is commonly accepted that the early theoretical base for an understanding of the relationship between the OR system and the associated decision-making system was due to Churchman and Schainblatt (1965). They proposed four possible models for such a relationship centered upon two key individuals: a consultant and a client.

A common form of relationship is the separate-function position. In this situation each party has its own responsibilities, which it carries out independently of the other. An OR analyst, or consultant, is responsible for carrying out an investigation of a situation and providing information about the situation on the basis of that work. A manager, or client, has a different set of responsibilities, which center on using that information to help in improving the situation of concern. Within this model, which was seen to be that most commonly arising in OR, it is not necessary for the consultant to understand what the client does or vice versa. The two functions are isolated from each other, and the relationship consists of only that which is sufficient to initiate and complete the project.

The second and third models place added responsibilities on the consultant. The persuasion position sees consultants as selling their work to a client. In order that sales can take place, the character of the client involved must be understood. Then results can be molded to be compatible with the client's view of the situation and so to increase the chances of their being acted upon. The communication position has a client being educated by a consultant during the course of a project. By making the client understand the reasoning behind the analysis, the analysis will, again, have an improved likelihood of being accepted. In contrast to the persuasion model, this form has the consultant molding the client's view of the situation.

The separate-function model is weak, according to Churchman and Schainblatt, because it ignores the nature of the important relationship which exists between consultant and client. This relationship is important because to understand a client and a situation fully a consultant must be aware of the client's perception of that situation. Thus a satisfactory analysis, as far as a client is concerned, can be carried out only by a consultant who understands how it is seen by the client. Equally, clients will fully appreciate what a consultant is providing them only if they can understand the nature of the investigation. Although the persuasion and communication models both go some way toward this ideal position, they are not sufficient to meet it. A fourth model, the mutual-understanding position, is necessary to define how both parties can be brought together in such a mutually beneficial relationship. In this model, interactions and communication between a consultant and a client occur regularly and are such that they encourage the mutual understanding necessary for satisfactory project completion.

The meaning of mutual understanding has been clarified by Polding and Lockett (1982) as having a sociological rather than an intellectual sense. Earlier work by Bean, Neal, Radnor, and Tansik (1975) and Huysmans (1970) had shown that the effects of clients gaining too much understanding of OR were detrimental to the implementation of results. Thus a naive interpretation of mutual understanding, meaning to understand how each other's mind works, does not appear to generate improved success of implementation. Polding and Lockett investigated an admittedly small sample of thirty projects in order to gather data on how projects were perceived by clients and consultants. They concluded, among other things, that mutual understanding is more of a goal for consultants than for clients. It would appear, therefore, that what consultants think is a useful aim is, in fact, detrimental to their broader aim of having their work used by clients. The need is to reconsider the meaning of mutual understanding, possibly to mean an appreciation of the roles, objectives, and constraints of the other actor rather than an in-depth grasp of how they operate.

Another aspect of the Lockett–Polding study focused upon the structure of the relationship between a client and a consultant (Lockett and Polding, 1978, 1981). The starting point for the investigation of the structure of the relationship is to note that the focus on a two-person relationship (consultant and client) omits consideration of the dynamics of organizational structure and the many other interactions which occur during the lifetime of a project. Further, the Churchman–Schainblatt mutual-understanding model implies that a common set of values and goals exists between the pair, which may not always be the case. In an attempt to develop the basic model to allow for these points, a richer model of the interactions in a project is suggested. This has a manager (client) as part of a system in which an executive and those people affected by the situation also exist. The manager communicates with both of these groups, which do not communicate directly with each other. Similarly, a modeler (consultant) is in communication with a management science executive and with other technicians who may help to support the work, for example, computer programmers. Communication between the two systems takes place horizontally and between adjacent levels as indicated in Figure 5.1. The Churchman–Schainblatt model is the special case, which concerns only the horizontal connection between manager and modeler.

By matching with this model the relationships found to exist in twenty-four of the projects studied, it was possible to examine the importance of the manager–modeler link relative to other structures. The first observation to make is that no common structure emerged in these projects. The manager–modeler link appeared often, but in only three out of the twenty-four cases was it significant, that is, one of a small number of relationships. Thus, while it was concluded that a strong relationship between the two sides was a powerful factor in favor of implementation, it was not necessary for this relationship to be between a modeler and a manager. What was found to be significant in affecting implementation was the existence of a diagonal link. This relationship between two unequal levels in the assumed organizational hierarchy bypasses the formal communication channels in the organization. In those projects which were deemed successful, such a link existed in some form. In three projects which were not implemented, a rectangular structure, based on the formal links, was present. Again, the sample is too small to suggest that any conclusive prescriptions for practice emerge from this analysis, but it does indicate some of the restrictions of the basic Churchman–Schainblatt approach.

Churchman and Schainblatt's work initiated an increased interest in the issue of implementation, that is, the nontechnical elements of OR which surround the modeling aspects of OR projects. *Implementation* is the term used to cover the varied activities which bind the technical parts of the OR process to the decision-making system it is serving. Schultz and Slevin (1975b) provide an early overview of the work in this

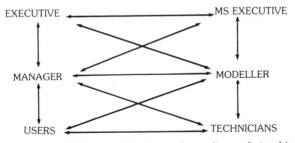

*FIGURE 5.1.* The Lockett-Polding model of consultant–client relationships (based on Lockett and Polding, 1978, 1981).

area, and more recent bibliographies and summaries are provided by Wysocki (1979), Schultz and Ginzberg (1984), and a special issue of *Interfaces* which appeared in 1987. The work in the area can be seen crudely as concentrating upon two related themes. One consists of empirical work, based upon methods of the behavioral sciences and designed to identify those factors which influence the implementation process. Surveys, questionnaires, case studies, and subsequent statistical analysis of the data collected are the hallmarks of this style of investigation. The second theme is the development of models of the implementation process, often based upon the results of empirical work, to provide a structure to the study and to generate hypotheses for testing. The inspiration for the more recent models is the general model of organizational change and development associated with Lewin and Schein. Each of these themes will now be considered in more detail.

*Empirical Models of Implementation*

There have been many studies of those factors which influence the way in which the results of an OR study are received by the clients involved. Many of the early examples are referred to in Schultz and Slevin (1975b), and Schultz, Slevin, and Pinto (1987) summarize five more recent studies which probably capture the core of current understanding. They identify several factors which are common to at least two recent studies of implementation and which between them point to the main influences on implementation success and are necessary for that success.

First, there should be clearly defined goals for the project which establish what it is designed to achieve and how it will be achieved. Failure to define the objectives of a project will make its management difficult and will hinder the project management's ability to adapt to changing circumstances.

Second, there need to be sufficient resources of staff, finance, time, and other necessary supporting activities available to ensure that the necessary work will be completed. Clearly, a lack of resources of any type will restrict the consultants' ability to undertake a full analysis and so increases the chances of certain elements of a situation being omitted from the study.

Third, top management support is seen as being important if a project is to have an increased chance of success. Any project which is in conflict with high-level management views is at a clear disadvantage in terms of achieving full implementation.

Fourth, a project plan into which deadlines and schedules are incorporated is seen as a useful aid to the completion of a project within a defined period. Projects which overrun and are late or incomplete by a completion date may fail to interlock with other projects and so may not be acted upon.

Fifth, competent project managers and team members who have the requisite experience, skills, and personal qualities for a particular project will enable a project to be tackled in the most effective manner. A lack of management skills or failure to include some skill in the group will be as disastrous for a project as the inclusion of people who are incompatible or who are unable to work in particular types of situations.

Sixth, there need to be adequate communication and information links within a project team and between the team and the remainder of the organization. It is important that the progress of a project be made available to all concerned on a regular basis; otherwise it is likely that decisions may be made which will run counter to the aims of the project.

Finally, there should be a capacity for feedback on the project to be given and for the project to respond to this feedback. This process will enable changes in the environment of a project to be identified and adapted to and consequently will lead to a more successful project which is capable of responding to clients and environmental alterations. Failure to be responsive may lead to the results of a project being inappropriate to the situation which prevails at its completion.

These factors provide a set of guidelines for the successful management of projects. They yield an interdependent set of issues which those people involved in initiating and managing projects can use as a basis for establishing and running project teams. The basis for these observations on the factors which will improve the chances of implementation of results is a series of empirical studies. Support for this range of management tasks is provided by Houlden (1979) and Miser (1985).

Houlden notes six areas where effective management is particularly important. First, the sponsor of a project, the person who will act on its outcome if it is deemed satisfactory, is crucial. The majority of OR projects are sponsored and are therefore related to live issues in the organization. Some work may be unsponsored, and this is likely to be concerned either with developing methods for possible future use or with identifying problems which will eventually be the basis of sponsored work. Sponsors should not be so high in an organization that they are divorced from the impact of a project and hence not sufficiently motivated to pursue it. Equally, they should not be so low that they do not have the authority to implement any actions which stem from the work. Second, the project leader and the team should be experienced in the skills necessary for the study in question. Third, the nature of the project should be carefully defined, and, if necessary, smaller subprojects should be used to impose a structure on the overall task. Fourth, the project should be planned and budgeted to provide an effective control mechanism. The specification of deadlines and review dates is an important element of this aspect. Fifth, presenting the results in a manner which is appropriate to the sponsor is important if they are to be understood. Finally, a completion report should be written which provides an overview of the project and its acceptance in the organization in order to guide future work and encourage consultants to reflect on their practice.

Miser poses a set of questions which he suggests a consultant should bear in mind at the start of a project in order to provide a sound basis for the work. These concentrate upon the nature of the decision makers being served and their organizational setting, the culture of the organization, the constraints upon the project, the level to which reporting should be made, and the relationship between the consultants and the remainder of the organization.

The experientially based observations of Houlden and Miser support the empirically based points discussed by Schultz, Slevin, and Pinto. Thus a strong level of agreement exists among different quarters over the important factors in implementation. The second theme in implementation research centers upon providing models of the implementation process within which these factors may be incorporated and which can be used to increase an understanding of their interactions.

*Change Agents and Process Consultation*

The basis for the models of implementation has shifted from the early normative and factor approaches which characterize the majority of the studies in Schultz and Slevin (1975b) to an approach based upon the Lewin–Schein process model of consultation (Batson, 1987; Srinivasan and Davis, 1987). Before considering this model, it will be useful to identify the role played by a consultant in an OR project. Eilon (1975a, 1980) suggests that researchers can take on seven possible roles, of which two are particularly appropriate for OR. The conventional view of the role of an operational researcher is that it is that of a puzzle solver. Puzzle solvers are technicians in the sense that they are concerned with the intellectual activity associated with solving well-structured problems (Eilon, 1975a). As a puzzle solver, operational researchers wait for a problem to be given to them, whereas the change-agent role has the prime objective of changing a given system. Within the change-agent role, an operational researcher may initiate involvement and may become more concerned with identifying problems. Eilon (1980) argues that OR should become more change-agent-oriented and should move away from the puzzle-solver role. As the Lewin–Schein model is firmly rooted in the change-agent paradigm, the use of this model of the implementation process will clearly lead to an understanding of OR which emphasizes an active role for OR in terms of problem seeking.

Within the general role of change agent, an OR practitioner will have several specific roles to play. Five have been identified by Batson (1987). One of the five roles, methodology specialist, is concerned with the technical aspects of modeling and related tasks. The other four roles are related to the consultancy process in which the modeling is embedded. A practitioner must be able to manage information about a project in the role of information specialist. By being a study process designer, the practitioner can plan and manage the project effectively. A key role is that of communication facilitator, which requires the encouragement of communication between the various people involved in a project. Finally, in the role of implementation assurance engineer, a practitioner can begin to ensure that the results of a study will be used. Each of these roles involves in some way ensuring that the different factors which aid in success will be incorporated into a project. Thus the general role of change agent, incorporating each of the above more specific roles, offers one way of understanding how an operational researcher acts within a project.

The dynamics of a project in which change agents participate are most widely accepted as being explained by the three distinct, sequential stages of unfreezing, moving, and refreezing (Lewin, 1947; Schein, 1969). The first task to be undertaken is to reduce any resistance to change which may be present. This resistance will be high in stable organizations, where commitment to the status quo protects the members of the organization from change and disequilibrium. Unfreezing the situation increases the desire of clients to learn about alternatives to the present state of affairs and establishes an environment in which change can occur. Moving the situation involves the acceptance of new ideas or methods by clients. In the OR context, this acceptance is, in effect, equivalent to the acceptance of the results of an OR investigation. Finally, it is necessary to reinforce the acceptance of the new situation by embedding it within the organizational culture. This refreezing stage involves making the new position the accepted one so that clients develop a commitment to it.

This model of the relationship between an OR consultant and the client has been empirically tested by Sorensen and Zand (1975). By studying 280 projects, they found that those were most successful in which unfreezing, moving, and refreezing were considered to have occurred. This observation led them to suggest that the three stages of the model are important indicators of ways to improve the implementation of OR projects. Thus a concern with opening up clients to the possibility of making changes, ensuring that the results of OR studies will be acceptable to the client (that is that they can be understood and are relevant to the client's concerns), and finally reinforcing acceptance of these results and the consequent changes during follow-up meetings are likely to improve the success with which results are acted upon.

Despite the shift toward process models which are inspired by this model of organizational change, questions have been raised about its universal applicability. Srinivasan and Davis (1987) have shown that the model is not relevant to use with studies of the implementation process associated with information systems. The basic assumptions of the model are not satisfied by current information systems consultants. The role of such consultants is not change agent but facilitator of the introduction of new systems. The need for unfreezing is reduced because resistance to new computer systems has been replaced by an acceptance that computer technology can benefit organizations. The process model assumes that the groups who will benefit from change are relatively homogeneous, whereas they are heterogeneous in most cases. Finally, the strictly sequential nature of the approach has been brought into question, and empirical studies have shown that in many cases a set of feedback loops between simultaneous stages has been present.

This assessment of implementation models with reference to information systems is part of a general trend toward focusing much of the recent implementation research on computer-based projects (Pidd, 1988). The validity of transferring the above critique to OR projects is weak, as OR practitioners often see themselves as change agents acting in situations where vested interests often encourage resistance to change. As Pidd argues, there is a need for further empirical work to test and develop models of the implementation process. This work can only improve the understanding of the various interactions which occur within a project. The above discussion has indicated the context in which projects occur, the factors which are usually seen as influencing the success of a project, and the set of tasks which a practitioner undertakes during the course of a project. This discussion has not considered the interactions which occur between projects and which give rise to a higher level of relationships between the OR group and its host organization. These are the focus of the next section.

## OR Groups in Organizations

*Reasons for Success*

The bulk of the work on implementation has been concerned with investigating single projects. As the majority of OR is carried out by inhouse groups, it is likely that factors at the group level have some impact on the success of individual projects. In the following, some of these factors are considered, and two examples of OR groups are used to exemplify one framework which seeks to structure these factors. In the next section the relationships between those factors acting at the project and the group level are explored, and a model of OR as a system of interventions is developed.

A rigorous analysis of the behavior of OR groups has been carried out by Whiteman and Wise (1981). Although this analysis is specifically concerned with those groups which are based in banks, there seems to be little reason not to view the points made as being applicable to groups in most types of organization. This attitude is reinforced by the fact that Whiteman and Wise found size and type of organization to be of little importance in determining behavior. Houlden (1979) has also commented on some issues which influence OR groups. A synthesis of these two discussions creates a comprehensive picture of the factors which influence OR groups.

Whiteman and Wise identify seven interrelated factors as being of key importance in the successful operation of an OR group. First, they recognize the perception and promotion of the role of an OR group to be important. The successful OR groups see themselves as playing a major role in tackling unstructured, large issues; seeking out issues to work on; adopting a more sophisticated set of techniques than those of classical OR; and recognizing how the complexities of organizational life interact with the managerial decision-making process they seek to support. The members of an OR group should expend considerable energy to promote this perception of themselves in the eyes of management.

Second, project selection is particularly important, a point echoed by Houlden. It appears that successful OR groups are entrepreneurial in their generation of projects, strive to ensure that their work will result in a high payoff to the organization, pay considerable attention to the management of projects and team membership, and develop a balanced portfolio of projects. Houlden gives particular attention to the mix of projects which an OR group should have at any time. Three aspects require balancing out: the need to have projects in different areas of an organization to avoid departmental bias, the need to have tactical and strategic studies so that long- and short-term organizational goals can both be allowed for in investigations, and the need to have long- and short-term projects to ensure that more difficult issues will be addressed while a regular supply of information to the organization is maintained.

The third factor influencing success is the type of staff which are present in a group. Intellectual and technical skills must be complemented by an ability to appreciate the role of management and to work with them. Houlden emphasizes the development of OR staff and suggests that they need to have a broad awareness of management in addition to the technical skills required for OR work.

Fourth, Whiteman and Wise recognize the need to have good communications between an OR group and the rest of an organization. Communications can be encouraged by arranging special meetings to address issues of concern, by involving management in the activities of an OR group, and by taking communication seriously. By seeking to build up the communications network between the OR group and its organization, learning can take place in the organization about the role of the group; such communication therefore helps to present a positive image of the group to those it aims to serve.

Fifth, successful OR groups seem to perceive the role of an OR manager in a particular way. They accept that the group does need to be managed and that this is a full-time activity. This perception is built on the fundamental view of the role of the OR group as an agent of change in the organization. If change is to be successful, then it needs to be coordinated, and the available resources must be used effectively. Those OR groups which are successful adopt this view of themselves rather than a perception of their work as being akin to scientists working individually on independent projects. This latter view reduces the management element of the work to an administrative function which does not add to the overall activity.

Not surprisingly, the attitude of senior management is seen to be the sixth important factor guiding success. The support and positive attitude of senior management toward OR will ease the introduction of OR to an organization and will influence how the activity is seen by the lower levels of management.

Finally, Whiteman and Wise recognize the location of the OR group within an organization as being important to its success. If the group is associated with another department (for example, computing or work study), the type of work done by OR may be seen as being restricted to an extension of that done by the attached department. How a group reports to the high levels of management can also restrict its impact.

Houlden argues that in reporting to a director with functional responsibilities such as production or marketing, an OR group may become constrained in its ability to work in all parts of an organization. Thus, in many cases, successful OR groups report to directors with nonfunctional responsibilities, such as deputy chairpersons and planning or similar directors.

## Modeling the Development of OR Groups

On the basis of their assessment of OR groups in European banks, Whiteman and Wise (1981) identify four possible stages in the development of OR groups. These can be recognized as being built around two indicators of the state of such groups. One indicator is the degree of sophistication associated with the methods used by the group. The second is the degree of confidence held by the management of the organization in the worth of the OR group.

Mature and successful groups score highly on both measures. They show a willingness to use methods of analysis which are broader in scope than the classical OR models and techniques. Such a perception of this type of group is supported by the high level of confidence in their work shown by management. The factors discussed above which influence success each help to maintain this confidence.

Groups which are characterized as having arrested development have not such a high score on the indicator of the methods used by the group. Such groups have a narrowly defined role, and they undertake this work with a high level of competence. Consequently, they have secured the support of management and score well in terms of the second indicator.

The third type of group is referred to as overdeveloped. These groups use sophisticated methods of analysis but fail to have the strong support of management. Unlike the first two types of groups, which are likely to survive, overdeveloped groups are likely to be disbanded because they place too great an emphasis upon the technical content of their work rather than on their relationship with the rest of the organization.

Finally, there is the type of group classified as having abandoned development. These groups have little management support and have available only standard OR methods. These circumstances limit the type of work the group can do and restrict its impact and so make it difficult for the group to establish itself. Consequently many such groups will not succeed unless they can improve their position.

It is appropriate at this point to mention an alternative approach to understanding the dynamics of OR groups in organizations that Conway (1989) and Holland (1989) built on Pettigrew's life-cycle model (1975) of specialist groups. Conway and Holland argue that following a period of prebirth and pioneering, an OR group may either be closed down or enter an period of self-doubt. Introspection by the group leads to a range of possible responses. The group may take actions which result in its adapting well to the host organization's needs, or it may fail in this adaptation. Actions which result in beneficial adaptation reflect the observations made above on the need for the group to be proactive in establishing itself in the organization and relating to management. Maladaptive responses correspond to a failure by the group to identify its strategic role appropriately and to see the group being absorbed by other functions, being closed down, or becoming a narrow, specialist service.

This model provides an alternative description of the development of OR groups to that of Whiteman and Wise and explains why OR groups may move between different values for the two indicators of the state of OR groups Whiteman and Wise proposed. Conway's and Holland's work emphasizes the important of strategic decisions in the management of OR groups; Whiteman and Wise indicate two fundamental factors which influence these decisions. Together the two analyses yield a device for understanding how OR groups evolve within an organizational context.

This framework can be used to explore the development, the current position, and the future options of OR groups. It captures those factors which are recognized as being important to the success of OR groups. Each of these factors contributes in some way toward increasing the value of the pair of indicators of the state of a group. In the remainder of this section, two examples of the development of OR groups will be explored with this framework as a guide. One group is that based in the National Westminster Bank with which Whiteman and Wise were associated. The second is the group attached to the Paris public transport service.

Whiteman and Wise identify four stages in the life of the Natwest OR group, from its inception in 1966 to their time of writing, 1981. The group remained in the late 1980s an example of a highly respected group within the OR community. The four stages were birth (1966–1968), childhood (1968–1971), adolescence (1971–1974), and adulthood (1974–1981).

The birth of the OR group occurred in a period when OR was making considerable progress in the industrial and business world. The potential of using OR in organizations was identified, and with the advice of Professor Samuel Eilon at Imperial College an OR group was established within the automation department of the bank. The group was headed by a banker, and selected recruits were trained by undertaking a one-year postgraduate course in OR. A set of projects was identified which were thought to be susceptible to OR analysis. The second stage of development (1968–1971) saw many projects being undertaken. Whiteman and Wise make several observations about the character of the group during this period. The group was heavily dependent upon the guidance of Eilon, who acted as a consultant to the bank for a period after the group's creation. There was little prior experience of using OR in banking, and thus the group had to establish itself and identify what its contribution might be. In the early days this lack of experience meant making use of standard OR techniques to tackle issues which were similar to those faced in areas where OR was better established.

The OR group was created with a fair degree of management support. The conservative nature of the banking profession meant that tension arose between the ambitions of the OR staff and the reaction to it by the banking management. Undoubtedly the guidance of Eilon and the commitment to the initiative by the top levels of management helped to support the group through its early years. By the early 1970s the group had become more self-confident and had succeeded in being accepted within the bank.

The move to adolescence is indicated by a change in the organizational setting of the group, which moved to the business development division, the head of the group being replaced by an operational researcher and the use of Eilon as a father figure declining. The work of the group altered as it began to learn about the banking business. A relatively well-defined set of projects were identified as being areas where the group could contribute. As the scope of these projects broadened, new areas of the bank became involved in the work of the OR group and again difficulties were encountered in convincing management of its value.

During this period the group slowly increased the range of methods of analysis it used. Those which were found to be particularly appropriate to the peculiar aspects of banking operations were advanced. The group concentrated upon achieving implementation in a few chosen areas and committed resources to this end rather than developing more speculative work. The group was becoming more generally accepted by the management of the bank and was learning how to present an acceptable image of itself.

In the second half of the 1970s, the group built upon the work of the previous decade and became more sophisticated in its methods of analysis, and its management was able to direct its work with more confidence as the group was accepted within the bank. The group had acquired a deep understanding of how it related to the organization and was able to take advantage of this in its work. The types of projects undertaken reflect this changing position and were concerned with issues which involved several parts of the organization and represented key areas of development for the bank.

If the emergence of this group is traced through the framework developed earlier, then one can recognize the importance of the initial phase. Here it would have been possible for the group to fail either because it did not succeed in gaining general support or because it focused on developing techniques instead of contributing to the organization. A diagrammatic representation (Figure 5.2) shows the path which brought the group away from that area where what is likely is disbandment, abandoned development, or overdevelopment to an area where stability was established. It can also be seen how strategic decisions made at key moments enabled the group to adapt to the host organization and to secure a niche within it rather than fail to survive.

The history of this group may be usefully contrasted with that of another, the OR group associated with Régie Autonome des Transports Parisiens (RATP), the Paris transport authority (Sitruk, 1983). The group was created at about the same time as the NatWest group in response to a particular issue, the scheduling of crews for buses. The group was part of a section devoted to economics and OR in the transport-planning and

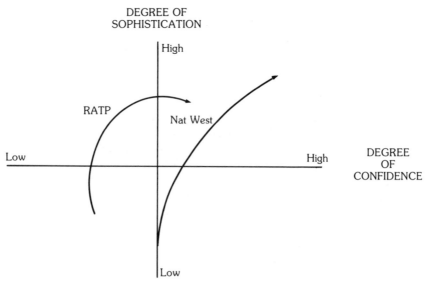

*FIGURE 5.2.* Development of two OR groups.

capital-investment department of the organization. Thus it was set up under different circumstances from the NatWest group. Rather than taking a conscious decision to adopt OR in the organization, OR emerged naturally as a means of tackling a particular issue. The group worked until 1972 on the crew-scheduling problem and was involved in constructing and perfecting a model and solution methods for this single issue.

In 1972 the organization began to expand its planning activities, and as a consequence the OR group found itself with more staff and more projects. Some projects were extensions of the bus crew problem; bus timetabling and metro crew scheduling were investigated. Other studies were concerned with energy supplies, bus routing, and maintenance center location. In each case considerable efforts were devoted to the construction and solution of mathematical models, with little regard being given to the organizational context in which the results might be used. Sitruk refers to this period as being tool-oriented and notes that a main criterion for the success of an operational researcher was technical ability.

By the mid-1970s the various projects had each had setbacks. Either the results had been found to be inappropriate to practical use, or technical difficulties were come across which meant that solutions were slow or impossible to find. These problems were accompanied by an economic recession, which placed the existence of the group in jeopardy. In response the group altered its style of working to take into greater account the organizational realities of the situation and to concentrate on providing useful aids to management rather than the previously sought optimal solutions to problems. In so doing, the group began to improve its reputation with the management of the organization and became involved in more projects influencing a wider part of RATP. The work of the group in the early 1980s was centered upon providing results to clients and managing the group to this end. The work came to be regarded more as the creation of change than as the application of technique. If the development of this group is considered, then a very different path from that of the NatWest group is seen (Figure 5.2). It can be seen from the diagram that the RATP group did not move away from the situations where disbandment was likely until it was threatened. It was then able to change direction rapidly and to respond to the threat. Other groups might not have been so fortunate. So adaptation did occur, not as the result of strategic decision making but as a response to crisis.

The conclusion of this analysis of OR groups is that in order to be successful, an OR group needs to be seen to contribute to an organization. It is of little value to measure success in terms of technical ability alone. As the RATP group demonstrates, being able to produce technically sophisticated results is of little value if management finds them of no use. This is particularly so in times of contraction. OR as a service to management must be seen to be providing a useful service; this is the criterion by which it will be evaluated by management. The development of methods allows the providing of more effective advice on a wider range of topics, but this development must not be made independently or at the cost of improvement in managerial perceptions of the OR group. Otherwise a group may find itself in the position of providing advice in areas which are not seen as being important by the organization.

It is clear that the above discussion overlaps in some ways with the points made earlier about successful project implementation. The two areas of focus are best understood as being related to each other and as contributing to a set of interventions in an organization by an OR group. In the next section this model is developed by bringing together the points made so far in this chapter within the framework of a systems view of organizations.

## The Systemic Nature of OR Interventions

### Organizations as Systems

The above consideration of how OR can be understood from an organizational standpoint has so far been fragmented. The relationships between projects and the OR group and that group and an organization have been implicit in the discussion. They will now be considered explicitly as the role of OR in organizations is examined. In keeping with the remainder of the present discussion on OR, a systems perspective on organizations is adopted. This is not to say that this framework is the only one which may help one to understand the organizational role of OR. Some comments on the limitations of this approach are made at the end of this section and will serve to indicate the assumptions which are being made here.

It is not the purpose of the current analysis to present a complete and rigorous description of the many variants of the systems approach to organizations. Instead, a summary of the commonly held attitudes, together with an overview of some of the more important contributions, will be provided. A comprehensive survey of the systems model of organizations and its intellectual foundations in functionalist sociology is given by Burrell and Morgan (1979). They identify a history of systems thinking in sociology and, in particular, in the sociology of organizations, dating back to Mayo (1933), Barnard (1938), and Roethlisberger and Dickson (1939), but receiving a major impetus from the work of Parsons (1951) and Parsons and Smelsner (1956). Other analysts such as Selznick (1948), the Tavistock group of sociotechnical systems theorists (Trist and Bamforth, 1951; Rice, 1958; Emery and Trist, 1965, 1972) and Katz and Khan (1966) have adopted systems ideas as being central to their work.

A common theme which runs through the more recent systems approaches to organizations is the notion that organizations are open systems (von Bertalanffy, 1950). This means that organizations are characterised by the way in which they exchange resources with their environment. Resources are imported and exported and, while inside the organization, are involved in a variety of transformation processes. Thus an input–throughput–output model of a system in its environment is created, with the added facility of feedback, by which the output can influence what future inputs may be. This model is often referred to as the *organismic analogy*, for it is assumed to be based upon an analogy between organizations and organisms. Burrell and Morgan (1979, p. 63), however, make the point that there are other possible analogies which inform the model. Mechanical, morphogenic, factional, and catastrophic analogies may also be recognized, although the organismic analogy remains the most widely understood.

A second theme which runs through the systems approach to organizations is the recognition that organizations have needs and that these are concerned with the survival of the organization. The contribution to the organization of its component subsystems is determined by the overriding need to maintain the viability of the organization. Thus each subsystem has a function which is related to the ability of the whole organization to survive. This concern with the function of the parts of a system and their relationship to their parent system's survival, which is particularly pronounced when the organismic analogy is adopted, led Burrell and Morgan (1979, p. 64) to connect this version of systems theory with the structural-functionalist school of sociology.

The open systems model of organizations provides some ideas about what an organization should embrace which act as a basis for diagnosis and improvement. Different versions of this model yield different insights. Parsons (1953) identifies four functional imperatives for the survival of any social system, including organizations (Burrell and Morgan, 1979, p. 54; Hamilton, 1983, p. 107). First, securing resources from the environment and distributing them in the system are necessary to allow the system to adapt in response to environmental change. Second, the system must resolve how to establish goals and how to use the resources present in order to attain them. Third, the system must be kept in as stable a state as possible, subsystems must be coordinated, and major disruptions must be avoided to achieve integration. Finally, there must be a set of activities which motivates the system so that structure may be maintained. These four components are usually referred to by the mnemonic *AGIL* (adaptation, goal-attainment, integration, and latency) and provide a way of assessing system performance and ways of improvement.

The sociotechnical systems approach was developed originally to address issues surrounding the interaction of technological and social factors in industrial production. Burrell and Morgan (1979, p. 155) cite the analysis of an Indian textile firm as a clear illustration of the prescriptive elements in this work (Rice, 1958). An industrial concern is driven by the need to survive within the industry of which it is a part. Any such concern will consist of social, technological, and economic subsystems, which should be mutually supportive if the organizational goal is to be achieved. This model then suggests that these three elements of an organization should be related as effectively as possible.

A third example of how the systems view of organizations can aid diagnosis is provided by Katz and Kahn (1966). They develop five necessary subsystems which will allow an organization to perform adequately. Production or technical subsystems are concerned with the throughput of an organization. Supportive subsystems ensure that resources will be imported or exported between the organization and its environment. Maintenance subsystems guarantee that the functional roles in the organization will be carried out. Adaptive subsystems are concerned with change in the organization. Managerial subsystems coordinate and control the other four (Burrell and Morgan, 1979, p. 158). This model again provides a blueprint against which an organization can be assessed and areas needing improvement identified.

*A Systems Model of OR Groups*

The generality of each of these examples of the systems approach to organizations is sufficient to indicate the potential of the approach as an explanatory and diagnostic device. It is also a reason for choosing not to use any of them as a basis for investigating the role of OR in organizations. The generality makes it difficult to being out adequately the unique nature of OR, which can become difficult to interpret satisfactorily within the above framework. OR has a role which can be seen as being useful in attacking each of the Parsonian imperatives; which facilitates the cohesion of social, technological, and economic subsystems within sociotechnical systems theory; and which acts across each of the five subsystems proposed by Katz and Khan. None of these three, or any other systems approach to organization, has developed a model which takes as its specific focus the OR group. If the systemic nature of OR is to be understood, such a model is necessary, and in the next part of this section, such a model is proposed. The inspiration for this model is the set of eight general principles around which the systems approach to organization is constructed (Burrell and Morgan, 1979, p. 63).

The first task is to define a boundary around the issues of concern. An obvious boundary is given by using organizational departments as the basis for a division between system and environment. This boundary definition causes difficulties, for, in a significant number of cases, OR is done by people in departments that, according to their label, are interested in other activities (ORS, 1986). For example, OR is done under the auspices of computing, corporate planning, and several other departmental labels in various organizations. The use of departments also suggests that OR will be undertaken in only one part of an organization, whereas it may actually be found in several. To overcome these problems, an activity-based definition may be adopted. The system in which we are interested consists of those activities which result in the provision of advice to decision makers in organizations about the nature of nonstandard and complex issues concerned with the management of the resources of that organization. This set of activities captures the work done by OR groups and may also include work done by other elements of organizations which are similar in character to OR.

At the level of the OR group, taken now to refer to the above set of activities, the process involved is based upon information. Information about the organization is acquired by the group and is analyzed to produce information in a form which is useful to decision makers as they address particular issues. Therefore the OR group can be seen as acting as an information processor. The input for the group is a mass of information, some purposely sought and some gained passively. This information covers a variety of organizational and environmental behavior. Changing production technologies, the effects of new employment legislation, new methods of constructing and solving models, and many other items will be absorbed by the OR group in an effort to maintain as contemporary an understanding of the group's organizational and wider environment as possible. Within the group this information is operated upon so that it results in an increased knowledge of the situations of concern. If there is insufficient information available, then more is sought from appropriate locations. The knowledge produced is structured so that it is made relevant to the decision makers' interests, and it is then output to the organization. It is this output which contributes largely to the image of the OR group in the eyes of the remainder of the organization. Decision makers will act upon the output, and this action will directly or indirectly alter the information which is taken into the OR group at a future date.

The motivation behind the activity of the OR group is the maintenance of its existence within an organization. Fundamental to this motivation is the belief that OR can improve the performance of organizations and can thereby contribute to their survival. A measure of the extent to which an OR group has been successful is the benefit to the organization of the information which it provides. An OR group can increase its effectiveness by ensuring that the information provided will be useful and regular. The NatWest and RATP cases show that, in the first case, effectiveness was improved by these two means, while, in the second, the OR group was unable to produce useful information regularly and so ran into difficulties. The OR group therefore needs to act as an efficient and continuous processor of information.

The behavior of an OR group as an information-processing system can be best understood by identifying its subsystems. These are the elements of the OR group's activity which enable the group to achieve its aims. The obvious candidate for forming the basis of the subsystems is the project. A project can be defined as that set of information-processing activities which is associated with a particular issue concerning organizational resources. The direct environment of a project consists of the set of other projects being undertaken within an OR group and the relevant parts of the organization and its environment. The information-processing activities of a project are focused upon the various stages of the OR process discussed previously. Information is gathered so that the situation may be formulated; analysis of this information is then undertaken so that relevant advice can be passed to the appropriate part of the organization.

The picture of the OR group presented here is that it is made up of a set of information-processing projects. Within this conceptualization, however, there is, at the moment, little notion of how the separate projects aggregate to produce the OR group. Keys (1989a) suggests that there are several interactions which bind the projects together and allow them to be seen as combining to produce a system. First, each project acquires information from similar, and possibly the same, sources. General background information on changes in the organization and its environment may be fed into each project simultaneously or, at least, by similar routes. Thus inputs are held in common. Second, outputs may also be common to several projects. When work is being done in different projects which all concern the same part of an organization, output from each project will be provided to the same decision maker or group of decision makers. Third, during the course of projects, interaction between projects will occur. Knowledge gained on one project may be thought useful to others and is transferred. Other projects may be used as potential sources of information for a particular project. Thus the projects are intertwined like the strands of a rope rather than independent like the strings of a violin. It is difficult to trace through the individual strands of a rope and separate each from its neighbors, just as it can be difficult to define exactly what separates one project from another. It is this complex of interactions which allows an OR group to be seen as a system of projects rather than as a set of independent activities. When one project is taken out of a group for investigation, the systemic properties are lost, for the crucial interactions between this and other projects cannot then be understood.

The implications of this model of OR groups are several. First, the points already noted above concerning the management of OR groups and projects can be interpreted within the framework. Projects should be managed so that together they generate a sequence of information which is diffused throughout the organization. This diffusion presents the OR group with a means of gathering information from the whole organization more easily than if it were not working for parts of it. It also enables the role of the OR group to be understood throughout the organization. Second, the OR group should establish mechanisms of gathering information of general use to the group and of making it available. This process will reduce the likelihood of people on different projects each seeking the same piece of background information. Third, the level of the interaction between projects should be high. Interaction can be encouraged by selecting suitably mixed teams for sets of projects and by using project leaders for mixed types of projects. While specialization is useful, if taken to extremes it may lead to the separation of projects rather than the interdependence which this model suggests is beneficial.

*Some Criticisms of the Systems Model*

It is appropriate at this point to outline some of the criticisms leveled at the systems model and which underline the above discussion of OR groups in organizations. Jackson (1985a) has summarized the main difficulties under three headings.

First, the systems model sees survival rather than goal attainment as the primary objective of organizations. This view implies that organizations respond to environmental change rather than create their own niche in the socioeconomic environment. In the case of OR groups the systems model emphasizes the need for an OR group to be aware of what the organization (its environment) is doing and to adapt to it. It is the case, however, that OR groups, as exemplified by the NatWest group, do identify those areas where they may be useful and go some way toward initiating action. Thus the above model is limited in this respect. OR groups should seek to impose themselves upon their host organization to a much greater extent than may be suggested by the systems model.

Second, systems models tend to reify organizations. Organizations are perceived to be possessors of the ability to think and act, whereas it is the people within them who have such properties. Reification does not allow the model to incorporate correctly the management processes which take place in organizations. For OR groups the difficulty posed is an inability to understand within the systems model the management of the group. The above discussion describes how the group is structured and should behave but fails to include any references to the decision-making processes which control these. The OR group has managerial processes, but these are not made explicit within the model. Hence it is not possible to assess the effectiveness of the management of an OR group from within this model and to provide guidelines for how it should operate. Yet effective management is needed to guide the group's work and to manage its staff, and is crucial to the success of a group.

Finally, the systems model can be said to place undue emphasis upon the interdependencies of the subsystems and their apparent subservience to the needs of the systems of which they are part. This emphasis makes it impossible for parts of organizations to have full or near autonomy and is contradictory to the fact that some departments or parts of organizations are able to act independently of others. This is not so much a problem for the systems model of OR groups, for it is in the nature of OR to be dependent upon the organization it is serving to some degree, and interactions are necessary for the group to be successful. At a lower level it has been seen that benefits accrue from having interactions between the projects undertaken within a group. When projects become independent of each other, information exchanges are reduced and efficiency is lost. Projects must also contribute to the aims of the OR group; otherwise the group's viability will be weakened.

Therefore, limitations can be found in the above model of how an OR group relates to its host organization. Alternative analyses may be able to provide a model which concentrates upon the management of

OR groups and, in so doing, to emphasize its ability to set and pursue goals. Such models may not bring out the complexity of the relationships between projects, OR groups, and organizations and show how they operate together in a systemic manner, each contributing to the effective performance of an organization. It is these aspects which can be appreciated by a systems-based model.

## Conclusion

The purpose of this chapter was to consider in greater detail than had previously been possible the interactions between the OR process and the remainder of an organization. This topic has been covered above at two levels. First, the relationship between analyst and client during a single project was considered. Second, that between an OR group responsible for many projects and the organization was explored. Finally, these two levels were brought together to yield a systems model of this situation which brings out some of the complexity involved. This model provides some guidance to the ways of making OR groups effective and thus acts as a prescriptive as well as a descriptive device.

# 6

## Systems, Science, and Technology

### Introduction

The previous two chapters have concerned themselves with presenting an image of OR as a system for solving problems of a particular type in a particular way which is embedded within an organizational environment. Systems ideas have been used to conceptualize the OR process. There has been no discussion of how systems ideas have been used within that process. The discussion in this chapter completes the consideration of systems in OR by looking at this issue. The previous chapter concluded with a model of OR as an information-processing system. The present chapter considers the use of systems ideas by this system.

There are four parts to this chapter. First, the conventional view of systems adopted by OR is considered and is seen to provide a way by which OR analysts can usefully understand the world to be structured. The process of inquiry into the world claimed by OR is scientific method, and the use of systems notions within OR highlights the second issue, which is whether OR is a systems science or not. In the third part the relationship between science and technology is considered, and then, in the final part of the chapter, the extent to which OR is a systems technology in relation to a systems science is assessed.

### Systems in OR: The Conventional View

There has been a connection between OR and systems ideas for almost all of the time OR has been a subject of interest. Equally, the systems literature has for a long time seen OR as a sister discipline. The use of systems ideas in OR goes back to the early days of the subject, and the accepted view of what systems means within OR has a long tradition. This conventional view has been referred to by Checkland (1983) as Paradigm I.

The first paradigm of systems thinking takes the stance that the real world contains systems and is systemic in its behavior. Anyone trying to understand such a world may use a systematic method to do so. This notion of using systems ideas both to structure the phenomena being investigated and to guide the process of inquiry was earlier referred to less rigorously by Kershner (1960), who used *systems* to refer both to an aggregation of similar or interrelated things and to a collection of rules for procedure or behavior. Caravajal (1982) identifies two usual means of describing systems approaches as being structural (problems are systems) or methodological (processes are systems) and so reflects the Paradigm I view that systems ideas can permeate both the entity under investigation and the process of investigation. As a starting point for the consideration of these interdependent aspects of the issue, the view that the world is formed of systems is tackled first.

There is no lack of support in the early writings on OR for the view that systems exist as phenomena in the real world. Churchman *et al.* (1957) see the setting for the type of problems with which OR is likely to become involved as "an organised system usually embracing machines as well as men" (p. 107). Roy (1960) shares this view and sees OR as being engaged "in the analysis of complex man and machine operations" (p. 23). The now-defunct statement of OR adopted by the British Operations Research Society refers to "the direction and management of large systems of men, machines, materials and money." It is still implicit in many OR texts that systems are natural or manufactured phenomena, both of which exist in the world. Cohen (1985), for example, uses the word *system* "to denote that part of the real world which is of interest in a particular problem and is therefore being modelled" (p. 2).

By seeing systems as existing in the real world, observers are able to take advantage of the theory of systems behavior to guide their investigation into that part of the world in which they are interested. Alternative sets of ideas are recognized as being important in the explanation of systems behavior. Checkland's focus upon holism, control and communication, and emergence and hierarchy has already been referred to in Chapter 4. Richards and Gupta (1985) prefer to see the concepts of synergy, open systems, purposefulness, and expansionism as being dominant, while Pidd (1979) refers to holism, teleological orientation, and openness as the three major features of systems approaches. Other systems thinkers have preferences for different language, and their emphasis is on different aspects of behavior. In general, several common features can be found to run through each of the above and other expressions of those factors central to an appreciation of the behavior of systems.

Churchman (1979) provides five basic considerations which help to identify the meaning of *system*. First, there are the objectives and performance measures of the whole system. The notion that systems have objectives and ways of seeing how close to these they are attaches to them a notion of goal-seeking, purposeful, or teleological behavior. Systems may be able to set objectives for themselves and so may be able to respond to events. Alternatively systems may be designed to achieve a specific purpose and may be unable to alter the target at which they are aimed. An example of a system able to set its own goals is an organization or part of an organization. Here objectives will be changed in response to factors internal in and external to the organization. A system which is designed to achieve an objective and is incapable of altering this objective itself is a room thermostat. While in many cases it will be systems with humans in them which are of the former type and machine-based systems which are of the latter type, the distinction is not as clear as this. A goal of artificial intelligence is to design machines which can set their own objectives and seek to achieve them. It is arguable the extent to which military personnel or workers on a production line can set their own objectives.

The second of the basic considerations is the presence of an environment for the system and the constraints under which the system must exist. This consideration forces an observer to recognize that a system does not exist in isolation from the rest of the world but is part of a larger entity and is constrained by it. Thus an organization exists within a market for its products and an economy which dictates its level of borrowing, pricing, and general financial behavior. A part of an organization has to exist within the remainder of that organization and must subscribe to the norms of behavior, the general objectives, and the methods of working acceptable to that organization. A machine must function in an environment which consists of the materials that the machine processes, the energy sources required to make the machine function (be these natural or manufactured), and the subsequent use to which the product of the machine is put. If the environment is not accounted for, the purpose of the system and its behavior cannot be fully understood. An organization can be fully understood only in relation to its market, its competitors, and its general socioeconomic surroundings. A machine takes on a different and more comprehensive quality when its purpose is understood relative to its inputs and outputs. A defining characteristic of the environment is that it is out of the control of the system.

The third aspect of the systems approach is the consideration of resources. These lie inside the system and are under its control. Resources can be brought into the system from its environment, and hence systems are said to be open to their environment. Once inside the system, resources can be used in various different ways to achieve different purposes. Thus the personnel of an organization can be deployed in a variety of ways, and each method of deployment will meet the objectives of the organization with a different level of effectiveness. A machine may be operated at different speeds and levels of accuracy to produce the finished item at different rates and levels of quality.

The fourth part of Churchman's systems thinking is the concept of components. These are the actions and functions carried out by the resources of the system which, when added together, will achieve the system objective. An organization can achieve its objectives only if products are made, the necessary raw materials are purchased, methods of sales and distribution are in place, and a means of receiving recompense is available. Without any of these functions being achieved, an organization will be unable to continue. It is no use being able to buy materials, to translate them into a product, and to distribute them to customers if no method of receiving payment exists. When each of the functions are implemented and operated, a synergy occurs and something new appears. An organization, a viable business, is created when the different, necessary processes coalesce to form a whole.

Finally, it is necessary to consider the management of the system. This involves planning how to use the system resources to achieve the system objectives and controlling the system to ensure that the plan will be correctly executed and to identify future changes which need to be planned for. A system which is not managed will not be able to function effectively in most cases. Only if the environment is stable and if the system is designed to work effectively in such conditions will management be a minimal activity, but, even in this extreme case, monitoring of performance is necessary, as complete certainty over future behavior will never be possible. An organization in which management does not occur or is ineffective will rapidly begin to fail to meet its objectives and will be unable to change course to improve the situation. A machine which is not managed will, literally, begin to go out of control.

Thus it is possible to identify, with the help of Churchman's considerations, a set of issues which appear to characterize the behavior of systems. They are purposeful and either have objectives imposed upon them or can impose them upon themselves; they exist in environments to which they are open and exchange resources; there is a form of hierarchy created by the synergistic addition of parts to form wholes which are different from their parts; and they need to be controlled, either internally or externally, if they are to function effectively. The conventional view of systems in OR emphasizes each of these features as being useful in helping to identify, structure, and understand the behavior of the world.

Implicit within this discussion of how to think about systems and to gain some understanding of their behavior is a particular notion of what these systems which exist in the world look like. Churchman (1979, p. 29) himself points out that management scientists seek to define *system* carefully as a set of parts coordinated to accomplish a set of goals. Beer (1966, p. 241) reinforces this view by drawing an equivalence between a system and a coherence of a number of entities called parts of that system and by emphasizing the need to acknowledge the relationships between these parts if a system is to be recognized. The earliest major OR text (Churchman *et al.*, 1957, p. 7) indicates that OR is an example of a systems approach because it can tackle problems involving the interaction of several parts of an organization for the benefit of the organization as a whole. The connection is made because *system* implies an interconnected complex of functionally related components. Rivett (1980) gives more detail on the nature of the relationships between the parts by identifying three characteristics of the reality with which OR deals. These are that it is observable, measurable, and systemic. By *systemic* is meant that there is a set of cause–effect relationships interacting in a complex and simultaneous manner. The relationships act in such a way as to enable a system to be seen as a set of entities. Each entity affects and is affected by at least one other entity in the set, and no partition into two subsets can be made without there being at least one relationship between an element of one and an element of the other.

Thus the perception of how systems ideas can be used in classical OR is that they describe the structure of the world. They prescribe how to understand reality; parts and relationships must be defined together with system objectives, an environment, and system–environment relationships. On the basis of this framework, analysis may then proceed. A second way in which systems ideas can be used within OR is to carry out this analysis systematically. The particular type of systematic analysis used within OR is seen to be based on scientific method. Attention is now turned toward an investigation of how closely scientific method can be used in OR studies in an attempt to begin to clarify the scientific character of OR.

## OR and the Scientific Method

*Preamble*

The connection between OR and the natural sciences has been explained from a historical perspective in earlier chapters. Here the connection is explored from a methodological angle. The OR process of investigating the world is brought into comparison with the systematic, rational, and rigorous methods of investigation associated with the sciences. Both sides of the comparison must be dealt with in a stylized manner. Just as no accepted specification of the OR process exists, neither does an accepted version of the scientific method. The two main versions of scientific method, the inductive-deductive approach and falsificationism, are treated here, together with Feyerabend's irrationalist picture (1975), which gives a useful balance to the usual formalized descriptions of scientific method. The extent to which OR can be said to be scientific within the appropriate frameworks is assessed. Finally, some general comments are made on the role of scientific method in OR.

A foundation of OR has often been seen as science or scientific method, and this view is held as strongly today as in the early days of OR. Mitchell (1980) notes "the binding belief among the OR community is that science is offerable, sensibly offerable, as an aid to problem-solving" (p. 460). Stainton (1984) sees that "the techniques of operational research are bound to the principles of scientific method, as it is traditionally expressed" (p. 146). The central role of science and scientific method in OR is reinforced by Haley (1984), who claims that these are "the only commonly agreed constituents of OR" (p. 193). In a thorough investigation of the OR community in Britain, the findings concluded "that most practitioners subscribe to the view that OR in practice uses, or seeks to use, methodology of a kind which would be endorsed by the scientific community" (ORS, 1986, p. 842). So the issue is not whether OR uses science but what form of science is involved and, following on from this, what this question implies for the relationship between OR and other sciences.

There are many sources of information on scientific method and general discussions of the philosophy of science. What follows is based upon a typical selection of these: Chalmers (1982), Pratt (1978), and Richards (1983). A more technical and advanced discussion of the material used here is available in Suppe (1977). Schmidt (1987) gives a useful summary of different forms of science in relation to organizational research.

*Induction and Deduction*

The central accepted goal of scientific endeavor is to provide proven knowledge about the world in which we live. The way in which such knowledge is acquired is debatable and forms a major focus for the philosophy of science. Historically the earliest attempts to formalize a means of investigating the natural world in order to derive laws and theories of behavior are due to Aristotle. Aristotle's logic allowed for observations to be made and, on the basis of these, a statement of behavior to be induced. The inductive method consists of observations followed by generalization to produce a statement about the phenomena under observation which is of wider applicability than those observations themselves. The reliability of this approach is based upon two premises: that observations are objective and secure and that the generalization itself is legitimate. Within this approach, observations are assumed to be made directly by the scientist and to act as an immediate input into the knowledge formation process. Generalization is seen as legitimate when a sufficiently large number of observations have been made under a wide variety of circumstances. The resulting general statement should not contradict any of the observations made in order to produce it.

As an example of how the inductive method would work, consider an investigation of the behavior of queues at checkouts in a supermarket. The inductive method requires observation of such queues and the recording of the information gathered. An example of this information might be as follows:

| Number of checkouts | Average length of queue | Day of week | Weather | Manager |
| --- | --- | --- | --- | --- |
| 4 | 10 | Mon. | Fair | Bill |
| 3 | 18 | Tues. | Wet | Joe |
| 4 | 12 | Wed. | Wet | Fred |
| 2 | 24 | Thurs. | Sunny | Bill |
| 4 | 11 | Fri. | Cold | Joe |
| 5 | 9 | Sat. | Snow | Fred |
| 0 | 0 | Sun. | Dry | — |

Central to the inductive approach is the belief that prior to observation, nothing is known of what factors will be important in explaining the phenomenon of concern. Thus data on all factors thought relevant should be collected. The next stage is to generalize from these data statements which capture the relationships contained within the data. In generalizing, the conditions necessary for induction to be legitimate should be met. Thus it might be deemed appropriate to suggest that, "As the number of check-outs staffed increases, the average length of queue decreases." This statement is made on the basis of six observations under different weather and management conditions over a week and is not contradicted by the observations made. It may be decided that six observations are insufficient and that more may be necessary; if so, these are made, and further general statements are produced.

Once the generalized statement has been produced, predictions can be made which would suggest what will happen in circumstances not previously observed. For example, by bringing together the general statement and the existing observations, it might be predicted that if one checkout was open, the average queue length would be in excess of twenty-four and that if five were open, it would be less than nine. These predictions can be tested by experimentation. Each experiment produces a further observation that can be added to those already made and, provided it does not contradict the general statement, that adds extra support to it. This process of prediction involves deducing the effect of applying the general statement to particular conditions. It is usual to see induction and deduction combined in scientific method to yield the inductive-deductive approach.

This example immediately opens up the difficulties of induction. First, there is the pragmatic issue of whether enough observations have been made under sufficiently wide conditions. In the above case, are 6, 60, 600, or 6,000 observations enough to support the generalization? Is the variety of weather conditions and management wide enough to cover all eventualities? Is it satisfactory to use only one supermarket, or should all of those in one town, region, or nation be considered? This somewhat obvious, but practically important, point leads into a connected difficulty of induction, which is its lack of logical proof. There is no way of guaranteeing that the next observation will not contradict the general statement. Attempts to prove that induction has a logical basis come to nothing, and reverting to previous successful uses of induction to give it credibility means using induction to prove itself, a logical flaw. Thus one of the underlying premises of induction, that generalization is legitimate, is shown to be of dubious validity.

The other premise, that observation is objective, is also open to criticism. Observation, within the inductive method, is the starting point of science and precedes theory building. However, it can be argued that in order to understand the observations which are made, a prior set of theoretical concepts must be in place. That is, in order to begin to understand the behavior of queues in supermarket, a conceptualization of that phenomenon must occur first. Only then can it begin to make sense to measure queue lengths and checkouts in operation. These observations make sense when the prior conceptualization is to see that part of the supermarket as a queuing system. If the situation had been structured by looking at the flows of money involved, a different set of observations might have taken place and might have produced a different general statement. Thus theories prescribe how observations will be interpreted, and observation is theory-dependent. This understanding of observations is in direct contrast to the inductive view of objective, unbiased observations made independently of any theoretical base whatsoever.

The inductive method is not defeated by these difficulties, and modifications are made to account for them. First, in response to the inability of inductivism to provide certain information, the inductivist retreats to probability. Rather than providing generalized statements which are certain, an element of probabilism is introduced. Thus the statement in the example above might be replaced by "As the number of checkouts staffed increases, the average length of queue is likely to decrease." As more observations are made in different circumstances, a greater belief in the validity of the statement emerges, while the probabilistic element remains to account for the possibility that the statement may be contradicted at some stage. Second, the condition that observation precedes theory can be relaxed while retaining the spirit of induction. Irrespective of where theory originates, science can still be seen as involving the collection of data and the assessment of the validity of a theory by an inductive process. Thus a modified, more sophisticated interpretation of inductivism remains as a valid and useful explanation of scientific method. The issue now is to examine how well it may be used within the OR process.

Several authors, including Goodeve (1952), Solandt (1955), Ackoff (1962), Rivett (1980), and White (1985), note that the OR process is an extension and modification of a scientific method which consists of observation, generalization, experimentation, and validation. The model of the scientific method which is seen to underpin OR is the inductive-deductive version discussed above. Therefore it is not difficult to draw analogies between the two processes. Within OR, observation of the problem situation is seen as the first stage, as this enables the problem to be formulated and data to be collected. Then general statements, in the form of models and the mathematical expressions embedded within them, are produced on the basis of these observations. Then the model is manipulated to predict changes, and these are then validated and, if appropriate, implemented. This process is clearly comparable to the deductive process, which acts as a test of the theory. If predictions prove not to be correct, the theory is modified in the light of possible further observations. Equivalently, in OR, if suggested changes do not work as expected, models are rebuilt and solutions are produced on the basis of the new model.

It is instructive to see what the criticisms of inductivism mean for the understanding of OR on the basis of the above analogy. The set of difficulties which are based on the premise that induction is a legitimate process raises issues having to do with the making of observations. Specifically it causes an observer to establish what observations should be made and when to stop them. Observations can be made continuously or at discrete intervals, and, if the latter, the length of interval must be specified. A choice must be made on the rate of observation. Decisions on what to measure, or to attempt to measure, need to be made. A stopping rule for the observations has to be specified, a predetermined number of observations may be made, or some other device for halting them may be introduced. There is no significant guidance in the OR process on how to make these methodological decisions.

The second premise of the inductive method is that observation is unbiased and objective, yet it can be argued that, in fact, it depends on prior theoretical frameworks. The difficulty that this point poses for OR is that it is possible to see theoretical frameworks enshrined in the standard models developed within OR. Thus a trained operational researcher who has knowledge of these models and their solution techniques will tend to see the world in these terms. When faced with a situation that takes on the structure of a queuing system, as in the supermarket example, the analyst will understand it in this framework and will make observations appropriately. This approach will limit the analysis and will prescribe how certain types of situation can be examined. There will be many situations which do not fall into the standard categories and that require more creative investigation. Even in these cases, however, the set of frameworks brought to bear by the analyst will influence how they are eventually perceived. The point here is not that standard OR models restrict and predefine how situations will be seen but a more fundamental observation. This is that models form a theoretical base which, once acquired, will dictate how situations are structured by the analyst.

Thus an argument can be made for OR to embody the inductive-deductive method. There is a strong equivalence between the OR process and this version of scientific method, as well as evidence to suggest that the OR process emerges from this. If this argument is accepted, then the criticisms of induction must be accepted also. It has been shown that these criticisms weaken the case for OR to be seen as an objective, empirical method of tackling problems, just as they weaken the case for inductive-based science to be objective and empirical. OR is unable to claim that it produces models which represent reality in a proven way for the generalization process, and the observations upon which it is based are subject to error. Further, the notion that OR produces models of situations which are guided only by the observations of those situations is invalid, for previous models influence the way in which future models will be constructed and situations perceived. Thus the position that OR is an objective, empirical process built upon the inductive version of scientific method is tenuous.

*Falsificationism*

In response to the fundamental difficulties of induction, an alternative explanation of scientific method has been developed. Originally dating back to the nineteenth century but associated mainly with the work of Popper (1972, 1977), falsificationism, or the hypothetico-deductive method, replaces induction by a process which starts by accepting those points which cause induction difficulty. Thus falsificationism takes as given that theory precedes observation and seeks to expound a method which is logically sound. The principle of falsificationism is that while a general statement can never be proved true, it can be falsified. Thus science is seen as a process which seeks to establish hypotheses and then attempts to falsify them. The more resistant a statement is to these attempts, the more credible it is. Hence theory precedes observation, for the hypotheses precede the observations made to test them, and there is logical support, for an observation which falsifies a statement disproves it conclusively. This approach therefore appears to overcome the difficulties which confront induction. The end result is the same—a general statement about some phenomenon—and so deduction can follow from falsificationism just as it does from induction and can lead to further observations to test the general statement.

The supermarket checkout example can be used to illustrate how falsification can produce knowledge. First, a hypothesis will be proposed which is essentially a guess at how the queues are behaving. Such a hypothesis might be "Queues are longer on wet days than on dry days." Observations are then made in an attempt to falsify this statement. By collecting data on queue length and weather, it will be possible to check the validity of the statement.

The advantages of this approach over the inductive method can be clearly seen. First, as soon as one observation of a queue being shorter on a wet day than on a dry day is made, the statement is proved false and must be discarded. Second, the statement guides the observations to be made. There is no concern with defining what to observe or for how long; the statement and the process clarify these issues precisely.

When a statement is falsified, it may be modified to make allowances for the observation which contradicted it. For example, when the above statement has been proved false, it may be thought that the days of the week also influence queue length, and so a modified statement such as the following may be made: "Queues become longer the wetter the weather and the later it is in the week." This statement then allows further observations to be made with a view to disproving it.

Falsificationism provides a very different view of science from the inductive approach and of the way in which knowledge is acquired. The inductive approach suggests that science is a steady accumulation of knowledge based upon an increasing number of observations. Knowledge is scientific if it is based on observations and is not contradicted by them. The falsificationist method, in contrast, sees science proceeding in a discontinuous fashion, with statements being continually changed as observations are made which contradict them. In particular, large changes in understanding occur if statements thought safe and uncontentious are proved false (the falsification of cautious conjectures), or if highly unlikely statements survive tests (the confirmation of bold conjectures). Knowledge is scientific if it is expressed as a statement which can be falsified.

This alternative to induction has its difficulties, however. These fall into two areas. First, the apparently sound logical basis for the method has some flaws. It is implicit within the method that observations are a true and accurate record of what occurs and that it is possible to include all relevant factors in the analysis. Both of these assumptions offer ways of retaining a hypothesis which has been contradicted by an observation. It can be argued that the observation was not accurate or that the method of observation was responsible for introducing an error. Equally, it might be claimed that the complexity of a statement makes it difficult to place the source of the error exactly. Thus, if the modified statement above were tested by observing queue length, weather, and days of the week and were still found to be false, two ways of retaining the statement are available. It can be argued that the difficulty of measuring the wetness of the day makes observations insecure. The time period over which measurement occurs, the area to be considered, and so on may each introduce elements of uncertainty. It could also be argued that an implicit statement about the independence of the weather and the days of the week may be the root of the invalidity, and it is this auxiliary hypothesis that needs further examination, not that hypothesis developed to explain queuing behavior.

The second area of difficulty is that on many occasions important scientific theories would have been ignored if the results of early observations had been taken as valid. Chalmers (1982) and Richards (1983) both give examples where theories with current substantial levels of support had earlier been shown to be false; the falsification had been ignored, and eventually the reasons for the falsification were found. Thus the logical strength of falsificationism can be circumvented if circumstances warrant, and thus the validity of the method is questionable.

Eilon (1975b) has drawn an equivalence between the OR process and the hypothetico-deductive method described above. The starting point of an OR process interpreted in this way is for an analyst to form a view expressed as a model of how the situation under consideration behaves. This process is equivalent to forming a hypothesis, which is then tested by collecting data and comparing model performance with actual performance. At this stage the model may be rejected or modified to produce a further hypothesis.

In a way similar to induction, the general difficulties of falsification are reflected in difficulties with the OR process when it is understood in this way. In particular, there is scope to continue with an existing model even though it may not reproduce behavior exactly. The problems of data collection and measurement in organizational settings provide plenty of opportunity for errors to be associated there rather than with the model and so protect the model from attack. The general lack of understanding of organizational behavior also makes it plausible to locate errors in those parts of the situation into which specific investigations have not been made.

Thus a case can also be made for understanding the OR process to be an example of falsificationist scientific method. The OR process can be interpreted as an attempt to falsify theories which are embodied in models. The implication for OR of taking this view is that it has an element of subjectivity built into it for the initial hypotheses, and that subsequent modifications are the creations of an observer and not a property of the object being observed. Neither is observation the prime element in the method. Thus OR is not an objective, empirical process when seen from within this perspective, just as it was difficult to hold this view within the inductive model.

This discussion of OR as interpreted within the two main schools of thought on scientific method suggests that it is neither objective nor empirical. The inductive method is severely flawed if one seeks to use this to provide a grounding for OR in scientific method, and falsificationism has to start from a position accepting subjectivity and the theory dependence of observation to overcome these flaws.

## Against Method

The discussion so far has sought to provide a foundation for OR in scientific method. The assumption that there is such a method, and that therefore science, and OR, has some systematic character in its process, has been questioned by Feyerabend (1975). It is useful to explore Feyerabend's work briefly in order to examine the extent to which his arguments have any validity for OR.

Feyerabend's arguments against scientific method are based upon the belief that whichever methodology of science is accepted, there has been no resulting set of rules to guide scientific activity. Both induction and falsificationism describe how knowledge may be gained but fail to prescribe how to gain it. The situation is such, according to Feyerbend, that it is unrealistic to expect a few simple methodological rules to account for the process by which theories are created or discovered. Such a complex process can be adequately understood only by a much richer analysis in which sociological, psychological, and historical factors are also borne in mind. The conclusion of this argument, at its extreme, is to say that any attempt to define the methods of science will be unable to capture fully the actual processes involved and that to attempt to do so is, therefore, a fruitless exercise.

The applicability of Feyerabend's argument to OR would suggest that OR cannot be adequately explained by either induction or falsificationism because they do not adequately explain science. The argument therefore offers one reason why attempts to understand the OR process by using the methods of science as a base have come to little. A consequence of Feyerabend's argument is that to understand OR as fully as possible requires a broader and more contextual analysis. In this, the OR process is embedded in a context which includes the social and organizational setting in which the process is being undertaken. If this broadening of the analysis is done, then the reality of the nature of the OR process relative to the scientific process becomes clear. In particular it emerges that the reasons for undertaking OR and the reasons for undertaking science are different.

If one views the OR process as part of a larger set of activities and identifies its function within that set, then the role of OR is seen to be the provision of information relevant to a particular decision-making or problem-solving situation. The scientific process has the function of providing understanding and knowledge about phenomena unrestricted by being relevant to any specific issue. Both processes may be undertaken in a systematic manner guided by experientially gained or methodologically based rules of behavior. There may be some overlap in these rules, as there is between OR and the inductive and falsificationist explanations of science, if one chooses to accept them. The reason for the overlap lies partly in the history of OR, where people trained in scientific disciplines moved into OR and used methods with which they were familiar and had been successful. The acceptance of scientific approaches to management problems was reinforced by the generally held view that science was a sensible and effective way to gain understanding. The danger is that the methodological similarities of OR and science may be seen to imply that OR is science. It is not science, for its prime goals are different from those of science. The goals of OR are much nearer those of technology.

Thus by adopting Feyerabend's antimethodological stance, it is possible to see the limitations of trying to match the OR process to a particular version of scientific method. The issue is not what version of scientific method is used within OR but whether OR is a science at all. What has been implied above is that OR adopts a scientific attitude but does not pursue the goals of science. Instead, it seeks to use scientific methods to address practical rather than intellectual matters. This point of view will now be clarified.

## Science, OR, and Technology

### OR as Not Science

Some early writers on OR were committed to the view that OR is a science. Johnson (1960) saw OR as being in a similar relationship to operational engineering as physics to electronic engineering. Ackoff (1956) notes that OR "is or is becoming a science and as such is defined by a combination of the phenomena it studies, its methods and its techniques" (p. 265). However, the view that OR is not a science slowly developed to provide strong arguments leading to the view that OR can be seen alternatively as a technology.

In the early 1960s both Lathrop (1959) and Barish (1963) were arguing that OR is not a science. Lathrop defined science as "that investigative activity which has as its objective the acquisition and communication of new knowledge regarding the world and universe around us" (p.

424). He was forced to conclude that science, "by itself, is useless to the world of decision" (p. 426) and thus, by implication, to say that OR, as it is relevant to decisions, cannot be purely a science. Barish defined science similarly as "accumulated knowledge systematised and formulated with reference to the discovery of general truths or the operation of general laws" (p. 389). OR was seen as being an applied science, in the sense that its purpose is to provide systems useful to humans.

The reasons for not seeing OR as a science were refined in the late 1970s. Dando and Sharp (1976) and Dando, Defrenne, and Sharp (1977) identify four characteristics of the mature sciences. These sciences have a focus on a defined set of phenomena, a working set of paradigms and associated languages, a system for testing theories, and the aim of producing explanations of "how parts of the system work which in total provide a coherent framework of understanding" (Dando and Sharp, 1976, p. 947). None of these elements are seen to be present in OR, and so it fails to meet the criteria for being a mature science. Only the final characteristic is felt necessary to define any science, and this is also found lacking, and so the conclusion is reached that OR is not an immature science. Bevan (1976) identifies two areas which concern him about identifying OR with science. First, OR fails to incorporate a proper critical attitude, and second, operational researchers try to influence people outside their community while scientists do not. Three differences between OR and science are identified by Bevan: OR is prescriptive, whereas science is descriptive; scientists determine "the truth," while operational researchers determine "optima"; and time is a major constraint on the OR process, whereas it does not have a significant impact on the scientist. Tomlinson (1981) identifies two significant differences between operational researchers and traditional scientists. The former are able to transcend the limitations imposed by a discipline and can draw on expert skills not their own, while these actions are less easy for the latter.

The sophisticated arguments of Dando, Defrenne, and Sharp led them to conclude that OR is a technology. The understanding of OR as technology is a view which Raitt (1979) did not think would surprise many practitioners. White (1970) had already suggested that a more appropriate title for an operational researcher or a decision analyst might be *decision technologist*. The cultural association between operational researchers and technologists has been expressed by Malin (1981), who argues that

the OR problem solving-solving approach is firmly wedded to the heuristic principles and passions of technological innovation and creativity and, as

such, is totally different from and conflicts with the intellectual principles
and passions involved in scientific discovery and creativity. (p. 958)

Rosenhead (1986) states clearly that OR "is best considered as a technology rather than as a science" (p. 338).

The process by which OR investigates the world is therefore systematic, guided to an extent by scientific method, but OR is being increasingly seen as a technology and not as a science. In order to understand more fully the processes and character of OR, it is necessary to develop this interpretation of OR and to explore the use of systems ideas within it. This is done in the following, where two models of the science–technology relationship and their implications for understanding OR are considered. It is necessary to examine technology relative to science if its character is to be fully brought out. Then the notion that OR is a systems technology is examined together with its relationship to systems science.

*OR as Technology*

The traditional model of the science–technology relationship is hierarchical in structure and sees technology as applied science. Barnes and Edge (1982, pp. 147–154), in discussing this model, recognize several important features which warrant attention. This model reflects the widely held distinction between science and technology in that science is concerned with the production of new knowledge, which is then applied in a routine and mechanical fashion by technology. Technological developments must therefore be triggered by a scientific discovery, and each scientific discovery will eventually lead to technological progress. The relationship is unidirectional, and technology is grounded in science. Therefore, to understand a technology, it is necessary to appreciate the science upon which it is based and from which it derives its impetus.

The various calls to see OR as a technology have sought to understand OR as a technology within this model. As early as the 1960s, Flood (1962) was visualizing OR as an applied science built upon a base of behavioral and systems sciences and using the methods of the experimental sciences to apply knowledge of human and systems behavior to problem situations. Dando *et al.* (1977) recognized OR to be a technology in need of a science of decision processes. Such a science would focus upon decision making in organizations, would use systems theories as the basis for its paradigms and language, would develop specific methods for testing theories, and would aim to produce general causal explanations of how decision processes work which would form a basis for the associated technology of decision-support design. Bonder (1979) wishes to see an operational science established which develops "knowledge, understanding and verified formal structures (theories) about these operational and management phenomena that are the components of the systems we study, analyze, plan and design in our practice" (p. 219).

Such a perspective has implications for OR which are significant and which pose severe problems for this model of technology. First, this model implies that a distinction between science and technology—between OR and its underlying body of knowledge—is possible. At the moment this distinction might be able to be conceptualized because no such science exists or is defined. In practice, however, the distinction will be difficult to achieve. While some people may be clearly at the science or technology ends of the spectrum, many are in a gray area in the middle, undertaking work which may be of both types simultaneously.

Second, the implication is that a single unified science will emerge to support OR, just as particular elements of the natural sciences support different types of engineering. In the case of OR the historical attachment to several disciplines and the nature of the situations it is involved with means that a multidisplinary theoretical base will be necessary. It is likely that the nature of the disciplines involved will prohibit the creation of a unified foundation. The quantitative approaches of some disciplines will prove incompatible with the qualitative attitude of others.

Third, this model suggests that technology cannot exist without a science to support it and that this science triggers technological change. Yet OR appears to have survived for at least half a century with no science being explicitly present to support it and has evolved to offer some sophisticated tools and techniques.

Apart from these difficulties with the relationship between OR and its scientific base, the model suggests that OR has a particular character, a suggestion that, when compared with OR practice, is found to be in error. The model would imply that OR consists of routine activities applying knowledge acquired outside OR to particular issues. Yet OR in many cases develops its own knowledge in order to tackle a specific case. The model also denies the creative element of OR, but again, successful OR requires creativity in various ways. Majone (1980) has developed a treatment of OR which emphasizes the craftwork aspect of the activity. The model prevents practical issues in OR initiating work in the theoretical areas which underpin it. However, many examples of developments in mathematics and computer science have initially been due to the need to solve a practical problem. Finally, the model sees the culture of OR as being determined by its underlying science and does not allow for a separate technological culture. It can again be noted that OR has developed its own professional attitudes, language, information networks, and structure, which have developed independently and have not been directly influenced by any science which underpins it.

These issues are not unique to OR, and Mayr (1976) and Barnes and Edge (1982) summarize similar problems when attempting to understand other technologies by the use of this model. In response to these general difficulties, an alternative, and now accepted, model of the science–technology relationship has emerged. This is referred to by Barnes and Edge as the symmetrical model, but it can be seen, in fact, to be a systems model of the science–technology pair. The modern understanding of the science–technology relationship emphasizes science and technology as separate bodies of activity which support each other in a mutually beneficial way but which are often difficult to distinguish from each other. Both parts of the relationship have their own particular cultures and are concerned with developing and enhancing them. The view that science drives technology is replaced by an alternative notion in which both science and technology create their own particular contributions to society: science contributes knowledge primarily, and technology contributes devices and mechanisms primarily. The work done within science and technology builds upon previous work in those areas, with only occasional use of resources and stimulus from the other party. In this modern understanding a greater amount of autonomy has been attributed to technology than was the case in the traditional model. Science, equally, is seen as not having the responsibility for causing major technological change which was attributed to it by the traditional model. Technological developments can occur without there being causal and prior scientific developments. Figure 6.1 provides a diagrammatic representation of the modern model of the science–technology relation.

The adoption of this model as an explanatory device for technology greatly increases the strength of the case for OR as a technology (Keys, 1989b). It removes the need to define or create a science to underpin OR. OR is free to draw upon and influence those sciences which are concerned in any way with the situations in which OR is involved at any time. Although there may be a core of such disciplines which influence OR on many occasions, there is no need for a formal connection between them, and OR need not concern itself with seeking to specify it. The paradox of OR as technology existing without a science is removed, for this model accepts that technologies have their own internal struc-

#### Chapter 6

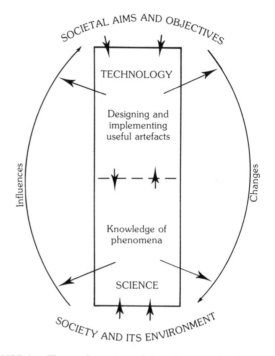

**FIGURE 6.1.** The modern view of the science–technology system.

ture and culture and can exist without a parent science. The routine, noncreative view of OR activity is replaced by a more realistic acceptance that technologies, including OR, involve nonroutine, creative enterprise. The initiation of scientific activity in response to a technological problem is allowed and hence can explain why problems faced within OR have led to developments at the scientific level. If the general model of Figure 6.1 is made specific to the OR situation then Figure 6.2 emerges, which presents a clear image of how OR relates, on the one hand, strongly, to the organizations in which it is involved and, on the other hand, weakly, to the various bodies of knowledge which influence its activity.

The specific issue now to consider is how systems is involved in this technological activity. In the next section a re-interpretation of the conventional view of systems in OR is developed based not on the view that OR is a science but on the view that OR is a technology.

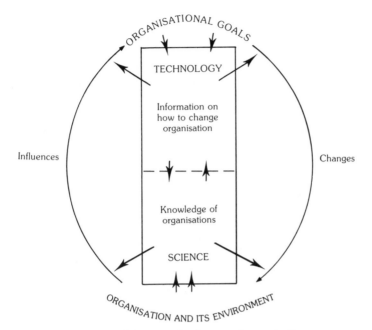

**FIGURE 6.2.** Science, technology, and organizations.

## OR as Systems Technology

In this final section some tentative observations on the technological character of OR are made. They are tentative because much more consideration of the issues needs to be undertaken before OR as technology can be convincingly used as a model for understanding the OR process. The starting point for the discussion is to accept that OR is a technology interpreted within the modern view of technologies. The focus for the discussion is to explore the influence and use of systems ideas within this technology, that is, to examine OR as a systems technology.

Two basic characteristics of any technology are its aims and the methods used to achieve them. The aim of OR is to produce information about methods which may be able to improve the effectiveness of an organization. In so doing, OR may investigate the relative benefits of prespecified methods, or it may be involved in the design of such methods itself. Thus OR may be asked to investigate the merits of a proposed production-planning schedule compared with the existing one, or it may be asked to design a schedule which is more effective than the existing method. In order to produce information on how to improve organizational effectiveness, it may be necessary to design methods to achieve this improvement. The methods which are used to produce the information are scientific in character. Although elements of craftwork appear in OR, they apply to the use of scientific processes of inquiry and do not form the process of inquiry itself.

These aims and methods give OR a unique character as a technology. Checkland (1981) has presented a typology of systems classes which serves as a useful starting point for placing OR within the set of technologies. Natural systems are those whose origin is in the origin of the universe and which result form the processes which characterize this universe. Designed physical systems are like natural systems except that they are the result of conscious design. They have been made to achieve some purpose. Designed abstract systems are those systems which humans have constructed to achieve a purpose but which are not tangible. The fourth class of systems are human activity systems. These are not tangible and consist of sets of human activities which are structured so as to achieve a purpose. Finally, there are those systems which cannot be understood, which, following Boulding (1956), Checkland labels transcendental. By matching the notion of technology to this typology, it is possible to see technology as the process by which designed physical and abstract systems are created.

OR, understood as a technology, is concerned with creating designed abstract systems which consist of information which is useful in the planning, organizing, controlling, and other activities necessary to the operation of an organization. In some cases OR may also create a designed physical system in the form, say, of a computer system to aid in planning or controlling. The part of the world which is served by the products of OR also helps to define the niche of OR in the set of all technologies. The creations of OR serve, primarily, an organization rather than society or an individual. Society may eventually benefit, but as a result of the organization's actions, which mediate between OR and society. An OR study may be carried out for an individual, but that person usually acts as a representative of an organization.

Thus OR is a technology which produces designed abstract systems and, as a result, may also produce designed physical systems, by scientific means, for use in organizations. The designed abstract systems take the form of information about different ways of improving organizational effectiveness, and the associated designed physical systems are methods of achieving these ends.

This view of OR does not contradict the conventional view of systems in OR. The objects of inquiry and analysis are systems, and the processes of inquiry and analysis are systematic. Checkland's Paradigm I model of OR still holds, as does the conventional perception of systems ideas and their use which is held by the OR community. What has altered is the framework in which these ideas are embedded. They have been interpreted above as forming a basis for a technology rather than for a science. In order to understand more fully how systems ideas fit into the technological model of OR, it is necessary to understand the general culture of technology and its dynamics.

A detailed account of the structure of technologies has been presented by Price (1969). Technologies, in general, are papyrophobic; there is no tradition of publication, such as exists in the sciences. A reason is that there is often a motivation to conceal results or products from competitors so that commercial success is not relinquished. Given this lack of a literature from which technologists can learn their trade, there are alternative mechanisms for developing and passing on methods, attitudes, insights, and knowledge. In part, this mechanism is found in the formal education taken by operational researchers. The well-defined route of a degree followed by an OR-related postgraduate degree (Beasley and Whitchurch, 1984; ORS, 1986), which is followed by a majority of operational researchers, introduces people to principles of logical thought, quantitative analysis, the standard types of OR problem, and methods of solution. Yet it is recognized that these courses do not adequately prepare analysts for doing OR. To be a successful OR practitioner requires "knowledge of, and skill in, social and political matters"; further, "many OR practitioners aspire to general management careers" and "comparatively little direct use is made of so-called OR techniques in OR practice" (ORS, 1986, p. 862). The gap between what is provided by formal education and what is necessary to do OR must be filled by an informal education gained on the job. A form of apprenticeship must be served to acquire the nontechnical knowledge necessary. This knowledge is then enhanced by experience and is eventually handed on to other people.

The use of systems ideas in OR is passed on in the above ways. To an extent, the use of systems notions is introduced by the formal educational system, and individuals then develop these notions as they feel is appropriate in the course of their careers. Price (1969) makes the point, however, that the interaction between science and technology is weak. Thus those aspects of systems which are introduced formally are likely to be those which were developed a generation earlier in the systems community. Thus the systems ideas current in today's OR community are the systems ideas which emerged in the 1960s. The more recent developments in the science of systems will be introduced within formal OR education only in the next decade. The lag between the development of ideas in science and technology and their transfer to appropriate technologies and sciences, respectively, is due to the separation of the scientific and technological cultures. The training of technologists involves only accepted and conventional elements of science, not the most recent, innovative, and more controversial elements. Equally, scientists receive information about those relevant technologies which is a generation away from contemporary thinking.

The influences upon technology which force it to change and develop are twofold. The strongest and most direct influence is that defined by the aims which the technology is to achieve. As the aims change, the technology adapts and develops so that it can meet them. The aims of an OR group are directly related to those of the host organization. Thus if the aims of that organization change or if different types of issues emerge which threaten the meeting of organizational goals, a group must respond. Thus changes in market conditions, the economy, or other elements of the environment of the organization influence the aims and objectives of the organization and may cause OR to adopt novel methods to tackle novel problems. Alternatively, change may be self-induced when the management of an OR group makes certain strategic decisions about the direction of that group.

A weaker, less direct influence comes from science and other technologies. Developments in ways of understanding relevant phenomena and the discovery of explanations for effects not previously understood are made in the sciences and eventually feed into those technologies which interact with the phenomena in question. Thus OR slowly accepts ideas from the sciences which study organizations in various ways. The social sciences, in particular, provide such knowledge, and in time these ideas are accepted, in a suitable form, by the OR culture. Other technologies also provide an infusion of ideas and concepts. Developments in engineering and production technologies will be found to be useful, in some form or other, to OR practitioners in the manufacturing sector. Recent innovations in computer and information technology influence OR greatly, as these are methods by which planning and controlling in organizations can be directly aided. In particular, developments in sciences and technologies which use systems ideas will feed into OR and so reinforce the use of systems ideas there. Those systems ideas which will be most readily accepted are those which are compatible with the existing view of systems held by OR. Thus aspects of sciences and technologies which deal with systems as parts of the real world can be incorporated into OR more easily than those which take other views of systems.

Thus OR is a systems technology in the sense that it deals with systems in a systematic way. It has within its culture a built-in understanding of systems as parts of the world which behave in certain ways. Operational researchers are able to conceptualize a system to the extent that it helps them with their task of understanding and analyzing situations. This conceptualization is not taught formally; rather, it emerges unconsciously via the education and training of OR analysts. It is reinforced by the day-to-day experiences and language used within the OR community. However, OR is also an economic technology, a mathematical technology, a political technology, and a sociological technology, among many others. Each of these bodies of thought have been accepted by OR. They each contribute something to the way in which an operational researcher perceives situations in an organization; yet on their own they are not seen as significant. OR might be said to be a technology system to which each of the pieces of knowledge contributes an element, but which makes sense only when the pieces are put together, and which is meaningless when they are seen in isolation.

## Conclusion

This chapter has focused upon the use of systems ideas in OR. It has shown that the conventional view, in which OR is seen to interact systematically with parts of the world which behave systematically, is compatible with the model of the OR process discussed earlier. Scientific methods are compatible with the OR process, and that process can be usefully interpreted as embodying either the inductive-deductive or the falsificationist version of scientific method. However, the purposes of OR are not comparable with those of the sciences, and the argument that OR is more like a technology is developed. By visualizing OR as a technology, insights into the character of OR are gained which present a different picture of the activity. In particular OR is seen as embracing systems ideas in an almost unconscious way. Thus OR might be said to be a systems technology, but it might also be said to be many other types of technology. The notion that OR is, instead, a technology system has some merit and warrants further consideration.

# III

# *Operational Research in Systems*

The purpose of the three chapters in this part of the discussion is to examine the place of OR within the broad context of those problem-solving methodologies that employ systems ideas. The previous chapters provided a rigorous examination of the use of systems ideas in OR. Because of space limitations, it will not be possible to present as deep an analysis of those problem-solving methodologies that are considered in the following chapters. Consequently, a broad overview of each is given where necessary.

The analysis proceeds in three stages. A starting point is provided by Chapter 7, where Checkland's notion of hard systems thinking is used to identify a family of methodologies to which OR belongs. The boundaries of effective application for this class of methodologies are then established. In the second stage, Chapter 8, a further set of systems-based problem-solving methodologies are considered in order to identify how they are different from hard systems methodologies and to explain why they can address issues outside the boundaries defined for those methodologies. In the final chapter, a framework is provided that imposes a structure on this range of methodologies and indicates a means of making choices between them. Some examples of this methodology for methodology choice are given.

# 7

## Operational Research and Systems Thinking

### Introduction

The focus of the discussion in this chapter is the concept of hard systems thinking and the nature and applicability of some of those methodologies which it generates. Hard systems thinking is one of two paradigms which Checkland (1983) argues are possible within the systems movement. The other, soft systems thinking, will be referred to here briefly in order to highlight the distinctions between them. The purpose of the discussion is twofold: first, to establish OR as a methodology grounded in hard systems thinking and to identify some other such methodologies and, second, to establish the limitations on the effective use of such methodologies, which arise from the fundamental assumptions of hard systems thinking. The starting point for this analysis is to consider what hard systems thinking involves.

### Hard and Soft Systems Thinking

Among the various different classifications of the systems movement, one which goes to the core of the discipline is that proposed by Checkland (1981, 1983, 1985). The identification of two paradigms of systems thinking is based upon the fundamental ways in which systems ideas are used to understand and intervene in the world. Thus it provides a structure for the systems movement which is useful in the many areas where the ideas find applications. The development of the ideas is fully expounded in Checkland (1981), and here only a review of their consequences for understanding OR will be provided.

Checkland's general model of how systems are used to guide interventions in the real world is one in which theory and practice are in continual and mutually beneficial interaction. A theoretical framework

169

is applied to a particular part of the real world by means of a methodology. This process provides insight into and knowledge about the world and, provided it is reflected upon appropriately, will also yield learning about the framework, the methodology, the real world, and their interaction. This learning can then be used to modify and improve subsequent interventions. The two paradigms of systems thinking have different ways of using systems ideas in this model.

Hard systems thinking is the "engineer's contribution" (Checkland, 1981); in the original discussion Checkland was particularly concerned with systems engineering and systems analysis. Within this paradigm it is accepted that systems exist in the world and hence that the world is systemic. The behavior of the world can be usefully understood by means of ideas such as hierarchy, emergent properties, connectivity, control, and other systems concepts. The methodology used to investigate the systemic world may be systematic, that is, ordered, rational, and logical in its procedures and techniques. The intellectual framework which supports this methodology has several features. The underlying purpose of intervention is seen to be goal seeking, that is, the efficient achievement of objectives which can be defined in advance of any intervention. The real world can be altered in order to achieve these goals. The nature of the world allows it to be modeled, and these models can be used to identify what changes need to be made. In hard systems thinking, problems have solutions which, when implemented, remove the problem.

The view held in the hard systems paradigm that the world is systemic is not accepted in the soft systems paradigm. This denial has several consequences which lead to a radically different way of using systems ideas. Rather than accept that the world can be known objectively, the soft systems paradigm takes the stance that the nature of the world can never be completely understood. Thus models are not of the world but capture the logic of the world. They are constructions which are useful in helping one to discuss and consider the world but are not direct representations of the world. Systemicity is switched from the world to the method of inquiring into the world. Given this approach to the role of models, the hard systems notion of using models to help find optimal solutions becomes meaningless. The emphasis in the soft systems paradigm is upon learning about the world via models and, on the basis of this learning, upon reaching some conclusions on how to proceed to resolve issues. As the world can never be fully comprehended, it is impossible to reach a stage where an issue is fully resolved, and so inquiry into it is never-ending, although there may be good pragmatic reasons why attention is shifted toward another issue at some stage.

The assumptions which underpin hard systems thinking and distinguish it from soft systems thinking can now be clearly recognized. A basic assumption is that the world can be understood objectively and that knowledge about the world can be validated by empirical means. This assumption supports the role of models in the hard tradition, which are seen to be representations of and which can be treated as proxies for the world. Methodologies based in hard systems thinking will reflect this assumption by placing great emphasis upon the modeling and validation processes, for these are central to the ability of the approaches to reproduce behavior in the models they involve.

A second assumption of hard systems thinking is the ability to define objectives and then to identify the best way of proceeding in order to achieve them. The notions of goal seeking and rational decision making depend upon this assumption, for if objectives cannot be defined, then a process which sets out to find the best way of achieving them is of no value. An associated assumption here is that it is implicitly the case that agreement on a set of objectives can be reached by any actors involved in the process. A consensus on what is to be achieved and the stability of this consensus are necessary within the hard systems paradigm. Hence great value is placed on the definition of objectives and the provision of ways of reaching them effectively.

One way of establishing whether methodologies are underpinned by hard systems thinking or not is to assess their compatibility with these two basic sets of assumptions and their consequences. Such methodologies will emphasize the stating of objectives, the modeling of the real world, the validation of models by empirical means, and the use of procedures to find optimal methods of reaching objectives. Methodologies which meet these criteria are grounded in hard systems thinking and may be referred to as *hard systems methodologies*. Four such approaches will now be considered.

## OR and Some Other Hard Systems Methodologies

### Operational Research

The methodology of classical OR has already been examined in earlier chapters, and there is no need to reiterate or expand on that discussion here. The contention that OR is a hard systems methodology does require some support, however, and that will be provided in the following analysis. The points that need to be considered are the extent to which OR incorporates the assumptions of hard systems thinking.

The first set of assumptions is concerned with models and their role in a methodology. It was shown earlier that models within OR are seen to be representations of what occurs in the parts of the world under investigation. Models are built of queuing systems, inventory systems, different ways of allocating resources, and so on. These models are then subjected to validation by comparison with real-world behavior before they are used to address specific problems. Central to models built in OR is the use of data collected from the real world, which are used to make as good a match between actual phenomena and model behavior as is possible. Once an acceptable model has been built, it is manipulated, by means of various procedures, to indicate what changes should be made in order to achieve a predetermined objective. The nature of the objective is variable, but it can generally be specified in quantitative terms, and hence it is possible, in principle, to compare alternative courses of action and to specify the best of these.

The second set of assumptions in the hard systems paradigm is built around the ability to define objectives. Within OR objectives play an important role. They are necessary if the methodology is to function, for without any objectives to be pursued, the OR methodology cannot provide solutions to problems. Objectives are therefore necessary, and their specification is given an explicit place in the OR methodology. It is not seen as being a problem, however, to define objectives. Little guidance is given on how to decide what objectives should be pursued, and the possibility of conflict over objectives is not recognized within the classical OR approach. The determination of objectives is not part of the role of OR; only the problem of how to reach them efficiently is seen to be of importance.

Hence OR incorporates the assumptions of hard systems thinking. It involves taking a view of the world which sees it as objective and as capable of being understood in a rational and proven way. Problems are defined by the objectives to be reached, and OR offers a way of finding out how to reach them in the most efficient manner.

*Systems Engineering*

Systems engineering (SE) is one of the two examples of hard systems methodologies which are considered by Checkland (1981). The history of SE has followed a path similar to that of postwar OR. Its beginnings lie in work carried out at the Bell Telephone Laboratories, and a formal course in the subject was taught at the Massachusetts Institute of Technology in the 1950s. A series of texts on the approach appeared during this period, notably those of Goode and Machol (1957),

Flagle, Huggins, and Roy (1960), Eckman (1961), Williams (1961), Gosling (1962), and Hall (1962). Of these, Hall offers the most sophisticated discussion of the SE process. More recently, Keys (1985) has discussed the relationship between OR and SE and argues that at a methodological level the two are similar, while the contexts of their application are different.

Hall provides a five-stage model of the SE methodology, which is based upon experience of many completed projects. The methodology is designed to create a system which can meet a set of needs. The SE methodology follows the creation of this system from the specification of the needs to the manufacture and implementation of the system. The first stage is called systems studies and involves a wide-ranging investigation of the current situation. Following this stage, exploratory planning is carried out, in which a particular area of need is identified and is given more specific attention. As part of this analysis, various ways of meeting the need are developed and compared, and a decision is made on which is to be taken further. Progress is made in the third stage, development planning, which is concerned with setting up the timetable and processes which will guide the development. This plan is put into operation in the fourth phase, which results in a prototype. The final part of the methodology sees the prototype modified as necessary and then put into full-scale use.

It can be seen from this brief outline of SE that it exhibits the basic assumptions of hard systems thinking. The concern of SE is almost exclusively with engineering systems, electrical components and equipment, machinery of various forms, and so on. Models are constructed within SE of these manufactured artifacts which indicate how they operate, how they are constructed, and their other general characteristics. These models are used to compare different designs on various criteria such as cost, efficiency, and reliability in order to show how well they meet the needs they must satisfy and to guide the choice of which design to pursue in detail. The specification of objectives is given a high status in the approach and is achieved by identifying the current position and the areas that need improvement. There is no mechanism within SE by which disputes over which objectives to set can be settled.

This adherence to the hard systems paradigm can be reinforced by examining how Hall uses systems ideas in SE. Systems ideas are used to describe the result of the SE methodology. The manufactured products are described as systems and exhibit systemic behavior, be they electrical, mechanical, or otherwise. A reason for this use of systems notions is the complexity of the items which are produced. These are typically large-scale complexes with many parts interacting in many ways. It is natural when considering such systems to use the idea of subsystems, hierarchy, and environment to begin to structure and understand what is being designed and built. The five-stage methodology devised by Hall also incorporates systems ideas. The five stages are linked together by various feedback loops which enable a high level of adaptation and change to take place. The methodology is systematic in that it provides a logical procedure for achieving the purpose for which it is designed.

Thus SE falls clearly within Checkland's hard systems paradigm. Its use involves viewing the world as being comprised of systems and using systemic procedures to intervene in the world. Objectives are set early in the process, are assumed to be agreed upon, and are not subject to major alteration, and models are built which represent parts of the world.

*Systems Analysis*

According to Quade and Miser (1985) systems analysis (SA) is "the multi-disciplinary problem-solving activity that has evolved to deal with the complex problems that arise in public and private enterprises and organisations" (p. 15). Checkland (1981) limits attention to RAND-style systems analysis, which emphasizes a holistic analysis of situations where decisions need to be made. Majone (1985) provides a broader overview of SA which places it within a historical progression after wartime OR and before the emergence of policy science in the 1970s. The specific focus of SA is more difficult to locate than is that of OR or SE. OR is concerned with operational procedures in organizations and SE with the production of complex manufactured artifacts; SA has a looser and less well-defined scope, which appears to reflect a concern with issues defined at a strategic level and which involves higher levels of managerial activity than either of the other two approaches so far considered.

The strict delimitation of SA, SE, and OR is not particularly useful in the current context. What is important is the methodology which characterizes SA. A framework for SA is provided by Findeisen and Quade (1985) which captures the spirit of the approach without being very detailed. They recognize five main components which are present in an SA study and which may be ordered in various ways. The procedure which they outline is described below.

The first stage involves formulating the problem. This formulation should provide a preliminary statement of the objectives to be pursued and how they may be measured, an initial specification of what courses of action may be fruitful, a definition of any constraints which are deemed to be present, an anticipation of what may result from each of the courses of action and possible criteria for ranking them, and a plan of how to proceed with the analysis. Problem formulation sets the boundary for what follows, and although it might be altered in due course, the momentum and direction of the analysis is largely set at this stage.

The second stage involves identifying, designing, and screening the alternatives. This element of the process requires creativity and imagination, for many of the situations being faced are unique and require novel approaches to their resolution rather than an application of existing methods. Thus existing alternatives are identified, new ones are designed, and this set is then examined so that infeasible or clearly weak courses of action will be removed from consideration. The remaining alternatives are then analyzed in greater detail.

Before proceeding to investigate the implications of a course of action in detail, further information on the likely future states of the world is sought. This results in a better understanding of the context in which the courses of action will operate. This process is followed by a detailed analysis of the chosen courses of action, which involves building and using models to predict the consequences of following each possible alternative. Models may take several forms, but they are always of such a type that an assessment of how each course of action will perform can be made as a result of the model's use.

In the final stage of the process, alternatives are compared and ranked by means of a suitable technique. This may be done on a judgmental basis in which the performance of the model is used to inform and guide opinion. At the other extreme, quantitative measures based on model performance may be used to yield a more objective measure of the alternatives. The knowledge generated by the overall procedure is then passed on to the decision makers so that it will be used as part of their procedures.

The SA approach outlined above has within it various iterative loops and mechanisms which allow an examination of progress and a modification of the analysis. Findeisen and Quade discuss these and other aspects in more detail, but for present purposes, the above level of description is sufficient.

The similarities between the above approach and SE and OR are clearly defined. The methodologies have a structural similarity which is reinforced by a common set of assumptions. The emphasis upon the use of models in SA to provide a basis for comparing the various courses of action is the result of an implicit assumption about the usefulness of such models. The approach relies upon models to provide it with a basis for the type of information it seeks to offer to decision makers. The models which are built are used primarily to compare alternatives, not to increase understanding of the situation at hand, which is a secondary purpose. Hence one characteristic of hard systems thinking is central to this approach. The other main assumption of the hard systems paradigm is also explicit in SA. The primacy of objectives in the methodology and the inability of SA to offer ways of reaching agreement on objectives are compatible with the view that objectives can be set and attained, which is at the heart of the hard systems paradigm. SA provides a means of identifying how to achieve a predetermined goal as efficiently as possible.

To Checkland's original consideration of SE and SA as hard systems methodologies can be added OR, as has been noted above. The distinctions between these three approaches lie in the context in which they are applied to a much greater extent than in the methodologies they involve. The classification of these three approaches as a family of hard systems methodologies has been noted by Jackson and Keys (1984), Keys (1987a), and other authors. There are other examples of problem-solving methodologies which might also be classed as hard systems methodologies. One of these which lies explicitly within the systems movement is system dynamics, which is now considered.

*System Dynamics*

The origins of system dynamics (SD) lie in the work of a group associated with Jay Forrester at the Massachusetts Institute of Technology. Bloomfield (1986) gives a useful summary of the intellectual and historical development of the approach. Forrester recognized two fundamental difficulties in OR as it existed in the early 1960s and set out to develop a method of examining issues which were incapable of being addressed by contemporary OR and other management science techniques (Bloomfield, 1986; Forrester, 1961; Wolstenholme, 1982). The basic problems lay in the modeling techniques used by OR at that time, which meant that only a small number of variables and only linear relationships between them could be expressed in models. By bringing together his knowledge of information feedback control theory, a belief that decision processes could be automated to some extent, an experimental rather than an analytical approach to model solution, and an understanding of the potential of digital computers, Forrester constructed a methodology which was capable of tackling more complex situations than had previously been possible. This increase in capability was the result of an understanding of how to build and solve more complex models than was then possible in OR. SD was developed as an approach to the modeling and analysis of system behavior which "focused upon dynamic, systemic behavior in a way that is more akin to those of the practicing manager than to the management science specialist" (Forrester, 1961, p. 9).

A description of how SD studies should proceed is given by Forrester in the first major exposition of the approach (Forrester, 1961). The first step is to identify the problem to be tackled. Then the factors which appear to be responsible for causing the symptoms of the problem are isolated. The various information feedback loops which relate decisions, actions, and information are then identified and modeled. The model's behavior is compared with actual performance and, if necessary, modified until it shows an acceptable correspondence. The model is then used as an experimental tool with which to explore possible alternative methods of improving performance. The results of these experiments are used to guide decisions on how to change the situation for the better.

This methodology shares its base with those of OR, SE, and SA. They each involve the assumption that a quantitative representation of the situation under study can be built and manipulated to yield information on how that situation will respond to changes. In the case of SD a particular type of representation is used which is manipulated by means of a specific technique. SD models are based upon a representation using levels and rates which is derived from engineering. A situation is characterized by the values taken by certain variables. These levels alter over time as resources flow between them. The rate of flow is affected by the values of the levels and other parameters. A computer-programming language called DYNAMO is used to construct and manipulate the models. A distinctive quality of SD is this reliance on a particular way of modeling the world. It is implicit within this approach, however, that models are representations of real-world behavior, although, because of the complexity of that behavior, they may not be particularly accurate. The SD approach takes the view that a partial analysis is preferable to no analysis and holds that modeling can indicate the direction of change and the magnitude of likely system states, if not absolute values.

Keys (1988a) shows how the SD approach which is described by Forrester also shares the hard systems paradigm's attitude toward objectives and goal seeking. No mention is made within the methodology of difficulties in defining objectives or of possible uses of the models other than in helping to identify how to achieve satisfactory change. Matters such as what change is deemed satisfactory and how to set the criteria for choosing between alternative changes are seen to fall outside the realm of SD, just as they fall outside OR, SE, and SA. The modeling approach adopted by SD sees models as being useful tools to help decision makers explore the consequences of different actions. They do this by providing an experimental laboratory in which decision makers can act freely without imposing change on the real world. There have recently been some efforts to expand the SD methodology to provide an approach which can help decision makers in a wider sense (Coyle, 1983a; Wolstenholme, 1982, 1983). This work is seen as being essentially different from the more traditional SD approach and will be discussed more fully later.

## The Boundaries of Hard Systems Methodologies

### Complexity

A key assumption underpinning the approach to problem-solving adopted by hard systems methodologies is the ability to construct and manipulate a model of the situation under study. A deeper analysis of this process of modeling and manipulating reveals characteristics which need to be satisfied so that the process is likely to be successful. A situation must be capable of being understood in terms of variables and the relationships between them if a model is to be built. Models of this form are the result of analysis. Ackoff (1974b, 1979a) associates analysis with machine-age thinking. This, as shall be shown, is equivalent to what Checkland refers to as the hard systems paradigm.

The analytic process involves breaking part of the world down into constituent parts which will be simpler than their aggregate. These smaller parts are then understood, and an understanding of the original focus of interest is gained by bringing these separate pieces of knowledge together. Thus, understanding a machine involves breaking it down into its parts, understanding what each of them does, and then understanding how they fit together to function as a whole. This process implies that the world is structured in nested hierarchies of systems, each level of which contains and is contained by an adjacent level. This view is equivalent to the hard systems paradigm view of the world consisting of systems and subsystems with systemic properties.

Machine-age thinking involves further assumptions about how to understand the world. The reductionist process which is followed suggests that there must be at some point a set of indivisible elements which are the basis of all higher level phenomena. Most of classical science can be understood as a search for these ultimate particles. Also embedded in machine-age thinking is the belief that the relationships between elements at fundamental and, by aggregation, at higher levels are those of cause and effect. Thus, in order to understand why a particular phenomenon occurs, an observer has to go back through a series of preceding causes until the original trigger event is identified. Understanding is to be gained by specifying appropriate elements and then recognizing how they are related by cause-and-effect mechanisms. The eventual consequences of any event can be found by establishing the chain of causes and effects which follow from it. If a way of achieving a particular effect is sought then relationships can be explored in reverse directions to find those causes which will eventually lead to the desired effect.

This approach to understanding behavior leads to the hard systems method of modeling. The elements are represented by the different variables in a model, which each take numerical values. The cause–effect relationships are then expressed as mathematical equations or their equivalent, which can be manipulated by algebra, computer-based techniques, or similar methods. The limitations of this approach emerge from the extent to which reductionism, cause–effect relationships, and the analytic process can be used to understand behavior. There are various ways of classifying these limitations, of which two will be considered here.

As part of a disassembly of complexity, Flood (1987) has identified various factors which make situations appear complex to an observer. Complexity is a root cause of the limitations of machine-age or hard-systems thinking. The recognition of a particular situation as being complex is a function of both the observer and the observed. People's interests, capabilities, notions, and prior knowledge influence the degree of complexity they attach to a particular situation. To an experienced mechanic a motor car engine is relatively straightforward when compared with the complexity associated with it by an apprentice. The same engine may appear simple to uninterested persons who are concerned not with how it works but only with its ability to make them mobile. Thus the observer has a role to play in determining how complex a situation may appear because complexity is not an objective quality. There are, however, some properties of a situation which influence the extent to which it may be seen as being complex. These each raise some issues about how possible it is to construct and manipulate models of the type used in machine-age and hard-systems thinking.

Flood (1987), following Yates (1978), notes five aspects of a situation which affect the perceived level of complexity. The first of these is the size of the situation as measured by the number of elements which are recognized. When an observer is able to decide which elements are included, size can be varied as desired. A motor car engine which is seen as including only a small number of parts—say, engine, carburetor, clutch, and gearbox—is much simpler than when it is perceived to include many more elements, including cylinders and a camshaft.

The second aspect is the number of interactions which occur between the elements. The number of elements determines the upper limit of the number of possible interactions, but there scope remains to identify any number of interactions up to this limit. A set of four elements may have up to sixteen interactions and a set of three elements up to nine. However, the set of four elements may, in fact, be seen as being simpler if the number of interactions included is chosen to be lower than for the set of three (see Figure 7.1).

The other three aspects influencing complexity are concerned with the structure of the situation rather than with its perceived size. First, relationships may be nonlinear. Nonlinear behavior is considerably more difficult to represent formally than linear behavior, and these representations are not easy to manipulate. Nonlinear models exhibit qualitatively

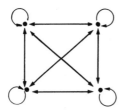 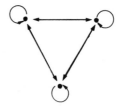

| 4 variables | is potentially | 3 variables |
|---|---|---|
| 16 possible relationships | more complex than | 9 possible relationships |

**BUT**

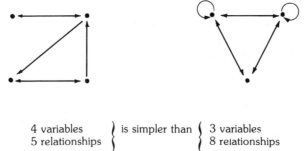

| 4 variables | is simpler than | 3 variables |
|---|---|---|
| 5 relationships | | 8 relationships |

*FIGURE 7.1.* Potential and actual levels of complexity.

different types of behavior from linear models, and this makes forecasts and model solutions more difficult to interpret. Second, not all aspects of a situation may be symmetrical. This asymmetry results in difficulties in analysis and uneven patterns of behavior. Some parts of a situation may have dynamics which function over a different time-period from others, and this causes difficulties in attempts to reconcile models of such situations. Finally, some parts of situations may have more autonomy than others, and the result is the setting of different goals and objectives. Again, there are difficulties in modeling such situations and in understanding the behavior.

This analysis reveals some causes of problems for the reductionist cause–effect approach. The number of elements and of the interactions between them and the nature of those interactions can each pose difficulties for an analysis based on reductionist principles. Another investigation, by Vemuri (1978), generates a further set of four difficulties for machine-age analysis.

First, even though it may be possible to specify an appropriate set of elements, they may not all be observable or be able to generate measurable quantities. In such a case the unobservable elements will need to be approximated by an alternative. Thus a decrease in the ability of the model to match reality results, and any analysis is also reduced in value.

Second, the stress placed upon deterministic cause–effect relationships in machine-age thinking is often too demanding. Relationships may be able to be defined only probabilistically, and thus a model based upon them will only be able to yield only likely, rather than exact, information on behavior.

Third, situations are in continual processes of change, so that relationships may be altered. The effects of environmental turbulence and natural evolutionary processes will be felt at some point and will be reflected in changes in the structure of situations. The assumption that elements and relationships remain static once they are identified is open to question, and models which incorporate such an assumption will not necessarily be valid for all time periods.

Finally, in situations where behavioral factors are significant, the political, cultural, social, and other aspects of these factors will be difficult to represent in a model. Consequently, any analysis will have to find other means of acknowledging these important influences on the situation.

Each of these four difficulties results in a situation being seen as more complex than if they were not present. Thus to Flood's five causes of complexity can be added the difficulties of observability, probabilism, evolution, and behavioral factors. As a set of issues they provide one major limitation on hard systems thinking and the methodologies based upon it. When situations are perceived as being complex, for any combination of the above reasons, difficulties arise in using a reductionist, cause–effect, analytical approach to understanding and thus in modeling such situations and manipulating such models. The need to build and use accurate models is at the center of the hard systems paradigm, and any restriction upon meeting this need severely limits the usefulness of this paradigm.

*Subjectivity and Power*

It has been argued above that the hard systems paradigm—or equivalently, machine-age thinking—runs into significant difficulties when the situations to be modeled are relatively complex. That discussion points to the limits imposed by one of the underlying assumptions of that paradigm. A second basic assumption of that approach concerns the ability to define objectives. It is accepted in hard systems methodologies that the specification and stability of objectives are not a problem. Once one has determined what goals are to be pursued at the beginning of an analysis, the issue is to identify how best to achieve them. How, not what, to achieve is an underlying focus of the hard systems paradigm.

In his discussion of complexity noted above, Flood (1987) recognizes that the interests, capabilities, and notions which individuals bring to bear upon a situation influence their understanding of that situation. Equally, the changes which they would like to see brought about to improve that situation are influenced by their background and their reasons for involvement. It is not necessary here to review the arguments which support this view, as the social sciences and management literature are replete with empirical and theoretical arguments (for example, Burrell and Morgan, 1979; Keat and Urry, 1975; Pratt, 1978). It will be taken that objectives and the reasoning behind the specification of objectives are subjective in nature. Of current concern are the mechanisms and conditions under which hard systems methodologies are compatible with this view and the limits which this compatibility imposes on the usefulness of these methodologies.

This issue is dependent upon the relationship which is deemed to exist between consultant and client in hard systems methodologies. It has already been seen that, within OR, what Churchman and Schainblatt (1965) call the separate-function position is often adopted. In this style of relationship the functions of consultant and client are kept as separate as possible. A consequence and/or reason is the inability of

OR to provide any means by which the consultant can help a client to recognize and understand the client's objectives. The most effective way for OR to proceed, therefore, is to take as given the objectives stated by the client and to work toward methods of achieving them without further considering their validity or rationale. During the course of a project, information gathering and questioning may reveal a reason to alter the objectives. The processes underlying this alteration have been discussed earlier when looking at the OR process. However, the investigation and possible changing of objectives must be seen as a secondary effect of the OR process, whose primary goal is to provide ways of reaching the goals set rather than to probe into the reasons for their being set.

The similar structure of other types of hard systems methodology suggests that they embody a similar attitude toward objectives. SA, SE, and SD each implicitly accept that objectives should, on the whole, be taken as given, as the approaches provide no real focus on which a discussion of objectives can be based. In Checkland's terms, hard systems methodologies concern themselves with cases where a single worldview is recognized. This worldview is that set of assumptions, beliefs, and knowledge which is compatible with the particular objectives which are adopted. Hard systems thinking cannot embrace a situation where more than one worldview is present when there is a need to reach an agreement or accommodation over the different perspectives which are then taken.

Eden and Sims (1979) identify the result of this particular situation as being one in which a "scientific aura" surrounds the consultant. This can be, and often is, reinforced by consultants maintaining a distance between themselves and a client. The acceptance of a scientific role by consultants provides them with a credibility which increases their authority and detached objectivity in the eyes of a client. It is in the interests of a consultant, therefore, and often in those of a client also, to maintain a position which ensures a high professional status for the result of the consultant's work. This situation has its difficulties, however. Eden (1982) suggests that it limits the creativity of consultants and leads to them being used to legitimize a client's position. It also introduces a degree of bureaucracy into the relationship between a consultant and a client which further separates them. The setting of timetables and deadlines makes it difficult to alter the course of a project once it has begun. Eden also notes that the existence of such a schedule makes it difficult for a consultant to influence management. Management retains its primacy in the relationship and employs rather than cooperates with consultants.

The process of hard systems methodologies is very much concerned with the ends to be achieved rather than with the means of achieving them. Ackoff (1976, 1979a) highlights the absence of the intrinsic value of means and the extrinsic value of ends in OR. By divorcing clients from the process of establishing means (that is, an involvement in the analytic process), the hard systems paradigm prohibits the gaining of satisfaction from this source. The achievement of ends is quite often also a means of reaching some other objective, so the clear distinction between means and ends limits the conception of problem solving and decision making.

An awareness of these difficulties and of the observations made concerning the place of objectives in hard systems methodologies allows the boundaries of the effectiveness of such methodologies to be explored. OR and other hard systems methodologies perform most satisfactorily in those situations where there is no room to question objectives, for several reasons. For example, if there has been considerable debate among the actors involved in making decision about what objectives to set and an agreement has been reached on this matter, then, provided all actors are prepared to accept the agreed upon view, it will be possible to use a hard systems methodology to assess how best to reach those objectives. Such an explanation is straightforward, for it implies that the problem-solving process is genuinely independent of the objective-setting process.

In other cases the consultant may implement certain procedures to encourage independence and to ensure a separation between objective setting and goal reaching. Then the task of the consultant is well defined and is concerned only with the assessment of how to achieve goals. Churchman (1970) suggests that consultants are involved in setting system boundaries and identifying the clients to be served at an early stage of the OR process. This task effectively defines what objectives are to be pursued, for, in deciding which clients to serve, the consultant is deciding which objectives to accept. The question of which client to serve is a difficult one for many reasons. The explanation above, where problem-solving is seen as independent of objective-setting, corresponds to the case where no decision on clients is made because the set of potential clients is in agreement. In other cases decisions on clients are made, and Churchman gives two possible ways by which a consultant may ease the problems of making this decision. One, determinism, is an impossible position to adopt for it involves the view that individuals have no control over their own actions, which are predetermined. Thus a consultant is "preprogrammed" to work with a particular client. A corollary is the view that planning, part of which is the role of the consultant, is itself of no value, and so the argument is self-defeating. The second, ethical relativism, is, according to Churchman, the position adopted by the majority of OR workers. This involves taking the view that people are able to decide what they want and that the consultant has no right to interfere with personal choice. Hence, having been told what objectives are wished by a client, a consultant should provide only advice and understanding and then leave the client to reach a final decision on future action. This view is totally compatible with the failure of OR and similar methodologies to provide methods to help determine what objectives to set in the first place, for it provides an argument for their not being involved in such matters.

Churchman's discussion operates at the level of the individual consultant–client relationship and offers explanations of why a consultant may choose to work with a certain client or group of clients. At a deeper level is the more general issue of the power relationships which exist in organizations, which support the role of management and hence, indirectly, the role of OR and other management advisers. Rosenhead and Thunhurst (1982), Tinker and Lowe (1984), and Rosenhead (1987) have argued that OR emerged to support and continues to support capitalism. Management, as an agent of the owners of capital, makes extensive use of those methods which enable it to enhance and reinforce its position relative to labor. OR and other hard systems methodologies developed because they were able to offer such methods in the years immediately after the Second World War. They are used to legitimize and promote the image of management by means of their scientific and objective character.

A reason why consultants may choose to work with some clients and to accept their objectives lies in the structure of the relationship between management, labor, and management advisers. Consultants have little to gain from working with those who hold little power and a lot to gain from those who have or expect to increase their authority. Consultants who need to work to support themselves will find it more beneficial to work for those who can reward them in the short run and who may offer them further work in the long run. The basis of the analyses of project management given by Houlden (1979) and Whiteman and Wise (1981) is the need to establish long-term relationships at an individual and group level between consultants and clients.

There is therefore a series of issues which converge to provide limits on the usefulness of OR and other hard systems methodologies. The subjective nature of objectives means that unless agreement is reached among several individuals, several different sets of objectives may be set for a given situation. OR provides no methods of helping to reach agreement in such cases. There are, however, several positions which help a consultant to minimize the likelihood of confronting a set of decision makers who hold varying objectives. Accepting that people have a right to decide what they wish to see achieved is one way of not becoming involved in a debate over objectives. A consultant takes on without question the task of finding out how to achieve the set objectives most effectively. This approach is reinforced by the underlying power relationships which exist and given authority to some and not to others. Consultants often serve their own best interests by serving those in authority. Subjectivity and power can therefore be added to complexity as sources of the factors which combine to impose limitations on the effective use of OR and other hard systems methodologies.

## Conclusion

The discussion above has placed OR within a local environment of systems-based problem-solving methodologies. The notion of hard systems thinking serves to unite OR, SA, SE, and SD into a family of hard systems methodologies. These approaches have common assumptions and similarly structured processes. The assumptions impose limitations on the usefulness of these methodologies, however, and complexity, subjectivity, and power have been identified as fundamental components of these limitations. These limitations can be overcome by alterations in the methodologies that relax the assumptions from which they derive. The following chapter considers some examples of how such alterations can be achieved. The set of systems-based problem-solving methodologies will thus be expanded outside the local environment to yield a larger environment in which OR exists.

# 8

# *Beyond Hard Systems Thinking*

## *Introduction*

The relationship discussed in Chapter 7 between OR and a set of hard systems methodologies places OR in a localized context by establishing a methodological connection between OR and a range of other systems-based problem-solving methodologies. The assumptions of this common methodological process provide a basis for identifying the boundaries within which hard systems methodologies can operate effectively. Outside these boundaries other methodologies are required which are able to overcome the restrictions present in the hard systems methodologies. It is the purpose of this chapter to present an overview of some systems-based approaches which can operate outside the boundaries of hard systems thinking.

The boundaries of hard systems thinking are fundamentally grounded in the complexity of the situations being addressed and any differences in worldview taken by various actors involved in a situation. A third dimension of the situation which also warrants attention is the power relations which characterize a situation and the implications of these for users of any methodology. The chapter is structured around these three themes. First, the issue of complexity is explored, and some approaches which claim to address aspects of complexity are considered. Second, the concept of pluralism and ways of tackling it are examined. Quite often, complexity is likely to imply pluralism, as situations which are inherently difficult to comprehend are prone to different perceptions. The complexity directly due to pluralism is different from the complexity inherent in a situation which may lead to pluralism due to differences of interpretation of the situation and requires different approaches if it is to be tackled effectively. Third, power and its implications for consultants working with a group of people with different amounts of power at their disposal are addressed.

## Dealing with Complexity

### Tools for Tackling Complexity

Complexity is an attribute associated with situations when they are perceived to be difficult to comprehend. Some reasons why this difficulty may be felt were mentioned in the previous chapter. Size, observability, behavioral processes, and dynamics each play a part in creating potentially complex situations. The emphasis in this discussion is on the ways in which systems ideas may be used to inform methods of addressing situations which appear to be complex.

The measurement of complexity is difficult, for complexity is the result of many different factors and has a subjective quality. A person may say that one situation is more complex than another but may find it difficult to explain why rationally. Complexity is implicitly bound up with uncertainty; the more complex a situation, the more uncertain an observer will be over the future of that situation. Predictability comes from an ability to establish cause–effect relationships and the use of these to trace rigorously the ultimate effects of an initial event. It is because of the nature of complex situations that this tracing cannot be done effectively, and predictability is lost and uncertainty replaces it. Hence the characteristics of complexity mean that methods of confronting complex situations and attempting to work effectively in them can be seen as methods of coping with uncertainty.

Three methods will be discussed below reflecting two responses to the complexity issue. One response which is appropriate when situations are sufficiently complex to prohibit detailed quantitative analysis but in which some structure can be identified is to construct qualitative models. These can then be manipulated and explored in order to increase the understanding of a situation and, possibly, to allow quantitative models to be constructed subsequently. An approach which follows this line is qualitative system dynamics (QSD). An alternative response is to accept that the complexity is such that there is no possibility of achieving a significant reduction in uncertainty. It then becomes clear that what is necessary is the creation of mechanisms and processes which allow adaptation to future unexpected change to take place and also to encourage learning from these experiences. Two methods which guide the design and implementation of flexible, responsive organizational structures are sociotechnical systems design (STSD) and a range of tools grounded in management cybernetics (MC).

*Qualitative System Dynamics*

System dynamics (SD) has already been discussed as an example of a hard systems methodology. A motivation for the creation of the approach was the inability of the contemporary management sciences to address strategic issues which were highly complex. The methodology of SD consists of qualitative and quantitative aspects, and recently an increased emphasis has been placed upon the qualitative dimension per se rather than upon the more usual use of a qualitative analysis to provide a basis for a quantitative model. An assessment of the relationship between the two aspects of SD and hard and soft systems thinking is given by Keys (1988a).

Wolstenholme (1982) represents the SD process as consisting of a systems description or a qualitative analysis phase and a quantitative analysis phase. This split is not emphasized in the conventional description of SD, but as a result of making explicit the qualitative component, it is possible to recognize and develop a different aspect of the SD approach than is usually presented. This approach will be referred to here as *qualitative systems dynamics* (QSD). The purpose of the qualitative phase is twofold: to provide a perspective on the observed problem or symptom and to provide a qualitative analysis on which to base recommendations for change (p. 548). The quantitative aspect has the usual hard systems purpose of providing a rigorous assessment of alternative courses of action.

The relationship between QSD, the conventional image of SD which emphasizes the quantitative aspect, and the decision-making process is revealed by Meadows (1980). The first part of the decision-making process is seen to involve the actors in gaining a general understanding of the situation they are addressing. Here modeling is useful as a means of generating understanding and structuring the investigation. Quantitative precision is not necessary when modeling is used in this way, and qualitative analysis may suffice. Second, it is necessary to move toward an understanding of how the situation can be improved. This policy formulation stage involves more investigation into specific aspects of the situation. The increased focus and greater depth of inquiry are accompanied by a need to become more precise, and hence more quantitative, in the analysis. Finally, a consideration of how to achieve implementation is needed. This involves specific and exact analysis and an even greater reliance upon rigorous, quantitative models.

This view of decision-making matches that adopted in the hard systems paradigm; it involves a choice between different courses of action. SD becomes useful in the latter stages of decision making, where it provides a particular means of representing situations. QSD is appropriate to the initial stages, where it provides a means of investigating ill-defined and poorly understood situations. The contribution of the qualitative element of SD is to provide a means of representing and analyzing situations without recourse to quantitative data and the manipulation of sets of equations or their equivalent. It does, however, retain the option for the analyst of constructing a quantitative model on the foundation of the qualitative model, which can allow this type of study to take place. This option is usually taken up in SD studies, where "the ability to provide qualitative analysis is, in general, taken for granted by practitioners of the subject" (Wolstenholme, 1982, p. 553). The QSD approach takes this ability and explicitly offers it as an independent methodology. As such, it can be seen as a method of tackling situations which are not amenable to quantitative analysis. The QSD methodology is most closely associated with the Systems Dynamics Research Group at Bradford and is described by Coyle (1983a,b), Wolstenholme (1983), and Wolstenholme and Coyle (1983).

The models which are used in QSD are built by means of signed digraphs as their representational device. Signed digraphs are, mathematically, a particular case of a graph in which the nodes represent variables and the arcs represent relationships between variables. The arcs have a sign (+ or −) which indicates the direction of the relationship. The theory of graphs—and in particular, signed digraphs—is well developed and reviewed by, for example, Roberts (1975). More important than the well-developed body of mathematical theory for the application of such models is the ease with which signed digraphs can be used to represent the structure of various situations. As a consequence they have found favor in many areas including political science (Axelrod, 1976), group behavior (Harary, Norman, and Cartwright, 1965), and geography (Cliff and Haggett, 1981). Signed digraphs (see, for example, Figure 8.1) consist of labels for variables which are linked by arrows depicting direction and sign of influence. Figure 8.1 shows a simple representation of how price, sales, income, and level of technology interact. As price increases (or decreases) the level of sales will fall (or rise), other things being equal. This inverse relationship is indicated by a −; a change in the variable at the tail of the arrow leads to a change in the opposite direction in the variable at the head of the arrow. Similarly, a + sign means that a change in the tail variable (the level of sales) leads to a change in the same direction in the head variable, (income), again provided that all other factors remain unchanged.

The natural dynamics of a situation may be represented by dia-

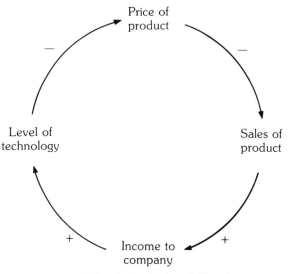

FIGURE 8.1. A simple signed digraph.

grams such as this. Wolstenholme and Coyle (1983) developed a methodology for constructing such representations in a logical and effective sequence of tasks. Analysis of the diagrams concentrates upon the cycles of arrows which lead a variable to influence itself and also upon chains of influences which relate variables which can be controlled to those which cannot but which are of importance. Such an analysis allows an understanding to be gained of the broad impacts which may result from any changes in the situation. Detailed assessment cannot result because of the qualitative nature of the model and the subsequent method of investigation. If such an assessment is thought necessary, then it is not a difficult step to build a quantitative SD model on the basis of the diagram provided the variables and relationships are amenable to quantification. There may be several reasons why a translation from qualitative to quantitative is not possible: lack of observability, inability to measure qualitative variables, the presence of behavioral rather than physical processes, and the natural dynamics of the situation, causing change which cannot be accounted for in advance. The reasons why a situation is seen as complex are the reasons why the qualitative model may not be able to be translated into a quantitative form. In the example of Figure 8.1, the level of technology may be difficult to quantify, as may the processes which underlie the response of consumers to price changes.

Thus QSD offers an approach which is capable of yielding and analyzing a model which captures elements of complex situations that cannot be represented in hard systems models. The approach does incorporate an attitude similar to systems ideas as embraced by hard systems thinking. Situations are characterized as interactions between variables, and systems are recognized as being present in reality. The difference is the level of information which can be obtained about them and its representation in a model. Thus QSD accepts the limitations of hard systems thinking in respect of complexity and seeks to provide a means of overcoming these limitations which is compatible with the underlying objective, rational, empirical basis of that paradigm.

*Sociotechnical Systems Design*

The QSD approach is a direct extrapolation of hard systems thinking into the areas where quantitative models are inappropriate and qualitative models of systems behavior are more useful. This methodology can work outside the boundaries of the hard systems paradigm, but it cannot overcome all the difficulties associated with complexity, for it still requires situations to be structured in terms of elements and the relationships between them. When complexity is great (for whatever reason), it will prove difficult to define with confidence the relevant variables and the relationships between them. In such situations a different attitude toward tackling complexity needs to be adopted. The concept of modeling systems so that their response to change can be predicted and the use of this information to guide decisions on change need to be replaced, for they will not yield useful information. If the actors in decision processes cannot obtain useful information about the effects of change in advance of making those changes, they must be prepared to respond to the effects of change after they have occurred. Methodologies which can be used to address situations of great complexity focus upon the provision of information which can guide adaptation to events which are not predictable rather than on information about events which are predictable. One such methodology is sociotechnical systems design (STSD).

This approach is based upon a body of theoretical and applied work carried out originally at the Tavistock Institute in London by Trist and his colleagues (Emery and Trist, 1965; Rice, 1958; Trist and Bamforth, 1951; Trist, Higgin, Murray, and Pollock, 1963). Subsequently the work has been developed and used in many different contexts (Pasmore, Francis, Haldeman, and Shani, 1978), and Pasmore (1988) gives a survey of the theory and methods which are collected under the label of sociotechnical systems theory and design. A central precept of the approach is the view that all organizations consist of social and technical systems acting in relationship to each other and to an external environment. The role of the environment is given particular importance, for organizational success is seen as being dependent upon the ability of the organization to be effective and adaptive in the presence of a highly complex environment. Sociotechnical systems theory is concerned with increasing the understanding of the nature of organizations within their environment, and STSD is concerned with making these theoretical insights operational with a view to designing effective and adaptive organizational structures. One understands the environment by examining its ability to change and the direction of that change. Organizations need to have an image of their environment and, within it, to be able to recognize opportunities and threats to their current position. Failure to take opportunities or to respond to threats can jeopardize the organization's existence.

The role of the social system in STSD is to be the source of "all adaptation to change, innovation, ideation and motivation" (Pasmore, 1988, p. 26). Social systems at individual, group, and organizational levels are the basis of the dynamics of evolution and development. These systems are essential, therefore, if an organization is to adapt to environmental change. An organization with no social system will not be able to respond effectively to the vagaries of the future. A key task is to design the organization in such a way as to allow the social system the freedom to bring about adaptation and change in as beneficial a manner as possible. STSD draws upon aspects of theory and practice concerned with individual motivation, group processes and performance, and organizational structure and culture to guide its approach to the design of social systems.

All organizations involve some technology, which may be simple or complicated but which certainly influences social behavior in the organizations. The view taken in sociotechnical systems theory (Trist *et al.*, 1963) is that the technology system is often the prime partner in this relationship. Social systems design often responded to technological change rather than it being the case that technology was fitted into a social blueprint. The technical system of an organization consists of the tools, techniques, devices, artifacts, methods, configurations, procedures, and knowledge used by organizational members to acquire inputs, to transform them to outputs, and to provide these to the environment (Pasmore, 1988, pp. 55–56). STSD is concerned with understanding the evolutionary processes which drive technological change and the implications they have for the people who are in contact, directly or indirectly, with that technology. A set of techniques for analyzing the technical system has been developed which specifically allows the place of the technical system in the rest of the organization to be understood. This analysis and any consequent design or redesign of the technical system are important for they not only determine the efficiency of the organization's ability to transfer inputs to outputs but they also lay down the parameters within which the social system will operate.

A methodology for using the ideas of sociotechnical systems theory to guide organizational change in such a way as to increase the adaptiveness of an organization to unpredictable future events has been developed by Foster (1967), Cummings (1976), and Pasmore (1988). This methodology can be summarized as a set of stages, the first of which involves establishing the boundaries of the process in financial and temporal as well as organizational terms. The environment is then scanned to generate an appreciation of what may occur in the future that may have an impact on the organization. On this basis, a vision of what the organization should be like in the future is drawn up. This marks the beginning of an educational phase in which members of the organization are exposed to the notion of change, the direction it will lead them in, and the process of achieving it. Within this phase the social and technical systems are analyzed and redesigned, and changes are introduced. These changes are not guaranteed to succeed, and continual improvement is necessary. Consequently evaluation of change and redesign becomes a continual process of adaptation to a changing solution.

STSD therefore provides a way of examining an organization with a view to increasing its ability to react to environmental and technological change. The analysis which is carried out is designed to improve flexibility and response and to bring out the most effective performance from the resources available to an organization. The concept of predicting changes that must be responded to is replaced by the concept of designing to respond to change. The organization is seen not as being able to control the environment but as being at the mercy of that environment.

The systems ideas which are used to guide STSD retain the hard systems perspective of representing what is seen to be in existence. Social and technical systems are analyzed as systems in relationships with their environment. What has altered is the analyst's ability to understand the structure of those systems and their relationships. Complexity does not allow the rigorous formal models of hard systems thinking to be built; they are replaced by a broader conception of an organization which is based upon the notion of open-systems behavior rather than the closed-systems perspective which is implicit in hard systems thinking.

This approach therefore incorporates an acceptance of increased complexity over that involved in QSD. The organizations which are the subject of the approach are seen as having to deal with high-complexity environments. They must therefore be designed to be adaptive and responsive to environmental change. The result of the approach is therefore a set of processes which can help organizations to tackle complexity rather than advise on how best to achieve a given objective.

*Management Cybernetics*

Cybernetics, the science of control and communication in the animal and the machine (Wiener, 1948) or the science of effective organization (Beer, 1966), can provide the necessary concepts and tools to enable extreme complexity and environmental uncertainty to be understood and tackled. The roots of the modern approach to cybernetics lie in the multidisciplinary efforts to address issues of control and communication in biological and electromechanical systems which took place in the U.S. in the 1940s. This work developed a conceptual framework which has since been found to have uses in other contexts, particularly in social rather than natural settings (Deutsch, 1963, McLoughlin, 1969, and Beer, 1981 being prime examples of cybernetic principles being applied to political, planning, and governmental issues).

The intellectual foundation of cybernetics lies in the relationship between several connected ideas. These have been reviewed from various perspectives by, for example, Beer (1959a, 1966), Strank (1982), Robb (1984), Clemson (1984), Jackson (1985a), and Espejo (1987), and there is no need to provide more than a summary here. The ideas have as a common theme a relevance to the study of extremely complex, probabilistic systems which exhibit self-regulatory behavior. The notions of variety, transformation, and feedback control allow the peculiar difficulties of analyzing and acting in such situations to be addressed.

The variety of a set of distinguishable elements is defined by Ashby (1956) as the number of distinct elements in that set or a logarithmic function of that number. For most purposes it is convenient to deal only with the former possibility. Situations of high complexity exhibit high variety, for they may be in one of many possible states, the possible states being associated with the elements in a situation of interest. As knowledge is gained, the perceived complexity is reduced, as is uncertainty over what future states may occur. Thus variety is a measure of complexity, uncertainty, and information gain. As a measure, variety is difficult to operationalize; only in specific cases can variety be measured in any meaningful way. Its benefit lies in the understanding it generates on how to tackle highly complex situations and a constraint which can be deduced about the extent to which such situations can be controlled. The key feature of this contribution is the law of requisite variety.

The law of requisite variety establishes a limit on the regulatory power of any device. A system's capacity as a regulator cannot exceed its capacity as a channel of communication (Ashby, 1956). Equivalently, and more commonly, the law is interpreted as meaning that only variety can destroy variety. Variety is the notion that links the complexity of what is to be controlled with the information-processing capability of the would-be controller. The reason why high-variety situations are difficult to confront is not their absolute complexity but the complexity they exhibit relative to that held by the controller. To inexperienced persons the task of mending a piece of electrical equipment is difficult, for they lack sufficient variety to deal with the variety of the problem posed. Experienced electricians possess higher variety, and the task is seen by them as being relatively simple.

The concept of variety provides an understanding of why situations are difficult to assess and a method of easing these difficulties. Variety engineering gives ideas on how to increase the variety of the controller and to decrease that of the controlled. Variety amplification and attenuation techniques are discussed fully by Beer (1979, 1981). Structural, planning, and operational tasks are interpreted as methods by which an organization may reduce the massive variety of the environment in which it exists. This reduction of high variety is reinforced by the structural, augmentative, and informational processes which can be used to increase the variety of the organization which seeks to control its environment.

Although variety and variety engineering capture the general problem of dealing with complex situations, they are insufficient on their own. Methods of responding to unexpected events and of understanding the behavior of complex systems are also necessary to help formulate decisions and strategies in complex situations. Cybernetics uses the notion of transformation to provide a representation of the dynamic behavior of complex systems. Rigorously analyzed by Ashby (1956), transformations correspond to a set of rules which prescribe how a system will move from one state to its successor. The processes underlying the change are not important, for they cannot, because of complexity, be fully understood. Transformations, then, are descriptions of change, not explanations of change. Use of the black-box technique allows transformation rules to be acquired by examining the input–output behavior of a system rather than probing into it to discover how inputs are changed into outputs.

Having established a path into the future, it is necessary to design and implement methods which minimize deviations from it because of unexpected environmental disturbance. Homeostatic devices, or error-controlled regulative feedback mechanisms, have been recognized to play an important role in the maintenance of biological variables within certain limits (Cannon, 1932; Wiener, 1948). Cybernetics accepts the generality of such systems, which compare actual with desired values, and initiates compensatory action if necessary to reduce any gap. The principles of design of simple and sophisticated control devices embodying the flow of information about a variable to a decision-making center are provided by cybernetics. For example, Bogart (1980) lays out designs for flows of information labeled *feedback*, *feedforward*, and *feedwithin*, which enable control to be exercised over variables in different parts of a system.

Cybernetics offers a rich source of insight into the nature and methods of tackling high-complexity situations. The usefulness of the ideas is perhaps best illustrated by the design of an organization which encompasses the necessary conditions for it to be viable provided by Beer (1979, 1981, 1985). In the viable system model (VSM), Beer develops from cybernetic principles a blueprint for an organization which is able to maintain a separate existence, that is, to be viable. The model can be used to diagnose organizations with a view to their redesign so that they are more capable of coping with their environment. The examples of the use of this model (see, for example, Britton and McCallion, 1985, and Walker, 1988, as well as the well-known application to the Chilean economy in Beer, 1981) show the diagnostic strength of the approach and suggest that cybernetics concepts can be utilized to provide useful practical insight.

An assessment of how cybernetics involves systems notions has been provided by Jackson (1985a, 1986) and Flood and Jackson (1988). There a comparison is drawn between the cybernetics contribution to management and organization theory and the more conventional view of organizations. The attitude toward organizations adopted within cybernetics is one which looks at properties of systems which maintain the status quo, are restrictive in their view of democratic processes, and concentrate upon goal seeking. Essentially it can be argued that there are many cybernetics concepts embedded in functionalist organization theory (Flood and Jackson, 1988, p. 29). This type of organization theory is that reflected by hard systems thinking and implies that cybernetics is grounded in the same fundamental beliefs as the hard systems methodologies discussed above but that it has built upon these foundations a set of concepts and methods appropriate to the level of complexity it sets out to confront. Thus cybernetics is an extension of the above set of hard systems methodologies which is capable of yielding insight and advice on how to understand extremely complex situations and how to design procedures to allow individuals and organizations to act as effectively as possible in such situations.

## Dealing with Pluralism

### Tools for Tackling Pluralism

An implicit assumption within the hard systems paradigm is that an objective to be pursued can be identified and agreed to by all involved. When this assumption does not hold, methodologies grounded in the hard systems paradigm will be inappropriate, and other approaches need to be found which do not invoke this basic premise. The assumption may hold in either of two basic cases. In certain cases the values, attitudes, perspective, and knowledge of all of the actors involved may overlap to such an extent that they can each support freely an objective which is developed from such a basis. Alternatively the actors may have different understandings of the situation which lead to different objectives, but because of the relationships between the people involved, some will have to accept that their objectives will be seen as secondary to those of other actors. Such power relationships exist to some extent in all social situations, whether they involve the family, informal groups, or, particularly relevant here, organizations. The presence and the exertion of power of one individual or group over others can lead to the acceptance of a single objective by all involved, even though it may not be everyone's preferred choice. When these situations do not exist, then pluralism results, each actor or group of actors bringing their own objectives to bear on a situation and these being explicitly recognized as being at variance and as being derived from different viewpoints. Pluralism cannot be tackled by hard systems methodologies, which require objectives to be stated and supported by all involved for their success.

Pluralism arises when significant differences between the worldviews of individuals are not dominated by the exercise of power by some of those individuals. It is this case which is explored in the following, where it is assumed that the supremacy of one party is not a significant issue and hence that power relationships need not be explicitly considered. Such a situation may result either from an unwillingness of those who can exert power to do so or from the absence of such relationships. A discussion of those situations where power is an issue of importance and consequently an influence upon the nature of the objectives will be undertaken later. The starting point for discussing methodologies here is that pluralism exists and is explicitly recognized to exist by those involved. Methodologies therefore need to provide mechanisms which can engineer an agreement over what objectives are to be pursued.

A necessary task in achieving this aim is to be able to find and use a representation which can reflect the various perceptions of a situation without prejudice to one type of perception. Such a representation should be able to be used by all actors, irrespective of background and knowledge, to an equal extent and should act as a neutral device for enabling each person to understand the views of the others. The extent to which a representation or its designer can be neutral is debatable, but neutrality is the ideal to be sought. A common theme throughout the methodologies described below is the use of language in the representations they involve. Natural language is the only modeling tool found capable of reflecting the subtleties of perception, but, even then, it can be seen as confusing, as words have relative value and interpretation. Methodologies based on natural language tend, therefore, to take as an important feature the need to expose as closely as possible the true meaning behind a word or phrase.

Pluralism of objectives is underpinned by the subjectivity of individual views, and methodologies capable of addressing pluralism effectively need to be built with the capacity to deal with subjectivity. Subjectivity, however, is a cause of complexity, and situations characterized by pluralism are, inherently, more complex than those where a single objective is underpinned by a single worldview. This extra complexity is due to the multiplicity of views on the nature of the situation. Irrespective of the nature of the situation, several views will always lead to a greater amount of complexity than a single perspective. As a consequence, methodologies capable of tackling pluralism are implicitly tackling a form of complexity, that deriving from an amalgamation of views of the same situation. This relationship between pluralism and complexity is important in discussions about the methodologies which can deal with pluralism. It must be recognized that methodologies which are capable of dealing with pluralism must also be able to deal with complexity, the complexity due to pluralism. Some may, in addition, be able to deal with the complexity of the situation which is independent of pluralism.

In the following, several methodologies capable of dealing with pluralism are discussed. This set of approaches is capable of addressing situations exhibiting different amounts of complexity. An indication of this capability is the extent to which the approaches involve methods of learning and adaptation to change. Those which have little or no such capabilities are best suited to use in relatively simple situations where complexity is largely the result of pluralism. Those methodologies which encourage continued learning about and adaptation to the environment are more suitable for use in cases where the situations of interest are inherently complicated in addition to showing complexity due to pluralism.

*Strategic Assumption Surfacing and Testing*

The first of the methodologies designed to tackle issues of pluralism which is considered here is strategic assumption surfacing and testing (SAST). It is most rigorously discussed by Mason and Mitroff (1981). In line with the above argument that pluralism is a form of complexity, Mason and Mitroff begin by recognizing the peculiar characteristics of problems associated with situations of organized complexity (Rittel, 1972; Weaver, 1948). Organized complexity can be usefully contrasted with disorganized complexity. In the latter there is no apparent structure underpinning the situation. The number of variables is large, but there appears to be no pattern in the relationships between them and hence no organization in them. Such situations can be explored very often by use of statistical techniques which can begin to cope with the apparently random behavior. Situations of organized complexity do possess an elusive structure and therefore contain more problems, as attempts to explore them lead the analyst deeper into the complex web of mutual influences and relationships.

The wicked problems of organized complexity (Webber and Rittel, 1973) exhibit a number of characteristics. First, they are highly interconnected so that changes in one area have direct and indirect impacts upon many other areas. Costs and benefits of changes cannot therefore be identified within a narrowly defined part of the situation but must be assessed throughout the situation. Second, they are inherently complicated, so that the desired effects may need to be achieved indirectly by changes being introduced in others parts of the situation. In some cases several changes spread across the situation may be needed to bring about the wished-for change at a further point. Third, they are uncertain, and this uncertainty creates a need to accept risk which may or may not be able to be calculated. In response to this uncertainty, decision makers must be able to act in a flexible and responsive way. Fourth, problems of organized complexity are ambiguous. That is, they can be perceived in different ways by different observers. The nature of such problems is such that they cannot provide empirical evidence to support a single, undeniable vision of what the problem is, and subjectivity of perception therefore exists. Following from these points, it is possible to identify the causes of conflict about how to proceed in such situations. The need to take risks and to consider wide-ranging costs and benefits, often by people who will see the situation differently, leads to fundamental conflict over values and goals. Pluralism is seen as an explicit consequence of the problems posed by situations possessing the characteristics of organized complexity. The constraints on reaching feasible and desirable solutions are social, organizational, political, and technological. Solutions cannot be constrained by the end to be reached because such a goal cannot be defined.

In response to this view of problem situations, Mason and Mitroff developed a methodology to help decision makers tackle them effectively. Their methodology is participative, adversarial, integrative, and "managerial mind supporting." That is, it involves the active participation of many individuals working in groups. The groups develop opposing arguments, as it is felt that a dialectical approach is most likely to generate the best judgments about a complicated situation. A result of such adversarial procedures is the expansion of the knowledge base, and in order to take advantage of this, a synthesis or integration is required. Finally, the emphasis is upon helping the decision makers to understand the situation more fully rather than providing them with information which they may use to help them choose how to proceed. The thinking process is being supported, not the decision-making process.

SAST involves five phases in an effort to meet these criteria. First, groups are formed which between them contain a wide range of people who may be expected to be able to contribute knowledge or expertise to the situation at hand. In forming groups it is essential to minimize the level of interpersonal conflict while maximizing the differences in knowledge and perception within each group. Each group will remain intact throughout the exercise and, as an initial aid to team building, is asked to give itself a name and to express its core concerns about the situation.

The second phase is assumption surfacing. The result of this is the identification of the assumptions which underpin each group's view of how to proceed in the situation. One means of locating such assumptions is, first of all, to identify the stake holders in the situation, those people who have a vested interest in it. Then the assumptions are identified which must be made about each stake holder so that the adopted strategy will be optimal. This process results in a list of assumptions about the key actors in a situation for each group. This understanding is then exposed to dialectical analysis.

The third phase is referred to as the within-group dialectic. Each group uses scaling methods to display the relative importance and certainty of each assumption. This is done individually, and this information is then brought together and debated so that a consensus is reached on the pivotal assumptions which form the heart of the group's understanding.

The fourth phase sees the groups being brought together in a series of between-group dialectical debates. Each group presents its assumptions and explains why its pivotal assumptions have been chosen as being central. Debate is then allowed, with a view to reaching agreement among all participants on a set of assumptions which are acceptable to all. This process creates a mood of cooperation and mutual understanding, which is vital to the final phase.

Synthesis and decision complete the SAST methodology. The acceptance of assumptions about the situation and of the reasons for the planning premises is increased, and in such conditions planning can be carried out effectively. The end result of SAST is that it has moved the set of decision makers from an unhomogeneous group with differing values and perceptions to a team that is committed to a common view of the situation and that is in a position to make decisions and to implement action in a coherent and unified manner. Thus SAST is effective in tackling pluralism and setting the scene for choosing strategies or determining action. It does not help decision makers to decide what plan to introduce or what action to take but creates an environment where these processes can take place more effectively than without its use.

Mason and Mitroff use systems ideas in two ways in their consideration of the nature of problem situations and how to tackle them. First, problems exhibiting organized complexity are understood as systems. Interrelationships between different parts of the situation and the continuing expansion of problems as they are investigated more deeply are insights derived from systems thinking. A second use of systems ideas is to inform the way in which actors are understood to relate to each other. The collected set of perceptions held by the individuals concerned is also seen as possessing systemic properties. The elements of the set interact with each other in a variety of ways, and the SAST methodology encourages this interaction to produce further insights. These insights emerge from the dialectical process used in SAST, which could be understood as an expansionist methodology, in the sense that it sets out to produce new and useful knowledge from the existing set of perceptions. Such an idea is based upon a systems view of individual and group behavior which emphasizes exchange, broadening, and emergent properties rather than focusing upon a narrow analysis of a situation.

*Strategic Options Development and Analysis*

Any consultant who is involved with a group of clients has to understand the psychological processes which motivate and distinguish each individual from the others. A natural extension of this necessary but often minimal involvement with individual behavior is to treat it as a serious component of the decision-making process. At this level the social psychology of group behavior and decision making takes on a particularly important role, for understanding this psychology offers one way of tackling the existence of pluralism. A program of work associated with Eden and his associates, based originally at Bath and more recently at Strathclyde University, has resulted in a methodology for aiding decision making built upon the conceptual base of social psychology. In particular the concepts of personal construct theory have been used, via the technique of cognitive mapping, to produce the methodology of strategic options development and analysis (SODA).

The model of individual behavior which informs SODA concentrates upon the interpretations or constraints through which individuals view their reality in order to give it order and meaning. The tool for making this subjective world available for scrutiny is the repertory grid (Eden and Jones, 1984; Kelly, 1955). Eden *et al.* (1983) give details of how repertory grids and other techniques of interviewing and eliciting information can be used to yield cognitive maps. These are signed digraphs similar in form to those used in qualitative system dynamics. Cognitive maps show the connections between variables which represent statements, beliefs, and visions about the world. Such statements are usually expressed as a pair (one set of words being the opposite of the other) in order to help clarify meaning. This opposition is necessary, as, for example, the use of *respect* by two people can easily be seen to take on different meanings when one person contrasts it with "treat with contempt" and the other with "ignore" (Eden *et al.*, 1983, p. 41).

Within this methodology, particular importance is given to the relationships between consultants who use the approach and the individuals who are the client group. Issues such as how to ensure that each individual will be able to take an equal role in the debate and what are to be the timing and management of meetings are given high priority so that the environment for reaching decisions will be as supportive as possible. A prime example is given by Eden (1985a).

The result of the first phases of the approach is a set of maps which represent the views of the individuals or groups who have been consulted. These maps are generally sizable and are stored and manipulated by means of a specially designed piece of computer software, COPE (cognitive policy evaluation). By means of COPE, maps may be analyzed and modified in a flexible manner. Areas of agreement and dispute can be highlighted, chains of explanation identified, and potential for change and development assessed. The results of the COPE analysis are used in various ways to inform the next stage of discussion, which focuses upon bringing the individuals together to create a consensus on how to make progress in the situation. Eden and Huxham (1988) note that the methodology "addresses that element of strategic management which emphasises consensus-building and team processes" (p. 889).

This approach tackles pluralism by studying the views of the world held by the individuals involved. The methodology, SODA, is seen as a process of interaction between a consultant and a client group which is designed to move a situation characterized by uncertainty and multiplicity of views to one characterized by commitment and consensus built around a vision of the direction to take. Within this process the techniques of cognitive mapping and the analytical power of COPE take a prime facilitating role in creating constructive debate.

The place of systems ideas in this approach is not apparent, for, at a fundamental level, the prime theoretical notions are those of social psychology. Indeed Eden and Huxham (1988) stress that "the basis for understanding how people construe their world is based in an 'action' rather than a 'systems' view of organisational life" (p. 891). Further, as Eden (1985b) notes, "systems thinking does lead to markedly different practice from thinking which is derived from the theories of psychology and social psychology" (p. 860). However, the cognitive maps which are used to represent how people see the world and to form a key part of the process are systemic in nature. Their analysis uses systems ideas such as hierarchy and connectivity and is considerably aided by this intellectual framework. An important issue is whether this systemicity emerges only at the representational level when cognitive maps are constructed or whether it is present in the assumed cognitive processes which the maps make explicit. In order to explore this point, the basic theory of personal constructs needs to be examined.

In establishing the philosophical position adopted by personal construct theory, Kelly (1955, p. 16) states that it is positivist, empiricist, rationalistic, monist, and neutral. Further, the existence of constructs is not denied, for "constructs are real interpretations of facts" (p. 136). Thus Kelly argues that constructs are produced by individuals as ways of construing the world, and that people act as scientists in continuing to improve their understanding by altering the set of constructs to provide a more useful picture. Personal construct theory is therefore deeply embedded in a subjective view of the world; each individual has his or her own constructs which guide his or her perception of and action in the world. The view of the world adopted by Kelly is that it is integral (p. 7). Each element of the world has an exact relationship with the others, so that "in the long run . . . the motion of my fingers, the action of the (typewriter) keys and the price of yak milk (in Tibet)—are interlocked" (p. 6). Thus constructs are considered an approximation of this complex of relationships. The systemicity of cognitive maps reflects a deeper systemicity of the personal constructs which they represent.

Kelly's systems thinking is based in the hard systems paradigm. The world consists of elements in relationship to each other which can be examined, in principle, by the use of reductionism. This view is reinforced by Kelly's discussion of prediction, which is built upon if-then (or cause–effect) relationships (pp. 119–125). It has already been seen that such a view of the world is limited in its ability to tackle situations of high complexity effectively. Thus a limitation of cognitive mapping and personal construct theory as a way of beginning to address problem situations is that it cannot bring out the full complexity of this type of situation. By its theoretical foundations in Kelly's personal construct theory, SODA is kept from being fully effective when it is used to tackle highly complex situations. It can deal with the complexities due to pluralism but not with the complexities of the situations being confronted. This failure is highlighted by the absence of explicit methods of learning and adaptation in connection with future activity. Learning and adaptation are discussed with reference to the cognitive maps of the actors and hence deal with this cause of complexity; they are not discussed with reference to a broader view of complexity.

*Strategic Choice*

The two approaches discussed above were built upon particular theoretical foundations: SAST upon a combination of Hegelian dialectic and systems theory and SODA upon personal construct theory. Strategic choice (SC) is a way of working with groups of decision makers which has been informed primarily by the observation of decision-making processes in the public sector. The approach has its roots in the Institute for Operational Research based at the Tavistock Institute, also the home of sociotechnical systems theory. A prime aim of the Institute for Operational Research was to expand the application of OR to broader policy issues (Friend, Norris, and Stringer, 1988), and an early and influential study was to observe the policymaking and planning processes of Coventry, an English city council, in the mid-1960s (Friend and Jessop, 1969). As a result of this experience the complexity of the decision-making processes and of the situations about which decisions were being made was recognized. Consequently an approach to helping with such processes was developed and subsequently refined. The methodology was labeled *strategic choice* to reflect the view that planning is seen as a continuous process of choosing strategically (Friend and Hickling, 1987, p. 1).

It was recognized in the studies of Coventry and elsewhere that certain dilemmas are regularly confronted by decision makers when they are faced with complex cases. Balances needed to be struck between a focused and synoptic treatment of scope, a simplifying and elaborating treatment of complexity, a reactive and interactive treatment of conflict, a reducing and accommodating treatment of uncertainty, and an explanatory and decisive treatment of progress through time. In response to such dilemmas the strategic choice approach goes against the more conventional norms of linearity, objectivity, certainty, and comprehensiveness. Instead the approach is designed to emphasize the need to work with cyclicity, subjectivity, uncertainty, and selectivity.

Like the other methodologies discussed here, SC has evolved a technique which is embedded in the approach and which facilitates it. The analysis of interconnected decision areas (AIDA) is a representational device for helping to focus debate and thought on key issues. The most recent comprehensive discussion of AIDA is given by Friend and Hickling (1987). A situation is recognized as consisting of or being related to a variety of decision areas. A decision area is an opportunity to make a choice, about location, product, size, technology, life span, or any other course of action. Decisions made about one factor—say, size—will influence and will be influenced by decisions on other factors, say, price, quality, or technology. A problem can be structured and understood by exploring the relationship between different decision areas and, in particular, by identifying which subset of all possible decisions within these areas is feasible. AIDA provides a means of achieving this understanding and also for generating a framework in which feasible choices may be compared. Once this framework has been developed for a particular case, judgments can be made on areas of uncertainty, and then decisions can be made on the actions and arrangements necessary to make progress. The process of identifying decision areas, choosing feasible options, and comparing them is used as a way of learning about the situation and of identifying where knowledge is lacking. Friend and Hickling (1987) provide a wealth of examples and advice on how to manage the process in which AIDA is embedded to bring out the full insight and understanding of those involved.

Friend and Hickling (1987) are keen to argue that SC is not an example of a systems approach, that it

> has no claims to be a "systems approach" in the commonly accepted sense: rather, it is a *process* approach in which the elements are choices which are

normally supposed to be of a transient nature, and the relationships between elements are not therefore expected to assume any systemic form. (pp. 47–49).

However, they compare SC with the conventional systems approach of the hard systems paradigm. Rightly, they note that the decisions which need to be made in the face of complex situations are fluid and complex in themselves and defy the use of a hard systems approach. They do perceive the set of decisions as understood by the actors involved to be systemic in character. In describing the nature of SC (pp. 85–108), they contrast the technology, organization, product, and process of this approach with more traditional decision-making and planning styles.

The technology adopted in SC needs to be as accessible to all involved as possible, and AIDA, as a piece of technology, is used in an open way. The focus on decisions helps to provide a common basis upon which all involved can act and participate in decision-making. The technology, be it computerized data and the associated software or flipcharts, is seen as being important in helping to encourage interaction and the sharing of opinions. The organization of a project using SC is designed to allow interactive participation and group, rather than hierarchical, connections. The creation of links across organizational boundaries is seen as being important also in the creation of synergy. The process of SC is characterized as being continuous and devoted to learning and understanding. Hence planning is an ongoing process which SC helps with in a particular phase. The complexity of the situations being dealt with and the ever-changing nature of the factors influencing decisions mean that plans cannot be made once and for all but need to be continually revised and updated. Finally, the product of SC is incremental progress and agreement on strategic projects, not solutions to problems and large-scale plans. The result is confidence in dealing with the future, not a fixed set of procedures to be followed in any event.

This vision of SC and its operation is rich in systemic quality. Decisions form a fluid, ever-changing focus of attention. Individuals need to be brought together to bring an outward-looking and synergetic attitude to bear on the situation of interest. Adaptation and learning are encouraged rather than solutions and analysis. Although the hard systems paradigm is incapable of providing a base for such ideas, the soft systems paradigm, which is compatible with subjectivity and complexity, can. The methodology of SC embodies aspects of the soft systems paradigm. Individuals are seen to perceive things differently and these perceptions alter in time. The methodology is built on this foundation and provides a representational device (AIDA) which can facilitate an exchange of views and generate a consensus of opinion on how to proceed. This device acknowledges the systemicity, not of reality, but of how individuals perceive that reality and deal with it. Thus, although SC is not a methodology grounded fully in systems ideas, it does exploit the language, imagery, and conceptual schema of systems thinking. These are used to understand the process by which groups of actors continuously tackle difficult planning and decision-making situations.

This methodology clearly provides a way of dealing with the complexities which arise as a consequence of pluralism. The presence of various views of a situation is accepted and is seen as a source of creativity and synergy. The use of AIDA provides a way of focusing on feasible options, which starts with many different ideas about what could be done and finishes with agreement on how to proceed. Although this agreement may not be in the direction of one particular option, it may be the way that leaves the most options open for later decisions. Rosenhead (1980) and Best, Parston, and Rosenhead (1986), for example, describe and use a method of analyzing the robustness of decisions which indicates the extent to which a decision restricts future options for decision makers.

The strategic choice approach also provides a means of dealing with situations which are inherently complex. An underlying premise of the methodology is that planning is continuous and needs to be so because the environment in which it takes place is changing in uncertain ways. The methodology is designed to provide learning experiences for those involved so that they are better able to make decisions in the future. There is no notion that once agreement has been reached, the matter is settled; agreement is a temporary state necessary to making some progress. This is a distinction between SC and SAST and SODA. Neither SAST nor SODA pays explicit notice to future problem situations. Although it is not denied that planning and deciding are continuous, the focus in both SAST and SODA is more on the present than on the future. SC concentrates on the present with an eye always on the future and hence seems more suited to use in situations which are themselves complex than either SAST or SODA.

*Interactive Planning*

One of the main figures in both classical OR and the newer forms of systems-based problem-solving is Ackoff. The particular approach developed by Ackoff in the 1970s is called *interactive planning* (IP). Based explicitly upon systems-age thinking rather than machine-age thinking, IP aims to provide a tool appropriate to the "messes" which now confront decision makers. Ackoff outlines his particular methodology in a variety of places (1974a, 1974b, 1979b, 1981a,b, 1983), and it has been assessed from different perspectives by, for example, Jackson (1982, 1987). Underlying the approach are three operating principles.

The first principle Ackoff labels the participative principle. This is based on the belief that a great benefit comes from being involved in the planning process. Classical OR concentrates upon the end result of the planning process rather than on the process itself, and IP seeks to redress the balance by placing emphasis upon the benefits of participation. Second, Ackoff notes that plans are always having to be changed because of unexpected occurrences. Hence planning should be continuous, a view enshrined in the principle of continuity. Planning is a cyclical process and should be explicitly seen as such. Finally, Ackoff introduces the holistic principle. This results in the premise that every part of a system and every level of it should be planned for simultaneously and interdependently.

These three principles reflect Ackoff's basic view that systems thinking, implying participation, dynamism, and holism, is preferable to analytic thinking, implying objectivity, stability, and reductionism. The principles are operationalized by Ackoff's procedure of interactive planning.

Formally, IP has five interrelated phases. The first of these, formulating the mess, involves imposing a structure upon the situation being dealt with. This is done not by identifying objectives and ways of achieving them, but by developing scenarios of what the future may bring if nothing is done to change it. Means–end planning is a key part of the approach, for it involves the creation of an idealized redesign of the system. This involves bringing the stake holders together to produce a statement of the policies, projects, and activities which they would like to see in place. The production of such a redesign helps to create consensus and momentum among those involved. Resource planning is, as expected, concerned with defining what resources are necessary to achieve the design and how they may be acquired and allocated. Organizational and management planning is, likewise, the specification of the systems for implementing and operating the idealized redesign, and for "effective organisational learning and adaptation" (Ackoff, 1979b, p. 191). The final element of IP is the design of the implementation and control mechanisms which monitor and act on the actions necessary to achieve the redesign.

The roots of IP in systems thinking are clear. It is an approach based upon systems thinking designed to tackle problems based in a world understood in terms of systems ideas. The holistic principle provides evidence of the conceptual link established between systems ideas used to understand the world and to aid interventions in that world. The other two principles indicate that IP is able to deal both with complexity due to pluralism and to that inherent in the situations being explored. The participative principle and the process of producing an idealized redesign offer theoretical and practical support to a way of dealing with pluralism. The principle of continuity and the creation of systems for the implementation of, among other things, a means of "effective organizational learning and adaptation" give a way of dealing with the uncertainty of future behavior due to the complexity of the situation.

*Soft Systems Methodology*

Finally, in this brief overview of some systems-based problem-solving methodologies which aim to overcome the limitations of hard systems approaches, attention is turned to that developed by Checkland: soft systems methodology (SSM). It was during the development of this approach that the notions of hard and soft systems thinking emerged. Checkland's is, therefore, the only approach genuinely derived from his notion of soft systems thinking, although, as shall be seen, it shares features with several methodologies discussed so far. The main ideas of SSM are developed rigorously in Checkland (1981), and they are also surveyed and summarized in Checkland (1983, 1985, 1987) and Wilson (1984).

For Checkland, systems thinking involves the basic ideas of emergence, hierarchy, control, and communication. Using these consciously in problem situations implies taking a systems approach to that situation (Checkland, 1987, p. 89). Both hard and soft systems thinking involve the use of such ideas; the difference lies in the purpose for which they are used. SSM is a process designed to facilitate the progression from finding out about a problem situation to taking action in that situation, during the course of which explicit systems thinking about that situation takes place (Checkland, 1985, p. 763). This systems thinking takes place within the context of conceptual models.

A conceptual model is "a systemic account of a human activity system, built on the basis of that system's root definition, usually in the form of a structured set of verbs in the imperative mood" (Checkland, 1981, p. 313). A root definition is a description of a system which serves to capture the essential qualities of that system. Use is made of the CATWOE mnemonic to define the six key characteristics: customers, actors, transformation, weltanschauung (worldview), ownership, and environment. By building different conceptual models based on different root definitions a variety of perspectives on the same situation can be considered. The construction of root definitions and conceptual models involves systems thinking based upon as deep an understanding of the situation as can be gained. The conceptual models are then compared with the situation. The purpose is to generate debate about possible changes which may lead to an improvement in the situation. This debate, undertaken by those involved in dealing with the situation, will lead to agreement on what action to take.

Systems thinking in this approach is undertaken to explore how the same situation can be perceived from different worldviews. The systems thinking that occurs is involved with perceptions of a part of the real world, not with the real world itself. As in IP, it is the subjective understanding of a problem which is of concern rather than those parts of it which can be objectively seen.

SSM can deal with that element of complexity due to pluralism. The explicit treatment of different views of a situation allows debate to take place over the relative merits of these and what can be learned from each of them. The intention is that the approach be used by those involved to encourage interaction and participation to the same extent as in SAST, SODA, SC, and IP. The approach is also able to tackle situations which are themselves complex. The result of an application of SSM is not the removal of a problem but a change in the nature of the situation. Learning has occurred, and decisions are made on the basis of this and other learning. However, as Checkland (1987) states, "it is a learning rather than an optimising system" (p. 94). Decision making and the process underpinning it are stages in a continual series of efforts to respond and adopt to the real world. SSM helps to improve the effectiveness of this process, but it cannot remove the need for the process.

## Pluralism and Power

In the introduction to the discussion on pluralism, it was noted that attention would be focused upon those situations where the superiority of one individual or group over the other actors involved is not a significant issue. This, it was suggested, would be the case if those who can exert their power choose not to do so or if there are no superiors in this sense. This assumption will now be considered further to explore the extent to which it can be justified and the implications that follow if the assumption is denied.

As Morgan (1986) notes there is no clear definition of power adopted in the study of organization and management. Two contrasting views are that, on the one hand, power is a resource to be used, while, on the other, power is a relationship defined between people and implying a dependency. When considering pluralism, the strict definition of power is irrelevant, for any exercise of power, whether as a resource or as a relationship, prevents the free exchange of views and the reaching of agreements, which each of the approaches discussed above seek to generate.

Morgan views the control of decision processes as one of the major sources of power in an organization. Three interrelated elements of decision making are recognized, each of which can be controlled and hence can become a source of power to the controller. The premise on which a decision is to be made is the first of these. Setting the boundaries of a discussion, the use of language, attitudes, and other actions can influence the starting point for any decision process, which therefore has a consequence for the subsequent discussions. Control of the processes by which decisions are made is also important. This can be achieved in various ways by managing the meetings at which decisions are discussed and by deciding upon who should be involved in making these decisions. Finally, it is possible to exercise power by influencing the issues and objectives to be considered. This can be done formally by stating the nature of the problem if someone is in a position to do so and informally by personal contributions to the debate, knowledge relevant to the situation, and the use of other means of influencing people. In considering this source of power, other aspects are brought into the analysis, such as power granted by virtue of position, authority, responsibility, knowledge, and control of resources.

Power is therefore not easy to define and is even less easy to express in a simple form. What does follow from the above is that power will always be present in situations where more than one individual is involved. It is a resource unequally distributed over a set of individuals which automatically gives rise to superior–inferior relationships of a complex nature. All of the methodologies which can deal with a variety of perspectives held by a group of people acknowledge that power is present, but they are not all able to offer ways of removing its influence. For example, Eden et al. (1983) provide useful ways of allowing each actor to make an equal contribution at an early stage of a study. Ultimately, however, they cannot deny the fact that those individuals in a relatively powerful position will be able to influence the way in which an agreed-upon course of action will be implemented if they so wish.

The conservative nature of several of the above methodologies (SAST, IP, and SSM) has been discussed by Jackson (1982). None of these methodologies are found to be capable of removing the existing biases due to power, and a suggestion is made that a means of negating the biasing effects of power should be used prior to the use of any of these methodologies. The consequences of following such a suggestion would be to ensure that an environment for open debate will be established, together with a means of ensuring that the agreements made in such a debate will not be altered as a result of a subsequent use of power. A methodology suitable for investigating the nature of power relationships in a given setting, which is explored by Jackson (1985b, 1987), is critical heuristics (Ulrich, 1983, 1987, 1988).

Critical heuristics provides a systems-based approach to the provision of "methodical help not only in formulating and justifying theoretical or practical propositions but also in rendering transparent the normative implications of these propositions in an envisaged context of application" (Ulrich, 1988, pp. 156–157). Thus it helps to facilitate the consideration of normative issues rather than policy or resource issues. Normative systems management has as a key task the management of conflict rather than the management of complexity or scarceness, which are the realms of strategic or operational systems management. What the critical heuristics methodology can do is to help individuals "to become self-reflective with respect to the normative implications of *any* standard of rationality" (Ulrich, 1988, p. 158). It is impossible to remove completely the effects of power; the best that can be achieved is to identify the boundary judgments that define where the exercise of power begins and the power of rational argument ends.

In order to help recognize the boundary judgments and the accompanying justification break-offs, Ulrich has established a set of twelve boundary questions (Ulrich, 1987). Organized into four groups, these questions guide an analyst and any other interested party through the normative content of a design and enable its underlying premises to be challenged. Thus the ways in which those responsible for the design derive their basic principles can be exposed. Each group of three questions concentrates upon one aspect of these underlying principles. The first looks at the sources of motivation: Who contributes and owns the purpose of the design? The second group explores the sources of control contained in the design: Who contributes and has the power to decide? Third, the sources of expertise are considered: Who has the appropriate skills to implement the design? Finally, the sources of legitimization are exposed by asking who represents the various concerns involved and how is this done. In each case the analysis is broader than to find out how these currently operate but asks how they ought to be supported so that a basis for constructive reflection is provided.

A crucial aspect of any attempt to develop a critical (i.e., self-reflective) approach is undistorted communication between those involved in the situation. This allows the maximum chance for rational argument to be successful. Methodologies such as SAST, SODA, SC, IP, and SSM have the potential to meet this need and form one possible foundation for a methodology of normative systems management.

Pluralism cannot be divorced from power, and Ulrich presents a picture of a methodology in which rational argument fills all the space inside a frame of power. The use of such methodologies and the natural evolution of the social world will have an effect on the nature of the power relationships and their evolution. Changes in these relationships will be slow and marginal and are unlikely to result in any radical shifts in the balance of power.

The role of management science (broadly interpreted) in maintaining the current distribution of power, at all levels, was discussed in the previous chapter. The contributions of Rosenhead and Thunhurst (1982), Tinker and Lowe (1984), and Rosenhead (1987) have made clear the inequality of access to "management science expertise," which is used by those with access to enhance their position relative to those without. Critical heuristics can do nothing to change this fundamental position, for it works within the existing framework of institutions and cultures. The only way of altering the balance of access to expertise is to offer it as a conscious decision to those normally without access. Thus Rosenhead and Thunhurst (1982) call for a "workers science" to serve the needs of labor in direct opposition to the "management science" which serves capital. The community OR initiative (Carter, Jackson, Jackson, and Keys, 1987) provides support to community-based organizations which are normally unable to afford the services of advisers.

The consequence of this discussion is to reinforce Ulrich's comment (1988) that "systems practice should not misunderstand itself as a guarantor of socially rational decision making" (p. 158). No methodology, systems-based or otherwise, can change the structure of the social world; only the individuals in that world can achieve that. Methodologies can be used to encourage debate between individuals within the parameters defined by social structure. They may also be used in the services of those who, as a result of the social structures, have relatively low amounts of power and influence. Both of these uses may lead to change in the social world; however, such change will not derive from the methodologies but from the actions of individuals, which may be informed by the use of the methodologies. Users and subjects of methodologies therefore should be aware of the assumptions and implications which are associated with any of the above methodologies concerning power and its role. Power is omnipresent, and its existence cannot be denied but merely exposed. Knowledge of what power exists, who holds it, and how it is exercised is useful in making people aware of how they may be acting in relation to it. Methodologies which can help in this area, such as critical heuristics, are potentially powerful. Their role is different from that of the other meth-odologies discussed above. Whereas OR, SA, and the rest are designed to support decision-making processes of different types in different ways, critical heuristics and any similar approaches shed light upon the nature of those processes and hence help to identify the range of ways in which support may be needed and provided.

## Conclusion

This chapter has presented a discussion of several systems-based methodologies which can operate effectively in situations where hard systems approaches run into difficulties. The boundaries due to the complexity of the situation being confronted and the complexity due to pluralism can be overcome by adopting different attitudes toward the purpose and style of the appropriate methodologies. The complexity of the situation needs to be addressed by developing learning and adapta-tive systems. Pluralism is reconciled by reaching agreements on which direction to proceed in. When entering a problem situation, a consultant needs to understand the nature of that situation in these terms and then to make an appropriate choice of methodology. Further, the consultant needs to make a choice about how to deal with the power relationships that will inevitably be present. In the next chapter, these issues are addressed within the framework of a classification of systems-based methodologies which provides a basis for a methodology for meth-odology choice.

# Systems Methodologies
## From Theory to Practice

## Introduction

The discussion in the previous chapter showed that there exists a range of systems-based methodologies capable of tackling situations which lie outside the boundaries of hard systems thinking. These boundaries, defined by the existence of complexity and pluralism, pose difficulties for hard systems thinking which can be overcome by altering the way in which systems ideas are seen to support methodologies. In this chapter the insights gained from the discussions in the previous two chapters are used as a basis for the development of a methodology aimed at helping analysts to understand the nature of the situations they confront and to choose or design an appropriate methodology with which to tackle those situations.

The chapter has three main parts. First the ideas underlying the earlier discussions are formalized into a framework that gives a simple but potentially powerful device for understanding the nature of problem situations. Second, this framework is used to support a methodology for methodology choice which can help in the diagnosis and the determination of the means of addressing problem situations. Some examples of the use of this methodology for methodology choice are given to illustrate its application. Finally, some reflections on this framework are made in order to suggest some further areas of development and clarification.

## Classifying Systems Methodologies

### Classifying Systems

The recognition that different forms of problem-solving methodology use systems ideas in a variety of ways to enable them to tackle effectively a range of situations prompts the question of whether a formal classification of systems-based methodologies can be produced. Classification schemes form a central part of many disciplines, for example, biology and zoology, where they serve to structure and direct attention to relevant phenomena. Within the broad discipline of systems, various classification schemes have been constructed. Beer (1959a), Boulding (1956), Checkland (1971), and Jackson (1987), for example, each propose a classification of phenomena understood in systems terms relative to some criteria. The purpose of these classifications tends to be related to the need to understand the nature of reality from within a systems perspective. The parts of the world exhibit different characteristics, which indicate something about their purpose and behavior.

This type of classification scheme is of little value for the current purpose, which has as its focus methods of interacting with the world rather than of passively observing it. The basis of a classification scheme relevant to interactions needs to reflect their purpose and behavior in the same way that a classification of the world should refer to its purpose and behavior. The discussion in the previous chapters suggests that a classification incorporating the notions of complexity and pluralism may be of value. These concepts indicate significant differences between the relative strengths of methodologies, and to ignore this insight may lead to an omission of some key factors from the schema.

*A System of Systems Methodologies*

In an attempt to provide an appropriate classification of systems-based methodologies, Jackson and Keys (1984) constructed a "system of systems methodologies," central to which are the concepts of complexity and pluralism. Methodologies are seen as being used within problem contexts consisting of three elements: the set of relevant decision makers, the situation about which decisions will be made and in which consequential actions will take place, and the problem solvers who will aid the decision makers in their task. A problem solver is confronted by two related factors: the decision makers and the situation under consideration. Decision makers are the source of pluralism, and a classification along this dimension is clearly related to this element of the problem context. The situation under consideration will be perceived by an observer as being complex to some degree, and a classification of complexity can be associated with this aspect of a problem context. Thus a classification of how problem solvers perceive problem contexts can be based upon the pluralism existing between decision makers and the perceived complexity of the situation under consideration.

The set of decision makers is understood to be either *unitary* or *pluralist* in character. A unitary set of decision makers will be in agreement over a set of goals to be pursued and will make their decisions in line with these goals. In contrast, if a set of decision makers is unable to reach agreement about goals and consequently cannot make decisions in line with a common objective, it is said to be pluralist. This two-way classification reflects ideal types and serves to focus attention upon an important distinction between the relatively easier case of unitary decision makers and the more difficult pluralist case.

The situations under study are perceived as systems possessing different degrees of complexity. Those with a relatively low degree of complexity are reasonably easy to understand, observe, model, and analyze. They may be understood to be systems functioning in a machinelike way, using reductionist methods of analysis and are referred to as *mechanical*. Situations which are more difficult to examine and hence are seen to be more complex are best understood by means of concepts such as holism, hierarchy, and emergent properties, and are referred to as *systemic*. This simple distinction draws attention to a significant difference between the more straightforward mechanical case and the more complicated systemic case.

These two dimensions, unitary-pluralist and mechanical-systemic, match the boundaries of the effective use of methodologies based upon hard systems thinking. The move from unitary to pluralist is compatible with a shift across the boundary caused by the difficulty that hard systems methodologies have in situations where objectives are not agreed upon. A pluralist set of decision makers will pose significant problems for someone using a hard systems methodology. The transition from a mechanical to a systemic situation corresponds to crossing the boundary where hard systems methodologies are unable to cope with high levels of complexity in the situations under study.

Only one of the four possible types of problem context (unitary decision makers and mechanical systems) falls inside the boundaries defining the limits of hard systems thinking. Within this class of problem context, the hard systems paradigm is appropriate, and methodologies such as OR, SE, SA, and SD will be effective. When a problem solver is part of a mechanical-unitary problem context an appropriate methodology to adopt will be one which has the characteristics of these or similar methodologies. Such methodologies provide a way of identifying how best to achieve a specified objective. In a mechanical-unitary case, the conditions under which this optimisation can be done effectively are satisfied.

The remaining three classes of problem-context (mechanical-pluralist, systemic-unitary, and systemic-pluralist) cannot be tackled effectively by hard systems methodologies. Each of them violates the boundaries around the hard systems paradigm in some way. In mechanical-pluralist situations, there is a need to combat the difficulties posed by the variety of objectives held by the different decision makers. Methodologies such as SAST and SODA provide guidance on how agreement can be reached and offer ways of operating across this particular boundary. The difficulty posed by systemic-unitary situations is the uncertainty resulting from the high amount of complexity which is found in such cases. The necessary learning and adaptation processes can be developed and supported by approaches such as QSD, STSD, and MC. Finally, in the most difficult cases of all (those in the systemic-pluralist class), agreement on goals needs to be reached and learning and adaptive procedures must be implemented. Systems-based methodologies such as SC, IP, and SSM meet these needs and provide guidance on how problem solvers should operate in such circumstances.

The Jackson–Keys framework offers a simple four-way classification of problem contexts which captures the major distinctions which affect the usefulness of problem-solving methodologies. The framework is to be used as a device for helping one to understand the nature of a situation and for providing indications of which methodologies may be useful in certain circumstances. A strength of the framework is its foundation in the rigorous analysis of methodologies, their structure, and their ability to deal with certain types of situation. However, the framework is not a definitive prescription for how to proceed in any given case or for how to understand the nature of that case. Methodologies not considered here may be appropriate in some cases; the methodologies which are mentioned may be used outside the classes in which they are seen as being particularly effective, and the use of pluralism and complexity as defining dimensions may not always be useful. Once it is stated that the approach is to be interpreted and used flexibly, it must also be stated that during its original and subsequent development the approach has been found to be of use in many practical cases, and this experience has led to a degree of confidence in its value. This practical use of the approach and a continued concern with its theoretical base have led to a deeper consideration of the way in which power relationships can be incorporated into the analysis.

In the previous chapter the relationship between pluralism and power was briefly considered, and it was argued there that the majority of problem-solving methodologies are inherently conservative in terms of power structures between decision makers. None of the methodologies mentioned above reveals or counters the deep-seated power relationships that may exist in any set of decision makers. This observation suggests that the limitation of the above framework to only two types of sets of decision maker, unitary and pluralist, is restrictive and that a refinement of the scheme to allow a richer consideration of power may be beneficial. Two directions have been taken in exploring this issue. One, noted in Jackson and Keys (1984) and subsequently pursued in Jackson (1987, 1988), involves extending the unitary-pluralist dimension to include a third possibility: coercive. The second direction, adopted in Keys (1988b), retains the dichotomy of unitary-pluralist and emphasizes the role of the problem solver in determining which actors to include as decision makers and by so doing making judgments on power and its effect on the situation.

## Unitary, Pluralist, or Coercive?

The extension of the unitary-pluralist dimension to become unitary-pluralist-coercive involves recognizing that situations which are unitary or pluralist may be so only superficially. Within any set of decision makers the exercise of power by one or several individuals over the remainder may result in an appearance of agreement over goals or a willingness to work toward and accept a consensus view. Thus, to the observing problem solver, such a set of people will appear to be unitary or pluralist, although this circumstance will not be the result of freely made decisions but of power being exercised. The extension of the framework to unitary-pluralist-coercive reserves the first two classes for situations where the cohesion is the result of genuine willingness. In coercive situations "any cohesion that does exist will be achieved by the exercise of power and by domination (overt or more or less concealed) of one or more groups over others" (Jackson and Keys, 1984, p. 483).

In coercive situations the conservative nature of the methodologies mentioned earlier results in a maintenance of the power structure if they are used. None of the approaches affects this aspect of the situation, as they do not offer the tools which can reveal or alter its fundamental character. The implication of explicitly recognizing this element of problem contexts is that it may under certain circumstances be seen as a legitimate target for a problem solver. The role of a problem solver is thus seen to include not only advising a group of decision makers on how to set objectives and reach them but also ensuring that this debate will not be biased by the existing power relationships. Hence problem solvers need to be able to identify and expose these relationships and move them toward some preferred pattern. Ulrich's critical heuristics appears to be the only systems methodology currently available which can offer any advice and support on how a problem solver might achieve these goals.

A problem solver who chooses to be guided by this extended framework may take on the tasks of, first, seeking out power relationships and, second, changing them. In deciding the character of the problem context, the problem solver has to choose the means of interpreting the perceived relationships of the set of decision makers. Coercion may be clearly present, and in this case the problem solver has to decide whether to explicitly acknowledge it or not. If problem solvers decide to address the coercive mechanisms, they must then be held responsible for any consequences of the ensuing analysis and change. If they choose to work within the existing situation, they are choosing to accept that some involved parties will not be able to contribute equally with others. This is a relatively clear-cut issue compared to that which confronts a problem solver when the nature of a set of decision makers appears to be unitary or pluralist. Then a decision has to be made about whether to investigate beneath the surface of the relationships which are perceived in order to assess their validity. A judgment needs to be made about the potential benefits of such an investigation relative to its costs. Advantages may follow by revealing previously unrecognized biasing effects which may be reduced to everyone's benefit. However, an analysis which causes disharmony and dispute in a previously coherent group is obviously disastrous for all.

This means of dealing with power and its consequences has its strengths. It draws attention to the presence of coercive processes and their consequences. The use of critical heuristics can reveal factors in a situation which were previously unknown. In certain types of situation, these may be useful factors. The Community OR initiative (see, for example, Carter *et al.*, 1987) has as a central theme the task of providing OR expertise to groups in the community who normally do not have access to it. In such cases an ability to become aware of and identify the means by which power operates against such groups can be beneficial. Attempting to identify coercive situations also has its weaknesses, primarily in the type of guidance it gives problem solvers. A problem solver using the above extended framework is presented with a means of classifying a problem context which suggests that a clear distinction can be drawn between the three categories which reflects differences in reality. In practice, however, because the conditions indicating "coercive" may be hidden behind those indicating "unitary" or "pluralist," a well-defined choice cannot be made between the three possibilities. Thus what appears to be a useful guideline to enable problem solvers to understand a situation confronting them is a source of uncertainty. This complication is manifested by the difficulties and hazards which are posed to a problem solver who has to choose between exposing coercive mechanisms or working within them and between accepting a perceived unitary or pluralist situation as being as it is and seeking to bring any possible hidden power relationships to the surface.

*Power and Negotiation*

The second way of incorporating power into this framework does so in a way which avoids the above difficulty by posing questions about the character of the set of decision makers in a different way. The emphasis in this approach to the issue is on retaining the original four-celled classification of problem contexts and to recognize that problem solvers will use it to guide their perception of the situation they are confronting. In particular problem solvers will choose whom they see as being involved in the set of decision makers and through this process can be recognized as addressing and making decisions about their treatment of power.

This method of incorporating power into the framework starts from the premise that problem solvers become involved in a situation by coming into contact with a client. The client(s) wish to achieve some change in the situation, and a problem solver is used to help examine the situation and to determine what changes may be suitable. Without the relationship between a problem solver and a client, the role and purpose of a problem solver becomes meaningless. By entering into an agreement with a client, the problem solvers immediately constrain themselves by the obligations which this agreement imposes upon them. A key issue in determining the character of the problem context, and hence of the set of decision makers, is the limits on the problem solver's tasks negotiated with the client. These limits and the process of negotiation which defines them are ways in which a problem solver can separate the issue of power from that of identifying the nature of the problem context.

The negotiation of what a problem solver is to achieve will be carried out within the constraints of what the client wishes to achieve. Within these constraints the client and the problem solver will negotiate the constraints to be placed on the analysis. These constraints will identify who is to be involved in discussions and who will be seen as having a legitimate role in proposing goals and objectives. The attitude of the client in these discussions may lie between minimizing the contributions of others and being open to involvement from any person. The client, therefore, is seen as having an important role in establishing the character of the set of decision makers. The problem solver may be prepared to agree to what the client suggests or may wish to establish a different, agreed-upon position. The chosen attitude will depend upon the circumstances of the problem solver, independent of and in relation to the client.

There are too many possibilities to explore the variety of these negotiations and their results fully; however, some common cases may be usefully mentioned here. At one extreme is the case where clients wish no one else but themselves to define goals and objectives and a problem solver is prepared to work within this constraint. Then the set of decision makers is unitary, and even if more people than the client are involved, their views will be dominated by those of the client. At the other extreme is the situation where clients are content to have an open and free debate over goals and objectives, perhaps because the clients are part of a group where this is an accepted norm of behavior or because the clients are asking the problem solver to work with a group of which they themselves are not a part but are responsible for. In this case a pluralist set of decision makers is recognized.

In between these straightforward extremes lie more difficult cases. The client in the first case above may find that problem solvers are not prepared to limit their concerns only to the goals of the client. Then either a compromise position has to be established or one or the other part must give way completely. If the client gives way, the problem solver may need to be aware of dominance being exerted subversively. If problem solvers give way, they may not be able to commit themselves fully to a project they are not fully satisfied with.

By concentrating upon the negotiations between client and problem solver, it is possible to recognize that problem solvers are not free agents in a situation, able to investigate and change power relationships at their own desire. Problem solvers are meaningfully involved in situations only with the agreement of a client or a client group. Power, as far as the problem solver is concerned, lies in hands of the client, who sets the boundaries of the problem solver's activities. Cohesion among a group of decision makers may not be genuine or may be overridden by more powerful actors in a situation, but if problem solvers enter a project under an agreement to ignore or overlook these issues, then they are breaking an obligation to the client if they choose to change these manifestations of a power structure. It is the responsibility of the problem solver to recognize the existence and use of power and to realize that by agreeing to work within its constraints, they are maintaining the relative dominance of the powerful over the powerless.

This approach to power and its treatment by problem solvers is essentially pragmatic and is grounded in the necessary relationship between client and problem solver. Its benefits lie in its pragmatism in that it emphasizes the responsibility taken by problem solvers when entering upon projects and negotiating their activities. This treatment of power, taken together with the advice offered to problem solvers by the four-celled framework, gives a useful picture of project activity to a problem solver. Its disadvantages also lie in the pragmatic view that problem solvers need to depend upon clients and hence are relatively less power-ful and therefore tend to support the status quo. A further disadvantage of this extension of the system of systems methodologies is that has no apparent place for methodologies, such as critical heuristics, which ex-plicitly explore power relationships. It is possible to overcome these limitations, and the ways of so doing require problem solvers to take posi-tive action in seeking out a different set of clients.

The conventional client base of operational researchers and similar problem solvers has been those who are in a position to bring about change. By definition these people tend to be those who are more powerful in society. Rosenhead and Thunhurst (1982) have made a powerful case for seeing OR as a support to capital in its domination over labor, and some reasons why this should be so lie in the above discussion of the negotiations between clients and problem solvers. Problem solvers, whose likelihoods depend upon successful projects, need to work for those who can remunerate them for their time and expertise. They will not therefore tend to be involved with those clients who are relatively powerless. The conservative nature of systems-based methodologies results not only from their inherent structure but also from the pressures which result in their use by problem solvers working for the powerful in society. By moving to clients who are relatively powerless, problem solvers can begin to alter the balance of power. This will be done not directly, but by strengthening the ability of less advan-taged groups to understand and tackle situations previously dominated by those with access to resources and skills.

The community OR initiative involves such a change of client base. People with skills and expertise not normally available to community-based organizations are encouraged to work in the voluntary sector and community organizations in order to develop their managerial and deci-sion-making effectiveness. Given the nature of such clients, a major interest is likely to be in understanding how power is exercised and therefore how it can be opposed and overcome. A methodology that helps in this direction is critical heuristics. Jackson (1988) cites one case where the approach was used to expose the underlying basis by which powerful groups were able to argue their positions in a case concerning nuclear waste disposal sites. In general, applications have been sparse, although the potential of critical heuristics within this initiative seems great.

Taken together, the work discussed above extends the original framework of four types of problem context considerably. It adds to the formal description of problem contexts the practical concerns which focus upon the social and political aspects of the problem solver's world. The analyses contribute to an understanding of how problem solvers relate to problem contexts and emphasize issues of practical importance. All of the way through this discussion, questions about how the above framework can be developed as a practical tool to aid the diagnosis of problem contexts and the choice of methodology have been raised. In the next section a rigorous consideration of these issues will be provided within the context of a methodology for methodology choice.

## A Methodology for Methodology Choice

*Definitions and Principles*

As a description and basis for analysis, the above discussion is valuable; it also provides useful guidance to a problem-solver on how to decide which methodology to adopt in a given situation, but lacks rigor in so doing. A formal methodology built upon the theoretical basis outlined above would be able to offer better guidance. The most detailed exposition of such a methodology is given by Keys (1988b) in a formal statement of the steps involved in a methodology for methodology choice, procedures for its practical use, and illustrations of the methodology's application.

The first stage in developing a methodology for methodology choice in a rigorous manner is to specify the various individuals and other elements which may be involved. As the focus is to be upon "methodologies," the notions of problem solver, client, and so on are relatively meaningless, as they are defined relative to a problem situation, not the means of tackling it. Two separate roles may be defined for individuals relative to methodologies. One is the role of *methodology user*. A person filling this role is able to use a set of procedures in order to bring about beneficial change. In other circumstances the person filling this role is likely to be called such things as a problem solver, a consultant, a management scientist, an operational researcher, or a helper. The task of a methodology user is to provide advice, understanding, information, and knowledge so that change may be achieved. The procedures by which this task is accomplished form a methodology. A key issue for the user is to decide what methodology to use in a given case. The second role is that of *methodology subject*. This role is filled by any individual with whom the user interacts while using a methodology. Thus clients, problem owners, sponsors, managers, decision makers, and so on are clearly methodology subjects, as are other individuals who are involved but who may not be in a position to act upon the work of the user, for example, shop floor workers, managers with other responsibilities, members of other organizations, and customers. Once people have been defined as subjects, they are assumed to be on an equal footing with all other subjects.

A *problem situation* arises when users and subjects come together in an attempt to bring about change. A problem situation consists of users, subjects, and the way in which they each see the world, in particular their perception of that part which is of concern. Methodologies are seen to act upon individuals' understanding of parts of the world. Part of this understanding consists of an appreciation of how other people perceive the same part of the world. Thus the understanding held by any individual consists of her or his own view on a problem together with an idea of how other people view the same problem.

Within this framework it is possible to consider some issues raised in the theoretical discussion of the previous section in a practical context. First, the perception of the user is crucial to the way in which the problem will be tackled. Within the above framework it is clear that the view held by the users in the situation is influenced not only by their own perception but also by that of the subjects. Users' understanding of a situation is developed from their understanding of how subjects view it. Therefore the users working with a single subject will have a different understanding of a situation than if they were working with someone else or a group of subjects. The choice of the set of subjects to work with can have a dramatic influence upon how users perceive a situation and how they begin to tackle it. Central to this choice is the attitude taken toward power by a user. This is a matter of concern for an individual user, but that taken here is in line with the second of the two possibilities discussed above. That approach emphasizes the importance of decisions made by the user in relation to determining the relationships which can exist between the user and the subjects. The adoption of this perspective is intended to make explicit issues of power and its exertion and the role of methodology users in the definition of who will be considered as subjects.

Second, having established the subjects and built up an image of how each of them understands the situation, the problem solver needs to consider only two factors in order to decide what type of methodology is appropriate. The sets of objectives held by each subject may be in conflict or not. The degree of uncertainty over how a situation behaves is an indication of its complexity. These two factors relate to the two dimensions of the system of systems methodologies developed above. It was argued above that these two dimensions capture the range of difficulties confronted by a user and are sufficient to allow a sensible choice of methodology. A user needs to establish where along these two dimensions a particular situation lies. A methodology for methodology choice needs to give guidance on how to make this assessment and how to interpret it.

Third, the systemic and recursive nature of the problem situation as defined above means that the individual perceptions of the problem under study will be highly fluid. A change in one person's view will influence everyone else's view, and this influence then leads to further changes. Thus a user needs to be continually aware of how subjects' views are changing. Any development may require users to change the methodology they are using or to retrace earlier steps as the nature of the situation demands. Agreed-upon objectives may change because of an alteration in one person's goals, cohesion may be lost as a group fragments into different factions, agreement may be reached and may move a problem context from pluralist to unitary, understanding may be gained and may thus reduce the perceived level of complexity, and so on. There are many possible trajectories which a problem-context may move through during its lifetime. A methodology for methodology choice should be able to reflect this fluidity and to suggest methods of monitoring and adapting to changes which a user can adopt.

These three observations result in principles which a methodology for methodology choice should follow. First, it should recognize the importance of the user's subjectivity. Second, it should incorporate methods of assessing the degrees of pluralism and the complexity of a situation. Third, it should represent the dynamic nature of problem situations. An example of a methodology for methodology choice which incorporates these principles is now given.

*Structure and Procedures*

The above discussion of the factors which are involved in a methodology for methodology choice and statement of some principles which underpin it can be formalized and translated into a specification of such a methodology. The first aspect is the specification by the user of a set of subjects. From a set of actors, $A$, each of whom may be a subject, $n$ individuals are chosen to act as subjects. This set of methodology subjects, $S$, consists of $n$ individuals, $s_i$, $i = 1, 2, \ldots$ , each of whom is a member of $A$. For each subject, $s_i$, the user creates a model, $m_i$, which indicates how $s_i$ perceives the problem situation. This set of models defines how the user perceives the situation through the eyes of the subjects. The user therefore deals with a set of $n$ models, $M$, which captures the variety of views held on the situation by the subjects. In addition to the understanding of the nature of the situation, the user also wishes to acquire knowledge about the objectives held by each subject. Each subject, $s_i$, will hold a set of objectives, $o_i$, which together form the set $O$. A user therefore has to generate four elements of knowledge about a problem situation:

$A$ = a set of actors
$S$ = $\{s_i; i = 1, \ldots, n, s_i \epsilon A\}$ = a set of methodology subjects
$M$ = $\{m_i; i = 1, \ldots, n\}$ = a set of models associated with $S$
$O$ = $\{o_i; i = 1, \ldots, n\}$ = a set of objectives associated with $S$

The second aspect of this approach is that a means of assessing degrees of pluralism and complexity should be developed. The degree of pluralism, $D_p$, is a measure of disagreement between the objectives held by the different subjects; it is therefore a measure of the elements of $O$. The degree of complexity, $D_c$, is a measure of the uncertainty in the behavior of the situation under study; it is therefore a measure of the elements of $M$. At present little useful work has been done in specifying such measures, although Keys (1988b) suggests that work done by Keeney and Raiffa (1976) and Klir (1985) may offer useful starting points and that influence diagrams, as used in QSD and SODA, may be an appropriate representational device.

The third part of the specification of the methodology centers upon the dynamic aspects of the problem situation. As methodologies are used and information is gained, the nature of $m_i$ and $o_i$ for each subject will alter. Thus the user will find that $M$ and $O$ change, and so will the values of $D_c$ and $D_p$. Thus the elements of $M$ and $O$ should be qualified by an indicator of time to reflect this. It should also be possible to change the set of subjects over time and to allow the user to expand or contract the number of people being considered. Thus the elements of $S$ should also be modified to indicate temporal factors.

On the basis of this formal specification of the components of the methodology, a five-phase procedure is developed which can be used to aid in the decisions about methodology choice.

The first phase requires the user to specify the set of actors, $A$, and from these an initial set of subjects, $S$. This specification will often be made as part of the negotiations with the client as to the boundary of the situation in which the user may work. It is clear that in specifying a set of actors, a user is, implicitly or explicitly, making decisions about how to treat the power structure in a situation. A set of actors which is limited to a small group limits the set of active participants (subjects) to that group. Hence these people are placed in a more beneficial position than others who are excluded from the set $A$. A large set of actors may suggest that a more open process of discussion is likely to occur, depending upon who is included and excluded. It is possible that a user may find a method of exploring conflict and power, such as critical heuristics, useful at this stage in determining what an appropriate choice of $A$ and $S$ may be in the first instance.

The second phase involves the user in identifying how each member of $S$ perceives the situation and feels about the objectives and goals to be pursued. These are then used to construct the set of models, $M$, and objectives, $O$. This is essentially a "finding-out" phase, and through it the users will begin to formulate their own understanding of the situation.

The third phase consists of making assessments of the degrees of pluralism and complexity associated with $O$ and $M$. Methods for doing this potentially range from the use of an informal assessment of the situation to the use of quantitative indicators, although to date only the former has been used. This appears to be satisfactory, as will be shown in the examples to follow, but many issues remain to be explored here.

In the fourth phase the user identifies and carries out the tasks indicated as being necessary by the values of the degrees of pluralism and complexity determined previously. Low degrees of pluralism and complexity indicate that action on deciding how best to achieve improvement can be taken immediately. This situation corresponds to the mechanical-unitary problem context, and methodologies such as OR, SA, SE, and SD may be useful here. A low degree of pluralism and a high degree of complexity suggest a systemic-unitary problem context in which action for designing and implementing procedures for learning and adaptation are needed in addition to finding out how to achieve goals. MC, STSD, and QSD are examples of useful methodologies here. A third possibility is a low degree of complexity and a high degree of pluralism indicating a mechanical-pluralist problem context. In such cases agreement needs to be reached as well as decisions made on how to achieve goals once they have been satisfactorily defined. Two existing methodologies appropriate here are SAST and SODA. Finally, there is the case of high degrees of pluralism and complexity, a systemic-pluralist problem context. Here, learning and adaptive procedures, methods of reaching agreement, and decisions on how to achieve goals are all needed. Approaches such as SSM, IP, and SC seem to offer useful starting points.

In addition to suggesting existing approaches which may be appropriate in each case, the methodology also provides an opportunity for users to design new methodologies or to combine parts of existing ones by indicating the need for fundamental problem-solving tasks (Keys, 1986). The determination of action, the engineering of agreement, and the design and implementation of learning and adaptive systems each have a role to play in different circumstances, and the methodology offers guidance to users on which need to be done in any given case. The choice of how to do them is not limited, and hence makes the approach as flexible as the users wish it to be.

The fifth phase emphasizes the dynamic nature of problem situations and requires the user to redefine $A$ and $S$, that is, to return to the first phase. Such a cycle allows a continual process of improvement and debate and emphasizes the fluidity of the problems. Users are reminded by this final phase that their work is biased and restricted by the initial choices of $A$ and $S$, and it offers an opportunity for the effects of those choices to be balanced by a later analysis involving a different set of individuals. It also allows a user to recognize that key people have previously been omitted and provides the opportunity to include them in the next iteration.

As in any formal statement of a methodology, it is not necessarily the case that all of the above phases need to be followed in sequence. They act as guidelines on what needs to be carried out if an effective way of choosing and using methodologies is to be pursued. The phases may be carried out in sequence, may be omitted if appropriate, or may be repeated if necessary. The methodology, although intended to be general, may not fit all cases and may need modification, in which case the theoretical base developed earlier should allow for modifications to be made in a consistent and progressive manner.

Although a strong theoretical case can be made for the methodology and its supporting philosophy, it is primarily a practical tool, and its value can be assessed only by its success in actual situations. Descriptions of its use have been given in Keys (1987b, 1988b), and here further examples are provided.

*Illustrations*

The use of the above framework will be illustrated by a description of a continuing piece of work carried out in conjunction with an organization based in the voluntary and community sector. Keys (1987c) has argued that the nature of management in such agencies is different from that in more conventional organizations and that this difference has consequences for the type of support that management needs. The participative ideal, strongly interwoven sets of individuals and organizations which form an environment, and problems in gaining resources result in management in community-based organizations being confronted with a different category of problem from that in organizations with strong hierarchical structures, which can focus on narrow and well-defined environments of customers, competitors, and suppliers, and which can generate resources directly by selling their products. Those issues will be touched upon during the following discussion, but it is felt that they do not narrow the applicability of the methodology for methodology choice as a general framework. The examples of the approach in earlier discussions (Keys, 1987b, 1988b) were based on interventions in organizations in the private sector.

The organization of concern here was initially conceived by a group of people based in various organizations but sharing a common concern with providing genuine employment for people with special needs. The core group of individuals who were the motivation behind the notion came from a local authority social services department, a council for voluntary service, political parties, and various organizations working for people with special needs. The broad agreement between these people was to establish an agency which would be responsible for setting up viable businesses which would employ a significant proportion of people with special needs. Several factors made this scheme different from the usual employment schemes for such people. The businesses were envisaged as being able to become independent, autonomous organizations. Subsidies, although probably necessary in the early stages, were not seen as being essential to the long-term viability of the organizations. Second, the employment to be offered was to be genuine and of a different order from sheltered workshops, where emphasis was placed upon work as therapy rather than as employment. The jobs to be generated were to be the next stage on from those based in sheltered workshops. Third, the businesses were to employ special-needs people as far as possible. Although many organizations offer positions to a small number of such people, they are often seen as peripheral to the main body of employees. The intention here was to offer opportunities where this would not be the case.

Despite this agreement over broad aims, there was no consensus on what types of business might be appropriate and no strategy around which those involved could combine to develop their ideas. The author, with the support of a postgraduate student, offered to work with the group in order to help them to make progress in this area. The offer was accepted, and the first task to be undertaken was to choose a way of approaching the problem. Although it was never made explicit, it was always accepted that the analysis would cover as wide a group of people as possible. There was no notion of the original group's dominating the project and hence restricting analysis to their own ideas.

When the above framework was used for guidance, the set of actors was seen to be large. Apart from the people associated with the core group, there were known to be many other people in similar organizations who could be expected to wish to be involved in any initiative. The variety of organizations involved in the care and support of people with special needs is great and ranges from fundamental care provision through education and training to wider social awareness activities. In addition, there is the group of people with special needs, who were also intimately involved in the proposed scheme and who could be expected to play a role at some stage in determining how it was to operate. From this large group of actors it was necessary to choose whom to work with, the methodology subjects.

In the first instance it was felt necessary to involve as many people as wished to be in the debate over the direction and structure of the Development Agency, as the organization was called at that time. Thus as many agencies, organizations, and groups as could be discovered were invited to send representatives to the first meeting to discuss how to proceed. A definite decision was made at this stage to omit people with special needs from the discussion because it was felt that there were sufficient people involved who had knowledge and understanding of the range of difficulties they suffered from and who could represent their views and needs adequately in the prevailing situation. On reflection there was sufficiently widespread concern over the particular status of special-needs people to justify this decision as not being to their detriment. The number of people involved altered over the various meetings, but nearly twenty people, representing many different interested parties, were seen during the course of the exercise.

After a group of methodology subjects had been identified, the first task was to elicit their general feelings about the ideas being proposed and from these to construct an image of their objectives and their understanding of the situation. It became clear from a set of interviews that three main purposes were attached to the initiative. Each of these led to a different set of tasks which were necessary to achieve it. The objectives and models of the methodology for methodology choice were taken to be the three broad objectives and the set of tasks necessary to achieve them.

One objective was to provide worthwhile employment for people with special needs. This required establishing jobs which could be done adequately by those people, setting up a business with its associated management structure and controls, and running this business effectively. A second objective was to provide a means of enabling people with special needs to participate in leisure and social activities. This involved identifying work-based leisure activities appropriate to such individuals and incorporating them within a suitable business organization. The management of such a business would be of a different type from that associated with the first objective, which was more conventional. Here the management would need to see employees as being in need of support in addition to working. The emphasis on work as being a basis for leisure posed a different set of issues from those involved in setting up a business. Finally, there was support for a view which saw the objective to be a means of increasing public awareness of the existence and special needs of the handicapped. This objective could be met only by recognizing the causes of isolation of people with special needs and positively seeking to design and introduce businesses which could overcome these.

In general, most of the methodology subjects felt that all three objectives were laudable, but conflict was felt to exist between them. For example, work-based leisure activities were potentially difficult to base in the same business as normal employment opportunities, and businesses which aimed to make the public more aware of special needs people were not necessarily the most economically sensible. The levels of complexity and pluralism associated with the views of the methodology subjects were thought to be high. Complexity was high because of the great deal of uncertainty over what business opportunities existed and how to implement any that were satisfactory. Pluralism was manifested in the different objectives which were recognized as being legitimate to pursue. In consequence an approach was needed which could facilitate debate over the relative claims of the three main objectives and that, at the same time, could shed light on the tasks which might be needed to achieve them.

Checkland's soft systems methodology was chosen, as it offered the potential to meet the needs of the situation and was also an approach with which the author and the student had some experience. On the basis of each objective and the interviews which had been carried out to generate them, three root definitions and conceptual models were developed. Analysis of the models led to a set of issues which would need to be addressed in the course of implementing any particular business idea. The methodology subjects were asked to think about these, and the understanding gained lead to a reduction in the uncertainty and hence the perceived complexity associated with the situation. Although answers were not forthcoming about such matters as legal requirements, volunteer availability and necessity, wages, and trade union involvement, they became understood as being important considerations, whereas previously they had been ill specified. The models also provided a means of reducing the pluralism and providing an agreed-upon set of specific areas where businesses might be based. Each model focused upon a particular benefit to be gained by setting up a business; ideally a business which could offer benefits in all three areas (employment, work-based leisure, and public awareness) appeared to be the ideal choice. Over twenty business ideas had been proposed at one time or another—furniture renovation, keyboard work, kennels, and curtain making, for example. Each subject was asked to assess each idea against criteria offered by the three models. At an important meeting the different responses were debated, and agreement was reached on those areas which seemed to be most widely thought of as meeting satisfactory levels in all three models. These were a bakery, a laundry, furniture collection and renovation, and a horticultural project.

At the end of this project the agency had formulated a strategy which centered upon pursuing these four areas in order to establish what each of them meant in terms of implementing a viable business. Pluralism had been reduced to a working consensus over these four possibilities. Complexity had also been reduced to the extent that more knowledge had been gained about where difficulties lay and what were likely to become key factors in any attempt to establish a business. In terms of the above framework, the situation had shifted from being systemic-pluralist to systemic-unitary. The nature of the task facing the members of the agency had also changed from being a problem of "how can we develop this good idea into practice?" to a matter of "which initiative do we take and how can we implement it?"

In subsequent pieces of work the author was able to help the agency members begin to resolve these difficulties by looking at two general problems of establishing viable businesses to employ special-needs people.

Before embarking on a description of these two pieces of work, it is worthwhile to describe some changes in the Development Agency which occurred immediately after the decision to focus attention as described above. The agency changed its character from an informal gathering of interested parties to a more formal organization with a constitution, but the peripheral members changed as progress began to be made toward definite ends. A part-time worker was employed who was responsible for developing the activities of the agency. Part of this task involved assessing the various opportunities in each of the four areas, and it was decided as a result that the bakery was the most likely to succeed and significant progress was made in identifying sites, attempting to generate resources, and so on. It was against this backdrop that the further two pieces of work were undertaken.

The first piece of work was concerned with the production of a method of understanding the particular requirements of employees with special needs and of developing a personnel-planning and -recruiting system to meet these goals. It was recognized that there would be particular aspects of the recruitment, training, and support of employees with special needs, and the aim was to design a complete personnel management package which incorporated these elements in an integrated fashion. As with the original piece of work, the agreement was to produce such a package by drawing upon any expertise and knowledge that could be gained from the appropriate people. The set of subjects involved here was more easily specified than in the first case. The contact person in the agency was the development officer, and, in addition, representatives of those organizations who were involved in the training and education of people with special needs were also included. It was expected that the usual route for employees would be from these organizations, and so it made sense to develop a staffing system based on their work.

The first stage was to identify the potential sources of employees with special needs and to construct a model of how these sources related to any business which the agency might set up. Although there were many sources and they each offered different types of person to the agency, the main picture was well defined. The key issue was to be able to specify the types of persons with special needs seeking to move into employment and then to use this information to assess their suitability for particular types of work. In addition, it was necessary to be able to appreciate what type and amount of support such a person may need while in employment, for example, the need for transportation and wheelchair access. The problem was recognized to pose little uncertainty, and there was agreement over what the end result should be. The task was therefore to design a method of gathering information about potential employees in a form which made it clear how they might be able to fit into a workplace environment.

Such a method was provided by developing a questionnaire in consultation with the various education and training agencies involved. This questionnaire was designed so that attention was drawn to the potential abilities of people with special needs and to the reasons why they wanted to move into a workplace rather than remain in a more sheltered form of employment. This questionnaire, when used alongside a more conventional interview–discussion session, was felt to be able to offer a structured set of information which, while being useful to those placing people in employment, was sympathetic to the particular needs of those people.

In addition to providing a personnel planning system for the agency, work is also currently in place on the task of designing appropriate structures for the businesses which it is to set up and their relationship to the agency. The need is for a set of guidelines for the agency on how to set up, in broad terms, businesses which can be autonomous as far as is possible but which can also remain under the control of the agency where necessary. As the future development of the agency and its business is unknown, flexibility without loss of rigor is required in this area. The methodology subject here is the development officer, who is the person charged with setting up the businesses. The agreement is to provide guidance to the agency and not to take into account, at this stage, the requirements of any businesses it may create. Hence a limited set of people are involved. The objective is clearly specified as being to define an appropriate set of procedures and guidelines for organizations which will be effective and useful in a variety of different types of business. Complexity is high here, not only because of the variety of types of business but also because of the uncertainty over how successful in the medium run the agency will be. Should it prove successful, then many businesses, possibly interconnected with each other, are likely to be involved and an integrated and consistent approach to their management and design is felt to be useful from the beginning.

The need here is for a methodology which can offer an adaptive yet rigorous approach to organizational design. Beer's viable system model (1979, 1981, 1985) is such an approach, and by incorporating the agency into this model at an appropriate stage, it will be possible to ensure that the Agency itself will adapt to changes in its environment. This work is currently in progress, so it is not possible to discuss its results. Conceptually it appears to be a fruitful line to take, and the agency and its businesses will be involved in a learning and adaptive exercise, which is necessary if they are to to be able to deal with the complex and ever-changing environment of which they are a part.

In all aspects of the work undertaken with the agency an awareness of the need to specify actors, subjects, models, and objectives and then to decide how to proceed in an informed manner has been found useful. Not only does it give a structure to the intervention process, but it also allows reflection during and after the intervention. The methodology for methodology choice provides a valuable base in which the more complex processes associated with different methodologies can be built. As it is used at the beginning of a project, it forces analysts to think about how they are to proceed at that stage rather than starting to use one approach and then finding that another may have been more appropriate. The methodology seems to enable the projects to begin from a starting point which is considered and has some rationale. In the course of projects it is then possible to assess progress in relation to this starting point and to modify or continue as necessary. Although the approach does not guarantee success, it does seem to draw attention to useful matters sufficiently early to reduce the risk of failure when compared to a more haphazard entry to a project.

The development of the system of systems methodologies and the methodology for methodology choice has been paralleled by work in related spheres. Here these strands of work are brought together, and their implications for the theory and practice of systems methodologies are explored.

## Reflecting on Methodology Choice

### Hermeneutics and Systems Methodologies

The starting point for this discussion is the attempt by Oliga (1988) to highlight the different modes of inquiry and practice which can be adopted within the systems approach. His analysis is based on a contrast of three methodological foundations of systems methodologies. Empiricism, and particularly positivism, takes the view that the underlying structures and processes of the world are independent of any observer, and hence that it is possible to acquire objective knowledge which can be shared by all observers equally. Such knowledge is characterized by theory neutrality and value freedom. Hermeneutics accepts a subjective element into methodology in two ways: a naturalistic methodology and historical hermeneutics. The naturalistic methodology retains the notion that knowledge is objective in character but recognizes that knowledge can be acquired only by understanding reality as it is seen by individuals. Historical hermeneutics goes one stage further and argues that understanding can be gained only through purely subjective activity. Finally, Oliga considers the critique as an approach which seeks to expose the social and individual processes at play in the world so as to allow the actors to understand more their behavior fully.

In relation to systems methodologies Oliga notes that empiricism and the naturalistic version of hermeneutics underpin particular classes of methodology, whereas historical hermeneutics and critique currently do not. The approaches of operational research, systems analysis, systems engineering, organizational cybernetics, and sociotechnical systems theory are supported by an empiricist methodology. Soft systems methodology, interactive planning, and strategic assumption surfacing and testing have a foundation in the interpretive approach offered by naturalistic hermeneutics. There is a poverty of methodologies underpinned by historical hermeneutics and critique; Ulrich's critical heuristics (1983, 1987) is the only example.

A consequence of this situation is that within systems methodologies the acceptance of received knowledge is reinforced by the dominant objective character of the methodologies themselves. A more self-reflective and critical approach is required if the issue of methodology choice is not to become a mechanical and trivialized process. This argument, when brought together with the pragmatic methodology for methodology choice and the relationship between that and the causes of complexity, reveals a stronger model of the development of systems methodologies and their application than is currently provided.

*Methodology Choice, Complexity Texture, and Self-Reflection*

A weakness of the methodology for methodology choice is, as correctly noted by Oliga, the level at which its closed loop operates. The dynamics of the approach encourage reflection by methodology users upon how they perceive the situation they are involved in. Figure 9.1 illustrates this point and shows how the methodology for methodology

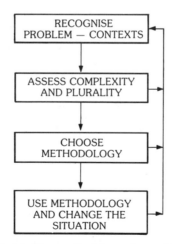

*FIGURE 9.1.* The methodology for methodology choice closed loop.

choice is internally closed and acts by intervening directly with the real world. Its use is influenced by various pieces of understanding, particularly those involving systems ideas. The weakness noted by Oliga is the failure to recognize explicitly that use of the methodology choice process can and does influence the user's understanding. By recognizing and developing this relationship, a more rigorous assessment of the methodology for methodology choice can be undertaken, and improvements in theory and practice may result, as illustrated in Figure 9.2.

The issue to be tackled, then, is to relate the methodology for methodology choice to a broader set of systems notions which allow for self-reflection and critical examination at an appropriate level of abstraction. There are many possibilities for this extension; the one developed here is based in Flood's disassembly of complexity (Flood, 1987), which shares some concepts with the framework of the methodology choice procedure and is therefore a convenient place to begin.

To Flood and Carson (1988, p. 19) systems science is about dealing with complexity, and systems notions are particularly valuable when individuals are confronted with something which appears to them to be complex. Flood's disassembly of complexity (1987) clarifies the view that

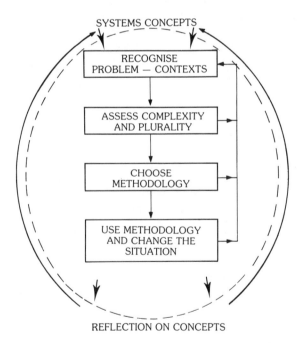

FIGURE 9.2. An embedding of the methodology for methodology choice.

complexity is a property of the object and the subject in combination and is a quality associated with difficulty of understanding. By disassembling complexity, Flood is able to establish the elements of complexity at several levels.

If one takes complexity as a whole to be the first level, two components constitute the second level: systems and people. As has already been noted, complexity is taken to be a consequence of observation, and people use systems ideas to help them conceptualize the world around them. Thus it is not the case that complexity exists in the world but that things, conceptualized as systems by individuals, exist in the world and that complexity is a function of how an individual chooses to perceive a situation. In unraveling this perceptual process, further clarification of the two components becomes possible.

The third level in the disassembly of complexity reveals the characteristics of systems and people which influence the extent to which a person perceives something as being complex. The system, which is used as an abstract device to make sense of the world, has a number of parts and a number of relations between those parts. At a simplistic level, complexity is a function of size as measured by these numbers. The more parts and relationships there are between them the more complex a system will appear. Deeper consideration of this observation suggests that the attributes of the parts and their relations are important, as are the observers' reasons for viewing the object of concern, their existing knowledge, and the set of concepts available to them. Thus two people will not necessarily perceive the same situation in the same way.

The disassembly of complexity gives a theoretical underpinning to the practical issues of assessing the complexity and pluralism in a particular situation. In assessing complexity, an examination should be made of the nonlinearity of processes, the symmetrical structure of situations, and the nature of any nonholonomic constraints which exist. These are suggested by Flood as being part of the underlying and essential causes of complexity. It is also appropriate to explore the reasons why the actors are involved in a situation, their capacity for observing, and the background knowledge which influences their perception. The interaction between these two groups of factors also contributes to an understanding of an actual situation.

This relationship takes advantage of general concepts to fill out and give guidance to a particular practical procedure. It is necessary to provide an indication of how to use that procedure, in turn, so that the general concepts may be refined and improved. In the current case of methodology choice the notions produced by disassembling complexity are given form by the assessment of complexity and pluralism. Thus the effectiveness of the concepts can be indicated by their contribution to the assessment of the degrees of complexity and pluralism. The ability of nonlinearity, asymmetry, nonholonomic constraints, and so on to assess complexity and pluralism will be an indicator of their value as general concepts. When they are used in such a practical way, their weaknesses and strengths become apparent, and subsequent strengthening of theory will occur together with improvements in practice.

This approach to developing the methodology for methodology choice reduces Oliga's fear that it will become a mechanical application of preset guidelines. The incorporation of theory development, methodological improvement, and practical application as outlined above encourages a self-reflective and critical attitude toward systems methodologies. Future work in this area needs to be concerned with this broader role for systems methodologies as a vehicle for theory developments as well as a means of aiding practical benefits, and Flood and Keys (1989) have gone some way toward defining this role.

### Conclusion

The discussion above has focused upon some practical issues associated with using the range of systems methodologies described in the previous chapter. In particular, it has indicated what factors need to be borne in mind when choosing methodologies. In relation to OR this emphasis on methodology choice leads to the recognition of when OR will be a valuable approach to use, and some guidelines are provided on when OR will run into difficulties. OR is not to be seen as an approach which can tackle all problems with equal effectiveness, but it has its strengths, which, when taken advantage of, can be of great value. The key practical issue is to be able to recognize when it is appropriate to take advantage of OR's capabilities and when to choose an alternative methodology.

# 10

# *Operational Research and Systems*
## Some Observations and Issues

## *Introduction*

In the laying out of the reasons for undertaking an analysis of the relationships between OR and systems in the first chapter, three issues were recognized as being worthy of attention. These centered upon the nature of theory and practice in OR and systems, the relationship held with scientific method by OR and systems, and the possible primacy of one of OR and systems over the other. The discussion in the above chapters has not addressed these topics directly but has built up a picture of how OR and systems are related to each other across a variety of dimensions. In this final chapter the above three topics are considered in the light of the above analysis, and some conclusions are reached as to their resolution. Unless otherwise stated, OR in the following will refer to classical OR as considered in the first part of this book.

The focus of the following sections can be clarified by considering Figure 10.1, where OR and systems are each broken into two related parts: theory and practice. In the first section below, the question of what constitutes theory and practice in OR and systems is addressed. The interactions between theory and practice are seen to involve method in some sense, and in the second section, the relationship between OR, systems, and scientific method is considered. A consequence of this discussion is an observation about the possible primacy of OR or systems in their relationship. The chapter concludes with an examination of the interrelationships between OR and systems in an attempt to assess this issue in more detail.

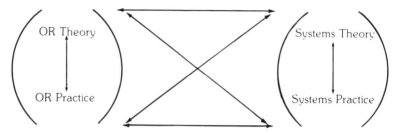

*FIGURE 10.1.* Interactions between OR and systems.

## Theory, Practice, OR, and Systems

A fundamental connection between theory and practice has been described by Checkland (1985) in relation to OR and the associated systems approaches. A set of ideas forming an intellectual framework is applied to an application area via a methodology. Reflections upon this process will generate learning about and modifications in all three components: the intellectual framework, the methodology, and the application area. When translated into the more simplistic language of Figure 10.1, the intellectual framework becomes a theory, and a combination of the methodology and the application area becomes practice. A key task here is to define in more detail what theory and practice refer to in both OR and systems.

The intellectual framework of OR comes from several sources. At an abstract level it is derived from an ability to represent phenomena and relationships in a logical way by using mathematics. This ability is related to an awareness that phenomena can be expressed in causal terms and can be understood to be the result of cause–effect relationships. Consequently, an ability is generated to represent reality by a set of mathematical formulae and by manipulating these to reproduce and predict how the real world behaves. Central to this framework is the need to be able to quantify phenomena and elements observed in reality so that the models of reality can be directly connected to the real world by their value. At a more pragmatic level the intellectual framework of OR is located in the set of standard models and techniques which are used by OR analysts. These offer a way of seeing the world and are a basis for understanding those situations which fall outside the range covered by standard models.

The practice of OR results from bringing together the application of the above intellectual framework and a part of the real world. The method of application centers on the process of model construction and involves understanding the nature of a situation and how to use a model to investigate it. The types of situation which can be explored are limited to those which are relatively simple and which can be fully observed, measured, and understood in terms of cause–effect relationships. Hence the practice of OR involves building mathematical models of situations which are amenable to investigation by using procedures grounded in reductionist, empirical methods.

Theory and practice interact in OR for various reasons. Possibly the most common reason is to draw upon the intellectual framework (theory) in order to secure an improvement in the real-world (practice) effectively. That is, the main emphasis in OR is upon achieving beneficial change in part of the real world and for it to do so effectively, a body of modeling techniques and the methods of using them are accessed. The intellectual framework which has emerged is that which has been found to be the most useful in tackling managerial problems. A second reason for theory and practice to interact in OR is the testing out of new components of the intellectual framework in real situations. Thus new algorithms, modeling approaches, or extensions of current methods will be tested out by being used on appropriate problems. A third reason for theory and practice to interact is to find the natural implications for theory which follow from a piece of practice and vice versa. The development of a new modeling approach or an improved algorithm will open up new opportunities for practical application. Equally, when a novel situation is being explored, the development of a new set of concepts which inform the modeling process may result.

The theory associated with systems centers upon a holistic view of the world embracing notions such as interaction, hierarchy, expansionism, and communication. This systems-age set of concepts is fundamentally different from that of the machine age and gives systems a different paradigm from which to operate than that associated with OR. The abstract notions of the systems paradigm are given form in a variety of models. The open-systems model, which emphasizes system–environment interactions, is one example of how systems thinking can generate applicable models. More specifically, Beer's viable system model gives a description of organizational form based upon systems ideas. Checkland's "formal system" is another example of how systems ideas are translated into general statements of how the world may be understood. Just as standard OR models and mathematical techniques provide a structure through which the world can be seen, the above and other systems models perform the same task.

When these concepts and general models are used to help understand and bring about change in reality, then systems practice occurs. Unlike OR, where a strong common core of a method of application can be recognized, the systems discipline has generated a variety of specialized methods, each often associated with a particular aspect of the intellectual framework. For example, Checkland's soft systems methodology is dependent upon use of that part of systems theory centered upon Checkland's view of how the world behaves and should be understood. Coyle and Wolstenholme's qualitative system dynamics approach is tied to their perception of the world as seen through a particular set of concepts and techniques. If one works with the full set of systems-based methodologies, then it is possible to recognize that the area of application of systems consists of those problems which are more complex in their nature than those addressed by OR. The restrictions placed on OR are relaxed by moving away from the need to model situations in a mathematical-quantitative way. However, restrictions remain on the areas where systems practice is effective, and these are connected to its limited ability to to address issues of power and dominance.

The reasons for the interaction of theory and practice in systems are similar to those for OR. The desire to improve a part of the real world requires the intellectual framework being drawn upon and the concepts chosen for use. The development of a new piece of theory may be tested by its use in a particular situation and involves practice being generated from theory. Additionally there are the more subtle implications for theory, which follow from reflections being made on a piece of practice, and for practice, which follow from a change in the intellectual framework.

The structure of OR and systems is thus seen to be similar when they are defined in terms of theory–practice interactions. What distinguishes them is the intellectual framework, which forms the theory, and the methods and areas of application, which form the practice. The divisions correspond to those discussed earlier which separate the hard and soft systems paradigms. An interesting insight is that the relationships between the respective theory and practice elements are of a similar form. This similarity suggests that, at a metalevel, OR and systems may be able to be seen as subdisciplines of a broader discipline. This discipline would have as a central feature the set of relationships which link theory and practice as discussed above, and OR and systems would be two of possibly several special cases. Figure 10.2 provides an overview of what such a core set of relationships might look like. If this metadiscipline could be rigorously specified, then it may provide a means of enhancing the currently available approaches.

The similarity of OR and systems recognized above and the differences between them, which are also apparant, have led to a degree of confusion over where a boundary between them lies, if one exists. This

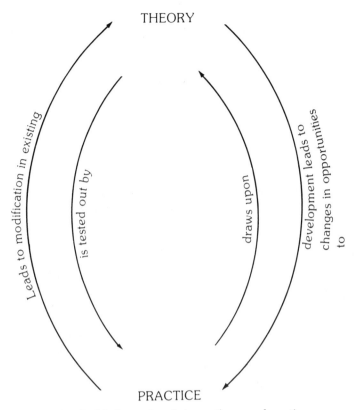

*FIGURE 10.2.* Interactions between theory and practice.

issue is considered in the next section, which explores how OR and systems relate to scientific method and the meaning of this relation in their definition.

## Science, OR, and Systems

OR has traditionally attached much importance to its adherence to scientific method. An earlier discussion explored the different versions of scientific method and how each of them relates to OR. Scientific method provides a basis for classical OR to relate theory to practice; hence classical OR is methodologically grounded in science. The methods used in systems, however, are not as closely related to science as are those used in OR. The methodologies used in systems are rigorous and well defined but differ in several fundamental ways from those of science. They cannot incorporate the same reliance on quantitative, empirical data as does OR, and model validation and manipulation both cause difficulties for the systems approaches. It has been argued above that the limits on the effective use of OR are related to the application of scientific method. As systems approaches offer a way of proceeding outside these limits, systems should be seen as being different from science. A problematic issue in the relationship between OR and systems is the form of this difference.

One possible basis for the difference is that one of OR and systems is a special case of the other. Such a view implies that one of scientific method and the set of systems approaches is a special case of the other and hence that one of hard and soft systems thinking is a special case of the other. One possibility is that systems is part of OR and hence that systems, the set of systems methodologies, and soft systems thinking are special cases of OR, scientific method, and hard systems thinking. This possibility can be reversed to suggest that OR, scientific method, and hard systems thinking are special cases of systems, systems methodologies, and soft systems thinking. There are basic problems with either of these suggestions, particularly at a conceptual level, where the differences between the two paradigms involved would seem to inhibit the embedding relationship being suggested.

This view can be understood, however, if a broader interpretation of OR or systems than has previously been given is accepted. Classical OR and systems, as discussed above, are seen to contribute different features to the general area of problem solving, but both could be subsumed under a broader umberella of operational research or systems if either term is taken to refer to the metadiscipline posited above. While this argument has some weight, and many proponents from either OR or systems argue it with genuine conviction, it serves only to disguise the differences between classical OR and systems and to draw attention away from the unique contributions that each can make. Therefore, while it is accepted that this is a popular view, it is not seen as adding anything meaningful to our understanding of how OR and systems are related. To argue that both the metadiscipline identified in the previous section and an element incorporated in that discipline can be labeled similarly is confusing and misleading and does not, therefore, aid in clarifying the relationships which are the subject of inquiry.

In denying that either OR and systems subsumes the other, it is also being denied that either scientific methodology or systems methodologies on the hard and soft systems paradigms is in a similar position of superiority. As has been shown above, in some cases an OR approach may be used and be perfectly effective. In others, a systems approach may be used to equal benefit. OR and systems—and hence scientific method and systems methodologies and hard and soft systems paradigms—are different and complementary. Each provides methods, concepts, and tools which are best suited to certain types of situation. The question of the existence of a boundary between OR and systems is a question not about a hierarchical relationship but about a horizontal one. It is a question about the relative strengths of the two approaches which leads to an appreciation of their potential contribution to problem-solving and decision-making situations.

A benefit of this complementarist view of OR and systems is that an opportunity is created in which other disciplines can also be brought into consideration. The metadiscipline in which OR and systems are embedded may also be able to accept other approaches, which can then be compared and contrasted with OR and systems in a meaningful way.

The conclusion to be drawn is that OR and systems, scientific method and systems methodologies, and hard and soft systems thinking are most usefully thought of as being complementary to each other. This conclusion goes some way toward addressing the third topic to be considered here: the nature of the interactions between OR and systems.

## Interactions between OR and Systems

As shown in Figure 10.1, three major types of interaction are possible between OR and systems. One is the exchanges which may occur at the theoretical level. A second is exchanges at the practical level. The third type of exchange may occur between theory in one discipline and practice in the other. The intention here is to consider these in turn and to suggest, where possible, ways in which the interactions may operate.

Consider first of all the interactions between OR theory and systems theory. Here exchanges can be identified which are concerned with identifying and defining the boundary between the two intellectual frameworks concerned. An increased understanding of the foundations of mathematical modeling may be used by a systems theorist to define the limits of the effective use of systems theory. The development of systems theory must proceed in a direction which parallels rather than crosses over that of OR theory if both are to progress effectively. Efforts to develop OR or systems theory in areas where the other is best suited are likely to result in less benefit than developments at the core of each approach. However, work must also be done to push back the limits of each body of knowledge so that increased knowledge of boundaries and their character can result. Thus research programs in OR and systems theory are needed which concentrate upon the mainstream issues of each discipline. These are largely already in existence. What is also needed is a more concerted effort to work consciously at the interface in order to identify the nature of that interface and to feed back its implications to the center of the disciplines.

Now look at the interactions between OR practice and systems practice. The exchanges here will focus upon a comparison of applications undertaken in each of the two types of approach. An OR analyst examining what occurs in a piece of systems practice may become aware of situations that cannot be tackled within the systems approach. The same holds true for a systems-based practitioner looking at a piece of OR practice. This information may be useful if it is accepted in the correct manner. The message it carries refers to the relative strengths of each of the approaches. An observer from the systems movement looking at OR applications should not decry that work because it fails to incorporate aspects which are seen as being important to systems practice. Reductionism and quantification may be perfectly appropriate in certain cases. The same point can be made in terms of an OR observer, who must realize that reductionism and quantification are not necessary for successful interventions. Exchanges of practice offer opportunities for practitioners to reflect on the experience of others as well as themselves. The need is for a framework which can guide this reflection and thus offer a way of using practical experiences to enable a broader appreciation of OR and systems practice to be gained.

Finally, there are exchanges between OR theory and systems practice and OR practice and systems theory to be considered. These can be used to enhance and reinforce the benefits gained from theory–theory and practice–practice interactions. The boundary between OR theory and systems theory can be illuminated by recognizing what happens when either of the theories is used to guide practice. Thus systems theory can benefit not only from an understanding of OR theory but also from an examination of OR practice. The same is true for OR theory, which can usefully draw upon both systems theory and practice. The benefits to practitioners of understanding what happens in other types of practice than their own specialty can be increased by an understanding of the intellectual framework which guides those practices. An OR (or systems) practitioner will benefit from an understanding of systems (or OR) practice but will benefit even more if it is supported by an understanding of systems (or OR) theory.

Thus, although OR and systems are separate, complementary approaches, the nature of their complementarity means that learning can take place between them to the benefit of each. The need is for a mechanism to encourage such learning to occur. This requires a culture being developed in the OR and systems communities where a positive view is taken of the relative strengths of each approach and where there is an appreciation of the fact that they each contribute unique qualities to the support of the problem-solving and decision-making process.

## Conclusion

This final chapter has sought to summarize the underlying argument of the earlier chapters that OR and systems, while being different, are mutually beneficial. It remains here to mention the next stages which follow from the above argument.

The notion of a metadiscipline is a potentially useful piece of theory to consider developing. It can provide a foundation for the framework developed above and may also provoke other questions concerning the process of OR and systems. At a practical level the need exists to provide ways and means of ensuring that OR and systems will be seen as being in concert rather than in conflict. Methodological tools and cultural changes need to be introduced to promote this view. In addition to the existing research programs within each discipline, research at the interface which services these needs is vital if OR and systems are to realize the mutual benefits each has to offer.

This book has contained some suggestions at how these further developments might proceed, some more fully worked out than others. Some may prove useful; others will not. What is clear, however, is that much more work is necessary if the full potential of OR and systems to contribute to society in all its aspects is to be realized.

# References

Ackoff, R. L., 1956, The development of operations research as a science, *Op. Res.*, 4:265–295.

Ackoff, R. L., 1957, A comparison of OR in USA and Great Britain, *Op. Res. Qu.*, 8:88–100.

Ackoff, R. L., 1961, The meaning, scope and methods of OR, in: *Progress in operations research*, Vol. 1 (R. L. Ackoff, ed.), Wiley, New York, pp. 1–34.

Ackoff, R. L., 1962, *Scientific method*, Wiley, New York.

Ackoff, R. L., 1974a, The systems revolution, *Long Range Pl.*, 7:2–20.

Ackoff, R. L., 1974b, *Redesigning the future*, Wiley, New York.

Ackoff, R. L., 1976, Does the quality of life have to be quantified?, *Op. Res. Qu.*, 27:289–303.

Ackoff, R. L., 1979a, The future of operational research is past, *Jnl. Op. Res. Soc.*, 30:93–104.

Ackoff, R. L., 1979b, Resurrecting the future of operational research, *Jnl. Op. Res. Soc.*, 30:189–200.

Ackoff, R. L., 1981a, *Creating the corporate future*, Wiley, New York.

Ackoff, R. L., 1981b, The art and science of mess management, *Interfaces*, 11:20–26.

Ackoff, R. L., 1983, Beyond prediction and preparation, *Jnl. Mgt. Stud.*, 20:59–69.

Ackoff, R. L., and Sasieni, M. W., 1968, *Fundamentals of operations research*, Wiley, New York.

Air Ministry, 1963, *The origins and development of operational research in the Royal Air Force*, HMSO, London.

Anonymous, 1980a, Obituary: Eric Charles Williams, *Jnl. Op. Res. Soc.*, 31:559–561.

Anonymous, 1980b, Obituary: Sir Charles Frederick Goodeve, OBE, FRS, *Jnl. Op. Res. Soc.*, 31:961–964.

Armytage, W. H. G., 1976, *A social history of engineering* (4th ed.), Faber and Faber, London.

Ashby, R., 1956, *An introduction to cybernetics*, Methuen, London.

Axelrod, R. (ed.), 1976, *Structure of decision*, Princeton University Press, Princeton.

Babbage, C., 1832, *On the economy of machinery and manufactures*, C. Knight, London.

Barber, W. J., 1977, *A history of economic thought*, Penguin, Harmondsworth.

Barish, N. N., 1963, Operations research and systems engineering: The applied science and its engineering, *Op. Res.*, 11:387–398.

Barnard, C., 1938, *The functions of the executive*, Harvard University Press, Cambridge, MA.

Barnes, B., and Edge, D. (eds.), 1982, *Science in context*, Open University Press, Milton Keynes.

Barth, C. G., 1922, Slide rules for the machine shop as a part of the Taylor system of management, in: *Scientific management* (C. B. Thompson, ed.), Harvard University Press, Cambridge, MA.

Batson, R. G., 1987, The modern role of MS/OR professionals in interdisciplinary teams, *Interfaces*, 17(3):85–93.

Beale, E. M. L., 1985, The evolution of mathematical programming systems, *Jnl. Op. Res. Soc.*, 36:357–366.

Bean, A. S., Neal, R. D., Radnor, M., and Tansik, D. A., 1975, Structural and behavioural correlates of implementation in US business organisations, in: *Implementing operations research/management science* (R. L. Schultz and D. P. Slevin, eds.), American Elsevier, New York, pp. 77–132.

Beasley, J. E., and Whitchurch, G., 1984, OR education—A survey of young OR workers, *Jnl. Op. Res. Soc.*, 35:281–288.

Beer, S., 1959a, *Cybernetics and management*, English Universities Press, London.

Beer, S., 1959b, What has cybernetics to do with OR?, *Op. Res. Qu.*, 10:1–21.

Beer, S., 1966, *Decision and control*, Wiley, Chichester.

Beer, S., 1979, *The heart of enterprise*, Wiley, Chichester.

Beer, S., 1981, *Brain of the firm* (2nd ed.), Wiley, Chichester.

Beer, S., 1985, *Diagnosing the system for organisations*, Wiley, Chichester.

Bell, J. F., 1967, *A history of economic thought* (2nd ed.), Ronald Press, New York.

Bellman, R., 1954, Some applications of the theory of dynamic programming—A review, *Op. Res. Qu.*, 2:275–288.

Bennett, P. G., and Huxham, C. S., 1982, Hypergames and what they do: A "soft" OR approach, *Jnl. Op. Res. Soc.*, 33:41–50.

Berg, M., 1980, *The machinery question and the making of political economy*, Cambridge University Press, Cambridge.

Best, G., Parston, G., and Rosenhead, J., 1986, Robustness in practice—The regional planning of health services, *Jnl. Op. Res. Soc.*, 37:463–478.

Bevan, R. G., 1976, The language of operational research, *Op. Res. Qu.*, 27:305–313.

Blackett, P. M. S., 1962, *Studies of war*, Oliver and Boyd, Edinburgh.

Bloomfield, B. P., 1986, *Modelling the world*, Basil Blackwell, Oxford.

Bogart, D. H., 1980, Feedback, feedforward and feedwithin: Strategic information in systems, *Behl. Sci.*, 25:237–249.

Bonder, S., 1979, Changing the future of operations research, *Op. Res.*, 27:209–224.

Boothroyd, H., 1978, *Articulate intervention*, Taylor and Francis, London.

Boulding, K., 1956, General system theory: The skeleton of science, *Mgt. Sci.*, 2:197–208.

Britton, G., and McCallion, H., 1985, A case study demonstrating the use of Beer's cybernetic model of viable systems, *Cyb. Sys.*, 16:229–256.

Burrell, G., and Morgan, G., 1979, *Sociological paradigms and organisational analysis*, Heinemann, London.

Cannon, W. B., 1932, *The wisdom of the body*, W. W. Norton, New York.

Caravajal, R., 1982, The dialectics of analytical and synthetic approaches, *Eur. Jnl. Op. Res.*, 10:361–272.

Carter, M. P., 1987, Preliminary findings of a survey of OR Society membership, *Jnl. Op. Res. Soc.*, 38:3–16.

Carter, P., Jackson, N. V., Jackson, M. C., and Keys, P. (eds.), 1987, *Community operational research at Hull University*, Dragon, 2(2):1–153.

Chalmers, A. F., 1982, *What Is this thing called science?* (2nd ed.), Open University Press, Milton Keynes.

Charnes, A., and Cooper, W. W., 1954, The stepping stone method of explaining linear programming calculations in transportation problems. *Mgt. Sci.*, 1:49–69.

Checkland, P. B., 1971, A systems map of the universe, *Jnl. Syst. Eng.*, 2:107–114.

Checkland, P. B., 1981, *Systems thinking, systems practice*, Wiley, Chichester.

Checkland, P. B., 1983, OR and the systems movement: Mappings and conflict, *Jnl. Op. Res. Soc.*, 34:661–675.

Checkland, P. B., 1985, From optimising to learning: A development of systems thinking for the 1990s, *Jnl. Op. Res. Soc.*, 36:757–767.

Checkland, P. B., 1987, The application of systems thinking in real-world problem-situations: The emergence of soft systems methodology, in: *New directions in management science* (M. C. Jackson and P. Keys, eds.), Gower, Aldershot, pp. 87–96.

Chiamsiri, S., Sculli, D., and Wong, J. Y., 1984, Determining number of serving points by discrete simulation, *Jnl. Op. Res. Soc.*, 35:289–295.

Chisholm, M., 1975, *Human geography: Evolution or revolution?*, Penguin, Harmondsworth.

Churchman, C. W., 1957, A summing-up, in: *Proceedings of the First International Conference on Operations Research* (M. Davies, R. T. Eddison, and T. Page, eds.), ORSA, Baltimore, pp. 514–520.

Churchman, C. W., 1970, Operations research as a profession, *Mgt. Sci.*, 17:B37–B53.

Churchman, C. W., 1979, *The systems approach*, Dell Publishing, New York.

Churchman, C. W., Ackoff, R. L., and Arnoff, E. L., 1957, *Introduction to Operations Research*, Wiley, New York.

Churchman, C. W., and Schainblatt, A. H., 1965, The researcher and the manager: A dialectic of implementation, *Mgt. Sci.*, 11:B69–B87.

Clark, S. A., and Wyatt, E., 1922, Scientific management as applied to women's work, in: *Scientific management* (C. B. Thompson, ed.), Harvard University Press, Cambridge, MA, pp. 807–834.

Clemson, B. C., 1984, *Cybernetics: A new management Tool*, Abacus, Tunbridge Wells.

Cliff, A. D., and Haggett, P., 1981, Graph theory, in: *Quantitative geography* (N. Wrigley and R. J. Bennett, eds.), Routledge and Kegan Paul, London, pp. 225–234.

Cohen, S. S., 1985, *Operational research*, Edward Arnold, London.

Collcutt, R. H., 1965, *The first twenty years of operational research*, British Iron and Steel Research Association, London.

Conway, D. A., 1989, Project based work groups and the organisation, in: *Operational research and the social sciences* (M. C. Jackson, P. Keys, and S. A. Cropper, eds.), Plenum, London, pp. 311–317.

Cooper, W. W., 1954, Presidential address, *Mgt. Sci.*, 1:183–186.

Coyle, R. G., 1983a, The technical elements of the systems dynamics approach, *Eur. Jnl. Op. Res.*, 14:359–370.

Coyle, R. G., 1983b, Who rules the waves?—A case study in systems description, *Jnl. Op. Res. Soc.*, 34:885–898.

Cummings, T., 1976, Socio-technical systems: An intervention strategy, in: *Current issues and strategies in organization development* (W. Burke, ed.), Human Science Press, New York.

Dando, M. R., Defrenne, A., and Sharp, R. G., 1977, Could OR be a science?, *Omega*, 5:89–92.

Dando, M. R., and Sharp, R. G., 1976, OR in the UK in 1977: The causes and consequences of a myth, *Jnl. Op. Res. Soc.*, 27:939–949.

Dantzig, G. B., 1951, Maximisation of a linear function of variables subject to linear inequalities, in: *Activity analysis of production and allocation* (T. C. Koopmans, ed.), Wiley, New York, pp. 339–347.

Dantzig, G. B., 1955, Linear programming under uncertainty, *Mgt. Sci.*, 1:197–206.

Dantzig, G. B., Fulkerson, R., and Johnson, S., 1954, Solution of a large-scale travelling salesman problem, *Op. Res.*, 2:393–410.

Davies, M., Eddison, R. T., and Page, T. (eds.), 1957, *Proceedings of the First International Conference on Operations Research*, ORSA, Baltimore.

Deutsch, K., 1963, *The nerves of government*, Free Press, New York.

Dubbey, J. M., 1978, *The mathematical work of Charles Babbage*, Cambridge University Press, Cambridge.

Eaton, R. J., 1955, Mechanising ticket printing and issue, *Op. Res. Qu.*, 6:65–73.

Eckman, D. P. (ed.), 1961, *Systems: Research and design*, Wiley, New York.

Eddison, R. T., and Owen, D. G., 1953, Discharging iron ore, *Op. Res. Qu.* 4:39–50.

Eden, C., 1982, Problem construction and the influence of OR, *Interfaces*, 12:50–60.

Eden, C., 1985a, Perish the thought! *Jnl. Op. Res. Soc.*, 36:809–819.

Eden, C., 1985b, Perishing thoughts about "Systems Thinking in Action," *Jnl. Op. Res. Soc.*, 36:860–861.

Eden, C., and Huxham, C. S., 1988, Action-oriented strategic management, *Jnl. Op. Res. Soc.*, 39:889–899.

Eden, C., and Jones, S., 1984, Using repertory grids for problem construction, *Jnl. Op. Res. Soc.*, 35:779–790.

Eden, C., Jones, S., and Sims, D., 1983, *Messing about in problems*, Pergamon, Oxford.

Eden, C., and Sims, D., 1979, On the nature of problems in consulting practice, *Omega*, 7:119–127.

Education Committee, ORSA, 1953, Report of the Education Committee, OR Society of America, *Op. Res.*, 1:248–251.

Education Committee, ORSA, 1956, Report of the Education Committee, OR Society of America, *Op. Res.*, 4:375–379.

Eilon, S., 1975a, Seven faces of research, *Op. Res. Qu.*, 26:359–367.

Eilon, S., 1975b, How scientific is OR? *Omega*, 2:1–8.

Eilon, S., 1980, The role of management science, *Jnl. Op. Res. Soc.*, 31:17–28.

Emery, E. F., and Trist, E. L., 1965, The causal texture of organisational environments, *Hum. Reln.*, 18:21–32.

Emery, E. F., and Trist, E. L., 1972, *Towards a social ecology*, Penguin, Harmondsworth.

Espejo, R., 1987, From machines to people and organisations, in: *New directions in management Science* (M. C. Jackson and P. Keys, eds.), Gower, Aldershot, pp. 55–85.

Feyerabend, P. K., 1975, *Against method: Outline of an anarchistic theory of knowledge*, New Left Books, London.

Findeisen, W., and Quade, E. S., 1985, The methodology of systems analysis: An introduction and overveiw, in: *Handbook of systems analysis* (H. J. Miser and E. S. Quade, eds.), Wiley, Chichester, pp. 117–149.

Finlay, P. N., and Wilson, J. M., 1987, The paucity of model validation in operational research projects, *Jnl. Op. Res. Soc.*, 38:303–308.

Flagle, C. D., Huggins, W. H., and Roy, R. H. (eds.), 1960, *Operations research and systems engineering*, Johns Hopkins Press, Baltimore.

Flood, M. M., 1962, New operations research potentials, *Op. Res.*, 10:423–436.

Flood, R. L., 1987, Complexity: A definition by construction of a conceptual framework, *Sys. Res.*, 4:177–185.

Flood, R. L., and Carson, E., 1988, *Dealing with complexity*, Plenum, London.

Flood, R. L., and Jackson, M. C., 1988, Cybernetics and organisation theory: A critical review, *Cyb. Sys.*, 19:13–33.

Flood, R. L., and Keys, P., 1989, Methodology choice, complexity texture and self-reflection, *Cyb. Sys.*, 20:401–415.

Ford, L. R., and Fulkerson, D. R., 1956, Solving the transportation problem, *Mgt. Sci.*, 3:24–32.

Forrester, J. W., 1961, *Industrial dynamics*, M.I.T. Press, Cambridge, MA.

Forrester, J. W., 1968, Industrial dynamics—A reply to Ansoff and Slevin, *Mgt. Sci.*, 14:601–618.

Foster, M., 1967, Developing an analytical model for sociotechnical analysis, *H.R.C. 7, 15,* Tavistock Institute, London.

Friend, J. K., and Hickling, A. A., 1987, *Planning under pressure,* Pergamon, Oxford.

Friend, J. K., and Jessop, N., 1969, *Local government and strategic choice,* Tavistock, London.

Friend, J. K., Norris, M. E., and Stringer, J., 1988, The Institute for Operational Research: An initiative to extend the scope of OR, *Jnl. Op. Res. Soc.,* 39:705–713.

Gallessich, J., 1982, *The profession and practice of consultation,* Jossey-Bass, San Francisco.

Gander, R. S., 1955, Letter to the Editor, *Op. Res.,* 3:215–216.

Gander, R. S., 1957, The state of operational research in the United Kingdom, in: *Proceedings of the First International Conference on Operations Research* (M. Davies, R. T. Eddison, and T. Page, eds.), ORSA, Baltimore, pp. 500–513.

Gantt, H. L., 1903, A graphical daily balance in manufacture, in: *Scientific management* (C. B. Thompson, ed.), 1922, Harvard University Press, Cambridge, MA, pp. 420–433.

Glen, J. J., 1986, A linear programming model for an integrated crop and intensive beef production enterprise, *Jnl. Op. Res. Soc.,* 37:487–494.

Gomberg, W., 1957, The use of psychology in industry: A trade union point of view, *Mgt. Sci.,* 3:348–370.

Goode, H. H., and Machol, R. E., 1957, *System engineering,* McGraw-Hill, New York.

Goodeve, C., 1952, Operational research as science, *Op. Res. Qu.,* 1:166–180.

Goodeve, C., and Ridley, G. R., 1953, A survey of OR in Great Britain, *Op. Res. Qu.,* 4:21–24.

Gosling, W., 1962, *The design of engineering systems,* Heywood, London.

Guetzkow, H., and Bowes, A. E., 1957, The development of organizations in a laboratory, *Mgt. Sci.,* 3:380–402.

Habakkuk, H. J., 1962, *American and British technology in the nineteenth century,* Cambridge University Press, Cambridge.

Haley, K. B., 1984, Techniques maketh OR, *Jnl. Op. Res. Soc.,* 35:191–194.

Hall, A. D., 1962, *A methodology for systems engineering,* Van Nostrand, Princeton.

Hamilton, P., 1983, *Talcott Parsons,* Ellis Harwood, Chichester.

Harary, F., Norman, R., and Cartwright, D., 1965, *Structural models: An introduction to the theory of directed graphs,* Wiley, New York.

Hertz, D. B., 1958, The international conference on operations research: A report, *Mgt. Sci.,* 4:344–347.

Hicks, D., 1983, The origins of operational research in the coal industry, *Jnl. Op. Res. Soc.,* 34:845–852.

Hildebrandt, S., 1977, Implementation of the operations research/management science process, *Eur. Jnl. Op. Res.,* 1:289–294.

Hildebrandt, S., 1980, Implementation—The bottleneck of operations research: The state of the art, *Eur. Jnl. Op. Res.,* 6:4–12.

Hill, I. D., 1973, Charles Babbage, Rowland Hill and penny postage, *Post. Hist. Intl.,* 2.

Hill, R., and Hill, G. B., 1880, *The life of Sir Rowland Hill and the history of Penny Postage,* Vol. 1, de la Rue, London.

Hirschheim, R. A., 1983, Systems in OR: Reflections and analysis, *Jnl. Op. Res. Soc.,* 34:813–818.

Hitchcock, F. L., 1941, The distribution of a product from several sources to numerous localities, *Jnl. Math. Phys.,* 20:224–230.

HMSO, 1916, *Report of the Advisory Council to the Privy Council on Scientific and Industrial Research, 1915–1916,* HMSO, London.

HMSO, 1935, *Report of the Department of Scientific and Industrial Research, 1934–35,* HMSO, London.

HMSO, 1937, *Report of the Department of Scientific and Industrial Research, 1935–6*, HMSO, London.

HMSO, 1949, *Report of the Department of Scientific and Industrial Research, 1947–48*, HMSO, London.

HMSO, 1950, *Report of the Department of Scientific and Industrial Research, 1949–50*, HMSO, London.

HMSO, 1958, *Report of the Department of Scientific and Industrial Research, 1957–58*, HMSO, London.

Holland, J., 1989, This little piggy revisited, *OR Insight*, 2:3–7.

Hollander, S., 1985, *The economics of John Stuart Mill*, Basil Blackwell, Oxford.

Holt, C. C., Modigliani, F., and Muth, J. F., 1956, Derivation of a linear decision rule for production and employment, *Mgt. Sci.*, 2:159–177.

Houlden, B., 1979, Some aspects of managing OR projects, *Jnl. Op. Res. Soc.*, 30:681–690.

Hovey, R. W., and Wagner, H. M., 1958, A sample survey of industrial operations research, *Op. Res.*, 6:876–881.

Howard, M. C., and King, J. E., 1985, *The political economy of Marx*, 2nd ed., Longman, London.

Howard, N., 1971, *Paradoxes of rationality: Theory of metagames and political behaviour*, M.I.T. Press, Cambridge, MA.

Huysmans, J. H. B. M., 1970, *The implementation of operations research*, Wiley, New York.

Hyman, A., 1982, *Charles Babbage*, Oxford University Press, Oxford.

Jackson, M. C., 1982, The nature of soft systems thinking: The work of Churchman, Ackoff and Checkland, *Jnl. App. Sys. Anal.*, 9:17–28.

Jackson, M. C., 1984, OR in systems: The alternative perspective, *Jnl. Op. Res. Soc.*, 35:155–161.

Jackson, M. C., 1985b, The itinerary of a critical approach, *Jnl. Op. Res. Soc.*, 36:878–881.

Jackson, M. C., 1985a, A cybernetic approach to management, in: *Managing transport systems* (P. Keys and M. C. Jackson, eds.), Gower, Aldershot, pp. 24–52.

Jackson, M. C., 1986, The cybernetic model of the organisation: An assessment, in: *Cybernetics and systems '86* (R. Trappl, ed.), D. Reidel, Dordrecht, pp. 189–196.

Jackson, M. C., 1987, New directions in management science, in: *New directions in management science* (M. C. Jackson and P. Keys, eds.), Gower, Aldershot, pp. 133–164.

Jackson, M. C., 1988, Some methodologies for community operational research, *Jnl. Op. Res. Soc.*, 39:715–724.

Jackson, M. C., and Keys, P., 1984, Towards a system of systems methodologies, *Jnl. Op. Res. Soc.*, 35:473–486.

Jackson, M. C., and Keys, P., 1985, Introduction, *Jnl. Op. Res. Soc.*, 36:753–755.

Johnson, E. A., 1960, The long range future of operational research, *Op. Res.*, 8:1–23.

Johnston, F. R., 1980, An interactive stock control system with a strategic management role, *Jnl. Op. Res. Soc.*, 31:1069–1084.

Jones, R. V., 1982, A concurrence in learning and arms, *Jnl. Op. Res. Soc.*, 33:779–791.

Kantorovich, L., 1958, On the translocation of masses, *Mgt. Sci.*, 5:1–5.

Karson, M., 1958, *American labor unions and politics*, South Illinois University Press, Carbondale.

Katz, D., and Kahn, R. L., 1966, *The social psychology of organizations*, Wiley, New York.

Keat, R., and Urry, J., 1975, *Social theory as science* (2nd ed.), Routledge and Kegan Paul, London.

Keeney, R. L., and Raiffa, H., 1976, *Decisions with multiple objectives: Preference and value trade-offs*, Wiley, New York.

Kelly, G. A., 1955, *The psychology of personal constructs*, Vol. 1, W. W. Norton, New York.

Kendall, M. G., 1958, The teaching of operational research, *Op. Res. Qu.*, 9:265–278.

Kepner, C. H., and Tregoe, B. B., 1965, *The rational manager*, McGraw-Hill, New York.

Kershner, R. B., 1960, A survey of systems engineering, in: *Operations research and systems engineering* (C. D. Flagle, W. H. Huggins, and R. H. Roy, eds.), Johns Hopkins Press, Baltimore, pp. 140–72.

Keys, P., 1984, The systems approach and OR: A linguistic analysis, *Jnl. Op. Res. Soc.*, 35:161–8.

Keys, P., 1985, A step beyond OR . . . , *Jnl. Op. Res. Soc.*, 36:864–867.

Keys, P., 1986, A framework for the design of problem-solving methodologies, in: *Cybernetics and systems '86* (R. Trappl, ed.), D. Reidel, Dordrecht, pp. 229–236.

Keys, P., 1987a, Traditional management science and the emerging critique, in: *New directions in management science* (M. C. Jackson and P. Keys, eds.), Gower, Aldershot, pp. 1–25.

Keys, P., 1987b, Planners, uncertainties and methodologies, *Pub. Pol. Admin.*, 2:23–34.

Keys, P., 1987c, Management and management support in community service agencies, *Dragon*, 2:19–45.

Keys, P., 1988a, System dynamics: A methodological perspective, *Trans. Inst. Meas. Ctl.*, 10:218–224.

Keys, P., 1988b, A methodology for methodology choice, *Sys. Res.*, 5:65–76.

Keys, P., 1989a, MS/OR projects and their interaction, *Omega*, 17:113–122.

Keys, P., 1989b, OR as technology: Some issues and implications, *Jnl. Op. Res. Soc.*, 40:753–759.

King, M., and Mercer, A., 1985, Problems in determining bidding strategies, *Jnl. Op. Res. Soc.*, 36:915–923.

Klir, G., 1985, Complexity: Some general observations, *Sys. Res.*, 2:131—140.

Lamson, S. T., Hastings, N. A. J., and Willis, R. J., 1983, Minimum cost maintenance in heavy haul railway track, *Jnl. Op. Res. Soc.*, 34:211–223.

Lanry, M., Malouin, K. L., and Oral, M., 1983, Model validation in operational research, *Eur. Jnl. Op. Res.*, 14:207–220.

Lathrop, J. B., 1959, Operations research looks to science, *Op. Res.*, 7:423–429.

Leontief, W., 1951, *The structure of the American economy, 1919–1931*, Oxford University Press, New York.

Lewin, K., 1947, Frontiers in group dynamics, *Hum. Rel.*, 1:5–41.

Lilienfeld, R., 1978, *The rise of systems theory*, Wiley, New York.

Lockett, A. G., and Polding, E., 1978, OR/MS implementation—a variety of processes, *Interfaces*, 9(1):45–50.

Lockett, A. G., and Polding, E., 1981, Organisational linkages and OR projects, *Eur. Jnl. Op. Res.*, 7:14–21.

MacDermot, E. T., 1964, *History of the great western railway*, Vol. 1, Ian Allen, London.

Majone, G., 1980, An anatomy of pitfalls, in: *Pitfalls of analysis* (G. Majone and E. S. Quade, eds.), Wiley, Chichester, pp. 7–22.

Majone, G., 1985, Systems analysis: A generic approach, in: *Handbook of systems analysis* (H. J. Miser and E. S. Quade, eds.), Wiley, Chichester, pp. 33–66.

Malcolm, D. G., 1954, Status of operational research in industry, *Op. Res.*, 2:211–213.

Malin, H., 1981, Of kings and men, especially OR men, *Jnl. Op. Res. Soc.*, 32:953–965.

Markowitz, H. M., 1957, The elimination form of the inverse and its application to linear programming, *Mgt. Sci.*, 3:255–269.

Mason, R. O., and Mitroff, I. I., 1981, *Challenging strategic planning assumptions*, Wiley, New York.

Mayo, E., 1933, *The human problems of an industrial civilisation*, Macmillan, New York.

Mayr, O., 1976, The science-technology relationship as a historiographic problem, *Technology and Culture*, 17:663–672.

McClintock, M. E., 1974, *University of Lancaster: Quest for innovation*, University of Lancaster, Lancaster.

McCloskey, J. F., 1954, Training for operations research, *Op. Res.*, 2:386–392.

McCloskey, J. F., and Trefethen, F. N. (eds.), 1954, *Operations research for managers*, Johns Hopkins Press, Baltimore.

McLoughlin, J. B., 1969, *Urban and regional planning: A systems approach*, Faber and Faber, London.

Meadows, D. M., 1980, The unavoidable a priori, in: *Elements of the system dynamics method* (J. Randers, ed.), M.I.T. Press, Cambridge, MA, pp. 23–57.

Mercer, A., 1981, A consultant's reflections on client management, *Jnl. Op. Res. Soc.*, 32:105–111.

Miser, H. J., 1985, The practice of systems analysis, in *Handbook of systems analysis* (H. J. Miser and E. S. Quade, eds.), Wiley, New York, pp. 281–326.

Mitchell, G. H., 1980, Images of operational research, *Jnl. Op. Res. Soc.*, 31:459–466.

Moore, P. G., 1986, *Basic operational research*, 3rd ed., Pitman, London.

Morgan, G., 1986, *Images of organization*, Sage, Beverley Hills.

Morrison, P., and Morrison, E. (eds.), 1961, *Charles Babbage and his calculating engines*, Dover, New York.

Morse, P. M., 1952a, The Operations Research Society of America, *Op. Res.*, 1:1–2.

Morse, P. M., 1953, Letter to the Editor, *Op. Res.*, 1:303–304.

Morse, P. M., 1955, Where is the new blood?, *Op. Res.*, 3:383–387.

Morse, P. M., and Kimball, G. E., 1951, *Methods of operations research*, Wiley, New York.

Oakley, A., 1984, *Marx's critique of political economy*, Vol. 1, Routledge and Kegan Paul, London.

Oliga, J., 1988, Methodological foundations of systems methodologies, *Sys. Prac.*, 1:87–112.

Operational Research Society, 1986, Report of the Commission on the Future Practice of Operational Research, *Jnl. Op. Res. Soc.*, 37:829–886.

Orchard-Hayes, W., 1958, Evolution of LP computing techniques, *Mgt. Sci.*, 4:183–190.

Parsons, T., 1951, *The social system*, Free Press, New York.

Parsons, T., 1953, *Working papers in the theory of action*, Free Press, New York.

Parsons, T., and Smelser, N. J., 1956, *Economy and Society*, Free Press, New York.

Pasmore, W. A., 1988, *Designing effective organisations*, Wiley, New York.

Pasmore, W. A., Francis, C., Haldeman, J., and Shani, A., 1978, Socio-technical systems: a North American reflection on empirical studies of the seventies, *Hum. Rel.*, 35:1179–1204.

Person, H. S., 1964, Foreword, in: *Scientific management* (F. W. Taylor, ed.), Harper and Row, New York.

Peterson, F., 1963, *American labor unions*, 2nd ed., Harper and Row, New York.

Pettigrew, A. M., 1975, Strategic aspects of the management of specialist activity, *Pers. Rev.*, 4:5–13.

Pidd, M., 1979, Systems approaches and operational research, *Eur. Jnl. Op. Res.*, 3:13–19.

Pidd, M., 1988, From problem-structuring to implementation, *Jnl. Op. Res. Soc.*, 39:115–121.

Pidd, M., and Wooley, R. N., 1980, A pilot study of problem-structuring, *Jnl. Op. Res. Soc.*, 31:1063–1068.

Pocock, J. W., 1954, Management consultancy and operations research, in: *Operations research for management*, Vol. 1 (J. F. McCloskey and F. N. Trefethen, eds.), John Hopkins Press, Baltimore, pp. 80–96.

Polding, E., and Lockett, A. G., 1982, Attitudes and perceptions relating to implementation and success in operational research, *Jnl. Op. Res. Soc.*, 33:733–744.

Pollard, S., 1968, *The genesis of modern management*, Penguin, Harmondsworth.

Popper, K. R., 1972, *Conjectures and refutations*, Routledge and Kegan Paul, London.

Popper, K. R., 1977, *The logic of scientific discovery*, Hutchinson, London.

Pratt, V., 1978, *The philosophy of the social sciences*, Methuen, London.

Price, D. J. de S., 1969, The structures of publication in science and technology, in: *Factors in the transfer of technology* (W. H. Gruber and D. G. Marquis, eds.), M.I.T. Press, Cambridge, MA, pp. 91–104.

Pugh, D. S., Hickson, D. J., and Hinings, C. R., 1984, *Writers on organisations* (3rd ed.), Penguin, Harmondsworth.

Quade, E. S., and Miser, H. J., 1985, The context, nature and use of systems analysis, in: *Handbook of systems analysis* (H. J. Miser and E. S. Quade, eds.), Wiley, Chichester, pp. 1–32.

Raitt, R. A., 1979, OR and science, *Jnl. Op. Res. Soc.*, 30:835–836.

Ramakrishna, H. V., and Brightman, H. J., 1986, The fact-net model, *Interfaces*, 16(6):86–94.

Rattensi, A., 1982, *Marx and the division of labour*, Macmillan, London.

Revans, R. W., 1955, Scale factors in the management of coal mines, *Op. Res. Qu.*, 6:91–107.

Rice, A. K., 1958, *Productivity and social organisation: The Ahmedebad experiment*, Tavistock, London.

Richards, L. D., and Gupta, S. K., 1985, The systems approach in an information society: A reconsideration, *Jnl. Op. Res. Soc.*, 36:833–843.

Richards, S., 1983, *Philosophy and sociology of science*, Basil Blackwell, Oxford.

Rittel, H., 1972, On the planning crisis: Systems analysis of the "first" and "second" generations, *Bedriftsokonomen*, 8:390–396.

Rivett, B. H. P., 1959, A survey of operational research in British industry, *Op. Res. Qu.*, 10:189–205.

Rivett, B. H. P., 1980, *Model building for decision analysis*, Wiley, Chichester.

Rivett, B. H. P., 1987, Donald Hicks, O. B. E., *Jnl. Op. Res. Soc.*, 38:111–113.

Robb, F. F., 1984, Cybernetics in management thinking, *Sys. Res.*, 1:5–23.

Roberts, F. S., 1976, *Discrete mathematical models*, Prentice-Hall, Englewood Cliffs, NJ.

Roethlisberger, F. J., and Dickson, W. J., 1939, *Management and the Worker*, Harvard University Press, Cambridge, MA.

Romano, R. M., 1982, The economic ideas of Charles Bbbage, *Hist. Pol. Econ.*, 14:385–405.

Rosenhead, J., 1980, Planning under uncertainty. II: A methodology for robustness analysis, *Jnl. Op. Res. Soc.*, 31:331–341.

Rosenhead, J., 1985, A system of systems conferences, *Jnl. Op. Res. Soc.*, 36:849–854.

Rosenhead, J., 1986, Custom and practice, *Jnl. Op. Res. Soc.*, 37:335–343.

Rosenhead, J., 1987, From management science to workers' science, in: *New directions in management science* (M. C. Jackson and P. Keys, eds.), Gower, Aldershot, pp. 109–131.

Rosenhead, J., 1989, OR at the crossroads: Cecil Gordon and the development of post-war OR, *Jnl. Op. Res. Soc.*, 40:3–28.

Rosenhead, J., and Thunhurst, C., 1982, A materialist analysis of operational research, *Jnl. Op. Res. Soc.*, 33:111–122.

Roy, R. H., 1960, The development and future of operations research and systems engineering, in: *Operations research and systems engineering* (C. D. Flagle, W. H. Huggins, and R. H. Roy, eds.), Johns Hopkins Press, Baltimore, pp. 8–27.

Saaty, T. L., 1957, Resume of useful formulas in queueing theory, *Op. Res.*, 5:161–200.

Schein, E., 1969, *Process consultation: Its role in organisational development*, Addison-Wesley, Reading, MA.

Schmidt, V., 1987, Four approaches to science and their implications for organisational theory and research, *Knowledge*, 9:19–41.

Schoderbek, C. G., Schoderbek, P. P., and Kefalas, A. G., 1980, *Management systems: Conceptual considerations*, Business Publications, Dallas.

Schultz, R. L., and Ginzberg, M. J. (eds.), 1984, *Management science implementation*, JAI Press, Greenwich, Conn.

Schultz, R. L., and Slevin, D. P., 1975a, A program of research on implementation, in: *Implementing operations research/management science* (R. L. Schultz and D. P. Slevin, eds.), American Elsevier, New York, pp. 31–51.

Schultz, R. L., and Slevin, D. P. (eds.), 1975b, *Implementing operations research/management science*, American Elsevier, New York.

Schultz, R. L., and Slevin, D. P., 1982, Implementation exchange: Implementing implementation research, *Interfaces*, 12(5):87–90.

Schultz, R. L., Slevin, D. P., and Pinto, J. K., 1987, Strategy and tactics in a process model of project implementation, *Interfaces*, 17(3):34–46.

Selznick, P., 1948, Foundations of the theory of organisations, *Amer. Soc. Rev.*, 13:25–35.

Simon, H. A., and Holt, C. C., 1954, The control of inventory and production rates—A survey, *Op. Res.*, 2:289–301.

Sitruk, G., 1983, A constantly evolving OR team, *Jnl. Op. Res. Soc.*, 34:183–191.

Smiddy, H. F., and Naum, L., 1954, Evolution of a "science of managing" in America, *Mgt. Sci.*, 1:1–31.

Snow, C. P., 1961, *Science and government*, Oxford University Press, Oxford.

Solandt, O., 1955, Observation, experiment and measurement in operations research, *Op. Res.*, 3:1–14.

Sorenson, R. E., and Zand, D. E., 1975, Improving the implementation of OR/MS models by applying the Lewin-Schein theory of change, in: *Implementing operations research/management science* (R. L. Schultz and D. P. Slevin, eds.), American Elsevier, New York, pp. 217–235.

Srinivasan, A., and Davis, J. G., 1987, A reassessment of implementation process models, *Interfaces*, 17(3):64–71.

Stainton, R. S., 1983, Editorial, *Jnl. Op. Res. Soc.*, 34:657–659.

Stainton, R. S., 1984, Applicable systems thinking, *Eur. Jnl. Op. Res.*, 18:145–154.

Stansfield, R. G., 1981, Operational research and sociology: A case study of cross-fertilisation in the growth of useful science, *Sci. Pub. Pol.*, 8:262–280.

Stansfield, R. G., 1983, Harold Larnder: Founder of operational research, an appreciation, *Jnl. Op. Res. Soc.*, 34:2–7.

Stansfield, R. G., 1986, The place of observation in OR methodology, 8th European Conference on Operational Research, Lisbon.

Sterling, F. W., 1922, The successful operation of a system of scientific management, in: *Scientific management* (C. B. Thompson, ed.), Harvard University Press, Cambridge, MA, pp. 296–365.

Strank, R. H. D., 1982, *Management principles and practice: A cybernetic analysis*, Gordon and Breach, London.

Suppe, F. (ed.), 1977, *The structure of scientific theories*, University of Illinois Press, Urbana.

Taha, H. A., 1976, *Operations research—An Introduction* (2nd ed.), Macmillan, London.

Tannenbaum, R., and Massarik, F., 1957, Leadership: A frame of reference, *Mgt. Sci.*, 4:1–19.

Taylor, F. W., 1911, Principles and methods of scientific management, in: F. W. Taylor, 1964, *Scientific management*, Harper and Row, London.

Taylor, F. W., 1912, Testimony before the Special Committee of the House of Representatives, in: F. W. Taylor, 1964, *Scientific management*, Harper and Row, London.

Taylor, F. W., 1906, On the art of cutting metals, in: *Scientific management* (C. B. Thompson, ed.), 1922, Harvard University Press, Cambridge, MA, pp. 242–69.

Taylor, F. W., 1964, *Scientific management*, Harper and Row, London.

Taylor, J., and Jackson, R. R. P., 1954, Application of birth and death processes to provision of spare machines, *Op. Res. Qu.* 5:95–108.

Thierauf, R. J., Klelkamp, R. C., and Ruwe, M. L., 1985, *Management science*, Charles Merrill, Columbus, OH.

Thompson, C. B. (ed.), 1922, *Scientific management*, Harvard University Press, Cambridge, MA.

Tinker, T., and Lowe, T., 1984, One dimensional management science: The making of a technocratic consciousness, *Interfaces*, 14(2):40–49.

Tomlinson, R. C. (ed.), 1971, *OR comes of age*, Tavistock, London.

Tomlinson, R. C., 1981, Some dangerous misconceptions concerning operational research and applied systems analysis, *Eur. Jnl. Op. Res.*, 7:203–212.

Tomlinson, R. C., Quade, E. S., and Miser, H. J., 1985, Implementation, in: *Handbook of systems analysis* (H. J. Miser and E. S. Quade, eds.), Wiley, Chichester, pp. 249–280.

Toynbee, A., 1927, *Lectures on the industrial revolution of the eighteenth century in England*, Longman, London.

Trefethan, F. N., 1954, A history of operations research, in: *Operations research for management*, Vol. 1 (J. F. McCloskey and F. N. Trefethen, eds.), Johns Hopkins Press, Baltimore, pp. 3–35.

Trist, E. L., and Bamforth, K. W., 1951, Some social and psychological consequences of the longwall method of coalgetting, *Hum. Rel.*, 4:3–38.

Trist, E. L., Higgin, C., Murray, H., and Pollock, A., 1963, *Organisational Choice*, Tavistock, London.

Ulrich, W., 1983, *Critical heuristics of social planning: A new approach to practical philosophy*, Haupt, Bern.

Ulrich, W., 1987, Critical heuristics of social systems design, *Eur. Jnl. Op. Res.*, 31:276–283.

Ulrich, W., 1988, Systems thinking, systems practice, and practical philosophy: A program of research, *Sys. Prac.*, 1:137–163.

Urwick, L., and Brech, E. F. L., 1949a, *The making of scientific management*, Vol. 1, Management Publications Trust, London.

Urwick, L., and Brech, E. F. L., 1949b, *The making of scientific management*, Vol. 2, Management Publications Trust, London.

Vemuri, V., 1978, *Modelling of complex systems*, Academic Press, New York.

von Bertalanffy, L., 1950, The theory of open systems in physics and biology, *Science*, 111(January 13):23–29.

von Neumann, J., and Morgenstern, O., 1944, *Theory of games and economic behaviour*, Princeton University Press, Princeton.

Waddington, C. H., 1973, *OR in World War Two*, Paul Elek, London.

Waddington, C. H., 1977, *Tools for thought*, Paladin, St. Albans.

Walker, J., 1988, Cybernetics in co-ops, *The new co-operator*, Autumn:7.

Weaver, W., 1948, Science and complexity, *Amer. Sci.*, 36:536–544.

Webber, M. M., and Rittel, H., 1973, Dilemmas in the general theory of planning, *Pol. Sci.*, 4:155–169.

Weinwurm, E. H., 1954, Letter to the Editor, *Mgt. Sci.*, 1:272–280.

White, D. J., 1970, A critique of "Research Methodology in the Management Sciences" by A. G. Beged-Dor and T. A. Klein, *Op. Res. Qu.*, 21:327–334.

White, D. J., 1985, *Operational research*, Wiley, Chichester.

Whiteman, R. P., and Wise, P. J. S., 1981, Lessons for OR from the world of banking, *Jnl. Op. Res. Soc.*, 32:519–534.

Whitin, T. M., 1954, Inventory control research: A survey, *Mgt. Sci.*, 1:32–40.

Wiener, N., 1948, *Cybernetics*, Wiley, New York.

Williams, E. C., 1968, The origin of the term "operational research" and the early development of the military work, *Op. Res. Qu.*, 19:111–113.

Williams, H. P., 1978, *Model building in mathematical programming*, Wiley, Chichester.

Williams, T. J., 1961, *Systems engineering for the process industries*, McGraw-Hill, London.

Wilson, B., 1984, *Systems: Concepts, methodologies and applications*, Wiley, Chichester.

Wolstenholme, E. F., 1982, System dynamics in perspective, *Jnl. Op. Res. Soc.*, 33:547–556.

Wolstenholme, E. F., 1983, Modelling national development programming—An exercise in system description and qualitative analysis using system dynamics, *Jnl. Op. Res. Soc.*, 34:1133–1148.

Wolstenholme, E. F., and Coyle, R. G., 1983, The development of system dynamics as a methodology for system description and qualitative analysis, *Jnl. Op. Res. Soc.*, 34:569–581.

Wolley, R. N., and Pidd, M., 1980, Four views on problem-structuring, *Interfaces*, 10(1):51–54.

Wooley, R. N., and Pidd, M., 1981, Problem-structuring—A lierature review, *Jnl. Op. Res. Soc.*, 32:197–206.

Wysocki, R. K., 1979, OR/MS implementation: A bibliography, *Interfaces*, 9(2):37–41.

Yates, F. E., 1978, Complexity and the limits to knowledge, *Amer. Jnl. Physio.*, 4:R201–R204.

Zuckerman, S., 1978, *From apes to warlords*, Hamish Hamilton, London.

# Index